SMALL STATES IN A GLOBAL ECONOMY

CRISIS, COOPERATION AND CONTRIBUTIONS

ECONOMIC ISSUES, PROBLEMS AND PERSPECTIVES

Additional books in this series can be found on Nova's website
under the Series tab.

Additional e-books in this series can be found on Nova's website
under the e-book tab.

ECONOMIC ISSUES, PROBLEMS AND PERSPECTIVES

SMALL STATES IN A GLOBAL ECONOMY

CRISIS, COOPERATION AND CONTRIBUTIONS

HILMAR PÓR HILMARSSON

nova publishers

New York

For permission to use material from this book please contact us:
Telephone 631-231-7269; Fax 631-231-8175
Web Site: http://www.novapublishers.com

NOTICE TO THE READER

The Publisher has taken reasonable care in the preparation of this book, but makes no expressed or implied warranty of any kind and assumes no responsibility for any errors or omissions. No liability is assumed for incidental or consequential damages in connection with or arising out of information contained in this book. The Publisher shall not be liable for any special, consequential, or exemplary damages resulting, in whole or in part, from the readers' use of, or reliance upon, this material. Any parts of this book based on government reports are so indicated and copyright is claimed for those parts to the extent applicable to compilations of such works.

Independent verification should be sought for any data, advice or recommendations contained in this book. In addition, no responsibility is assumed by the publisher for any injury and/or damage to persons or property arising from any methods, products, instructions, ideas or otherwise contained in this publication.

This publication is designed to provide accurate and authoritative information with regard to the subject matter covered herein. It is sold with the clear understanding that the Publisher is not engaged in rendering legal or any other professional services. If legal or any other expert assistance is required, the services of a competent person should be sought. FROM A DECLARATION OF PARTICIPANTS JOINTLY ADOPTED BY A COMMITTEE OF THE AMERICAN BAR ASSOCIATION AND A COMMITTEE OF PUBLISHERS.

Additional color graphics may be available in the e-book version of this book.

Library of Congress Cataloging-in-Publication Data

ISBN: 978-1-63463-032-0

Published by Nova Science Publishers, Inc. † New York

To my mother and father

CONTENTS

Preface   ix

Acknowledgments   xiii

Acronyms and Abbreviations   xv

Introduction   xvii

Chapter 1   Small States during a Global Economic, Financial
                 and Social Crisis - Successes, Failures and
                 Vulnerabilities. Did They Own Their Reform
                 Programs? The Case of Latvia and Iceland   1

Chapter 2   Iceland's Cross Border Banking Expansion:
                 Dishonesty or Incompetence?   33

Chapter 3   Small States As Contributors to International
                 Development Cooperation. Can the Baltic States
                 Make a Difference Globally and if so How?
                 What Lessons Can They Learn from the
                 Scandinavian Countries?   71

Chapter 4   Small States and the Global Transition to Clean
                 Energy: Can Iceland Make a Difference in
                 Developing Countries in Partnership with
                 International Financial Institutions?   107

Chapter 5   Small States in a Global Economy.
                 Discussion, Lessons Learned, and Conclusion   143

Book Endorsements   163

Contents

About the Author   **167**

Index   **169**

PREFACE

In an era of globalization no country can be an island disconnected from the rest of the world and small states are now integrated in the global economy. The analysis in this book shows that the experiences of small states can be valuable for other countries but at the same time small states can be vulnerable. The book discusses several issues that are of global importance and analyses how small states are affected, why they can be vulnerable and how their experiences can be beneficial globally, including for larger states. The issues discussed include the 2008 global economic and financial crisis; governance issues and vulnerabilities in small states with small institutions and limited administrative capacity; international development cooperation; and how small states can contribute to the global transition to clean energy. Each chapter is a case study. Following the introducion the book is divided into five chapters as follows:

The first chapter (Small States during a Global Economic, Financial and Social Crisis – Successes, Failures and Vulnerabilities. Did They Own Their Reform Programs? The Case of Latvia and Iceland) examines the interaction between small states and external forces/actors during times of crisis. Those external forces include international organizations, especially the European Union and the IMF; other countries, especially the Scandinavian countries, and major central banks. To what extent were the governments of Iceland and Latvia in control of the situation during the 2008 economic and financial crisis and to what extent did they follow, or did they have to follow, the advice or instructions of outside forces, multilateral and bilateral? This chapter will also examine what role internal forces/actors played in responding to demands from larger nations, namely the Netherlands and the United Kingdom (UK), that were supported by the EU. This included two national referendums in Iceland, unprecedented in its history. This chapter will also critically evaluate the post crisis situation in Latvia and Iceland in terms of both economic outcomes and social progress.

The second chapter (Iceland's Cross Border Banking Expansion: Dishonesty or Incompetence?) examines the consequences of the privatization of Icelandic banks, followed by aggressive cross border expansion. The chapter will examine action and inaction by the Icelandic government to prevent the collapse of the banks as well as issues of economic integration, namely the EU allowing cross border banking expansion without host country bank supervision. It will also discuss the reactions of major central banks, including the Bank of England, the European Central Bank (ECB) and the Federal Reserve, as well as the Nordic central banks, when the Central Bank of Iceland sought their assistance before the crisis hit. Issues discussed include possible dishonesty and incompetence of the Icelandic government and the international community in reacting to this expansion both pre crisis and when the crisis hit.

The third chapter (Small States as Contributors to International Development Cooperation. Can the Baltic States Make a Difference Globally and if So How? What Lessons Can They Learn from the Scandinavian Countries?) discusses the international development cooperation of the Baltic States. Theory predicts that small states are more likely to work through international organizations than are larger states. This chapter discusses the bilateral development cooperation in which the Baltic States are engaged with their priority countries, as well as their participation in international development organizations. Reference is made to the Scandinavian countries, which remain very prominent contributors to international development cooperation in spite of their small size and that are also active in shaping the policies of international development organizations.

The fourth chapter (Small States and the Global Transition to Clean Energy. Can Iceland Make a Difference in Developing Countries in Partnership with International Financial Institutions?) discusses Iceland's potential to engage in geothermal energy projects in developing[1] and emerging market economies. Iceland has made the transition to clean energy, electricity production and space heating, which has received international attention. Clean energy projects, including geothermal and hydropower, tend to be large, capital intensive and long term, while Iceland, post crisis, does not have ambulant capital for cross border investments. Given the size and complex

---

[1] In this book, the term "developing countries" includes both low and middle income countries, while "emerging countries" are also developing countries but which tend to be in the middle income category.

nature of cross border energy projects in developing countries, this chapter discusses funding and risk mitigation for cross border energy projects in developing countries in partnership with international financial institutions.

The fifth and final chapter (Small States in a Global Economy. Discussion, Lessons Learned and Conclusions.) is the concluding chapter and discusses what lessons can be learned from the previous chapters, the challenges small states are faced with in a global economy, and how they can contribute constructively to the development and well being of other countries globally.

ACKNOWLEDGMENTS

In this book I draw on my experience in working for the World Bank for 12 years in three continents, from 1990 to 1995 and again from 1999 to 2006. I also benefited from serving as a Special Advisor for the Minister for Foreign Affairs in Iceland from 1995 to 1999. Since joining academia in 2006 I have also greatly benefited from interacting with students and faculty members at the following universities, while teaching, giving seminars or speaking at conferences: Aalborg University, American University Washington DC, Bifröst University, Bucharest Academy of Economic Studies, Copenhagen Business Academy, Cornell University, Georgetown University, Kaunas University of Applied Sciences, Klaipeda University, Odessa National Academy of Food Technologies, Pacific Lutheran University, Riga Stradins University, Stockholm School of Economics in Riga, Södertörn University, Tallinn University of Technology, University of Akureyri, University of California Berkeley, University of California Los Angeles, University of Iceland, University of Illinois at Chicago, University of Latvia, University of Mauritius, University of Porto, University of Tartu, the University of Washington, University of York, Vytautas Magnus University and Yale University.

Earlier versions of the following chapters were presented at the following conferences or seminars: Chapter 1 at the Baltic and Scandinavian Studies conference at Yale University on March 15, 2014. Chapter 2 in seminars at Cornell University on March 3, 2014; University of California Berkeley (UC Berkeley) on May 7, 2014 and University of California Los Angeles (UCLA) on May 3, 2014. The seminar at UC Berkeley was co-sponsored by the European Union Center of Excellence; the Institute of European Studies; and the Institute of Slavic, East European, and Eurasian Studies. The seminar at UCLA was sponsored by UCLA Scandinavian Section. Chapter 3 was presented in a seminar at Cornell University on March 4, 2014. The Seminar was sponsored by Cornell's Earth Energy Institute, IGERT. Chapter 4 was discussed at the 23rd Conference on Baltic Studies at the University of Illinois at Chicago on April 26, 2012. At all these conferences and seminars the author benefited greatly from questions asked and comments made by participants.

Listing all the students and faculty members whom I have interacted with over the years would be too long but I would like to single out Thráinn Eggertsson, Professor of Economics, University of Iceland and Adjunct Professor, Hertie School of Governance, Berlin and Mr. Magnús Óskar Ingvarsson at the Sudurnes Comprehensive College, true friends and advisors for more than three decades. I would also like to thank my language editor Mr. Christopher Goddard for a careful review and editing of the text.

ACRONYMS AND ABBREVIATIONS

BIS	Bank of International Settlements
BOT	Build-Operate-Transfer
CBI	Central Bank of Iceland
CEO	chief executive officer
COFACE	A French company specialising in export credit insurance
CV	curriculum vitae
DFI	Development Financial Institutions
DPL	Development policy loan
DPO	Develop policy operation
EBRD	European Bank for Reconstruction and Development
EC	European Commission
ECA	Export Credit Agency
ECB	European Central Bank
EEA	European Economic Area
EFTA	European Free Trade Association
EIB	European Investment Bank
EKN	Exportkreditnämnden (Sweden)
EU	European Union
FDI	Foreign direct investment
FME	Fjármálaeftirlitið (Icelandic financial supervisory authority)
FY	Financial Year
FYR	Former Yugoslav Republic
GATT	General Agreement on Tariffs and Trade
GDP	Gross Domestic Product
GGDP	Global Geothermal Development Plan
GIEK	Garanti-instituttet for eksportkreditt (Norway)
GNI	Gross National Income

GNP	Gross National Product
HQ	headquarters
IBRD	International Bank for Reconstruction and Development
ICSID	International Center for Settlement of Investment Disputes
IDA	International Development Association
IFC	International Finance Corporation
IFI	International financial institutions
IMF	International Monetery Fund
MIGA	Multilateral Investment Guarantee Agency
NT2	Nam Theun 2
ODA	Official development assistance
OECD	Organization for Economic Cooperation and Development
PBA	Programme-based approach
PCG	Partial credit guarantee
PM	prime minister
PPP	Public-Private Partnership
PR	public relations
PRG	partial risk guarantee
PRI	political risk insurance
SIC	Special Investigation Commission (Iceland)
TRÚ	Tryggingardeild útflutnings (Icelandic export credit agency)
UK	United Kingdom
UN	United Nations
US/USA	United States /of America
VAT	value added tax
USSR	*Union of Soviet Socialist Republics*
WBG	World Bank Group
WEF	World Economic Forum
WTO	World Trade Organization

INTRODUCTION

SMALL STATES IN A GLOBAL ECONOMY – CRISIS, COOPERATION AND CONTRIBUTIONS

This book discusses small states in the global economy. It focuses on several recent small state issues that could also have global implications. These include how two small states, Iceland and Latvia, were affected by the 2008 global economic and financial crisis; how the government of Iceland failed in its response to excessive pre crisis banking expansion, which eventually resulted in the collapse of the banking system, and how the international community reacted; how small states like the Baltic States – Estonia, Latvia, and Lithuania – can draw on their own recent transition experience to contribute to the development of less advanced emerging countries; and finally how Iceland can contribute to the global transition to clean energy, drawing on its leadership in utilizing geothermal energy. During the discussion reference is made to other small states that Iceland and the Baltic States cooperate with, especially the Scandinavian countries: Denmark, Norway and Sweden.

Given the diverse issues addressed in this book, its theoretical approach is multidisciplinary, drawing on theories in economics and business administration, including finance; public administration and policy, as well as political science. This broad approach also reflects the author's academic training in business administration, economics and public administration, as well as diverse experience, including as a staff member of the World Bank Group for twelve years based in three continents, having been in government as an advisor to the Minister of Foreign Affairs for four years, and finally in academia for eight years lecturing, giving seminars and speaking at about 30 universities around the globe, including some of the world's leading universities.

As its title, *Small states in a global economy - crisis, cooperation and contributions*, suggests, the book discusses small state issues from different angles. Small states can be vulnerable during times of crisis, as the 2008 economic and financial crisis demonstrated in both Iceland and Latvia. They can also serve globally in a constructive way by cooperating and sharing their experience and reforms with other countries. An example of this is when Latvia assists less advanced states, such as Georgia, Moldova and Ukraine, in their transition. Small states can also be contributors and leaders in certain areas, for example Iceland in clean energy, and their contribution can be of global significance.

Small states may sometimes be discouraged to engage globally, given their limited resources and human capacity. This book argues that small states can play an important and constructive role in the international community. Partnership with international organizations and larger states could often make their global contributions more meaningful, as will be discussed in the following chapters on international development cooperation and on the transition to clean energy. The chapters on the economic and financial crises also show that small states can be vulnerable if other larger countries or international organizations seek to impose conditions on them to serve the interests of larger countries or a group of countries that hold a dominant position *vis-à-vis* small states.

What Is a Small State?

Since the focus of this book is on small states, the question arises: what exactly is a small state? Many authors have addressed this question (see, for example, Crowards, 2002, Thorhallsson, 2006, and Maass, 2009), but no consensus has been reached on a single definition. This question will perhaps never be settled, and some have queried whether there can, or should be, a single and universal definition of a small state. One criterion for determining whether a country is small is to look at the size of its population, its land area, productive capacity (the size of the economy as measured by gross domestic product (GDP)) and military capacity (size of the military) (East, 1975, p. 160). More recently some scholars have introduced additional variables to determine whether or not countries should be classified as small (see, e.g., the comprehensive analysis by Thorhallsson, 2006).

Countries can also be small in one sense and not in another. Sweden, for example, may be classified as a small state in Europe if one considers its population and the size of its economy; but Sweden is large in Europe if one considers its geographical size. Smallness can also be viewed differently in different regions of the world. South Korea, a high income economy with 50 million people and a strong military regards itself as a small state (Maass, 2009, p. 79) while Vietnam with a population larger than Germany, the most populous country in Europe, may consider itself a small state given its proximity to China, with the largest population in the world.

Small states can also be large in certain activities. For example, the Scandinavian countries, Denmark, Norway and Sweden, are all considered small in the small states literature. However, these countries are not small if one considers their absolute contributions in international development cooperation. This is because they contribute a larger share of their gross national income (GNI) to international development cooperation than any state that is considered large.

Small states can also possess special knowledge and experience that is valuable globally, thus making small states important. The Baltic States are small in international development cooperation if one considers their financial contributions, both in absolute and per capita terms. But they have made a transition from being provinces of the USSR to becoming modern states in a short time. Their transition experience can be especially valuable to other more fragile states in Europe and Central Asia that share a similar history. Iceland is a small state, but it has extensive experience in the utilization of geothermal energy, which has received international attention. This experience is valuable globally during times when many nations want to make a transition to clean energy for environmental reasons, and forms part of the global fight against climate change.

Among European Union (EU) countries, Germany, Britain, France, Italy, Spain and Poland are traditionally classified as large states while the remaining 22 EU member states are classified as small. According to these criteria countries like Iceland (a non EU member) and the Baltic States, discussed in this book, are all small states. The Scandinavian countries referred to are also considered small states here.

A final issue to mention is that small states can be influential if they cooperate in groups. One example that will be discussed in this book is how the Baltic and Nordic[1] countries cooperate in the Bretton Woods institutions, i.e., the World Bank and the International Monetary Fund (IMF). For example, arguably these countries are more influential in the World Bank than their size would suggest because some countries in this group are more generous in their support for international development cooperation than large states while some countries in this group have unique transition experience.

Small States and Multilateralism

As stated above the issues discussed in this book include the 2008 global economic and financial crisis; governance issues and vulnerabilities in small states with small institutions and limited administrative capacity; international development cooperation; and how small states can contribute to the global transition to clean energy. Key issues in this regard relate to how small countries work with international organizations, as well as other countries, when crisis hits (Iceland and Latvia); how they organize themselves when they contribute to the development and transition of other countries, and if they emphasize bilateral cooperation or partnership with others, including multilateral institutions (the Baltic States). There is also discussion about how a small country (Iceland) can contribute globally to the transition to clean energy in cooperation with international financial institutions.

Multilateralism is the international governance of the many. It opens up the possibility for small states along with larger states to participate in international decision making. According to Thorhallsson, the small states literature generally claims that it is beneficial for small states to concentrate on multilateral relations within international organizations (Thorhallsson, 2005). When discussing multilateralism Kahler states that "Smaller, weaker states were believed to be disadvantaged by bilateralism..." and "[i]n their formal institutional design at least, most postwar multilateral institutions incorporated a larger role in decision making for states that were not great powers and could not aspire to be" (Kahler, 1992, p 681). When discussing small states as aid donors, Hoadley predicts high levels of participation by small states in multilateral agencies (Hoadley, 1980, p.129). More recently, Evans and Newnham argue that small states are said to show limited involvement in

---

[1] In this book reference is made to the Nordic countries which are: Denmark, Finland, Iceland, Norway and Sweden. Reference is also made to the Scandinavian countries which are: Denmark, Norway and Sweden.

international affairs, favor international governmental organizations, are strong advocates of International Law, shy away from the use of military force and in general have limited, mostly regional, foreign policy priorities (Evans and Newnham, 1998, p. 500–501). Finally, Maass states that "[m]embership and participation in international governmental organizations is not only a frequent priority of small states, but it has also been discussed as an indicator of independence, and as such as a secondary definitional requirement for small states in particular" (Maass, 2009, p. 69). A group of small states can also be influential as Ingebritsen argues, when discussing Scandinavian countries, that "these states exercise collective authority beyond their borders that exceed their military or economic might" (Ingebritsen, 2006, p. 1). She also argues that Scandinavians are likely to be found in groups that seek to strengthen international institutions. Keohane suggests that we focus on the systemic role that state leaders see their countries playing and their impact on the international community. These are the following: *System-determining* when a state plays a critical role in shaping the international system; *System-influencing* are states that cannot expect individually to dominate the international system but may be able to influence it through unilateral or multilateral action; *System-affecting* states are those that cannot affect the international system if acting alone but can exert significant impact on the system if working through small groups or alliances or through universal or regional international organizations; and finally *System-ineffectual* states are those that can do little to influence the system-wide forces that affect them, except in groups which are so large that each state has minimal influence (Keohane, 1969, pp. 295 - 296).

How can this categorization contribute to the behavior of small states in international organizations? As Keohane observes, "...a major function of international organizations – perceived by many small and middle powers – is to allow these states acting collectively to help shape developing international attitudes, dogmas and codes of proper behavior" (Keohane, 1969, p. 297). The Baltic States and Iceland, acting alone or in partnership with a very large number of other countries, are likely to have little impact and would probably be classified as *system-ineffectual*. These states could probably do little in most cases to influence system-wide forces. However, situations do exist, including international development cooperation, where small countries that work in partnership such as the Nordic-Baltic group can become *system-affecting*. This is because the Nordic countries, especially Denmark, Norway and Sweden, are leaders in international development cooperation and can, as a group, have significant impact globally. Although it is useful to review the small states literature, one must keep in mind that no universal formula explains how small states act in international organizations. This varies depending on many issues, including how these institutions are organized, what the issues are, and other factors. For example, the World Bank Group, often referred to in this book, consists of five institutions each with its own structure and instruments. Small states in Europe can also respond differently to international events from small states in Asia or Africa. The Scandinavian countries may act differently from other small states in Europe, for example, because they are relatively rich and deploy strong welfare systems for their citizens. Small states may also behave in a certain way, not because they are small states, but because of something else that needs to be explained.

Multilateral Institutions Discussed in the Book

An overview of the multilateral institutions or international organizations discussed in this book is shown in Table 0.1 below. The broadest term used for multilateral institutions is international organizations.

Table 0.1. Multilateral Institutions/International Organizations discussed in the book

International Organizations		
EU, NATO, UN, and International Financial Institutions (IFIs)	*IFIs*	
	Bank of International Settlements, *IMF, World Bank Group and Regional Development Banks*	*Regional Development Banks*
		African Development Bank, Asian Development Bank, European Bank for Reconstruction and Development (EBRD) and Inter-American Development Bank
EU		
IFIs: Bank of International Settlements, IMF, World Bank Group, as well as the Regional Development Banks, i.e., African Development Bank, Asian Development Bank, EBRD and Inter-American Development Bank.		
NATO		
UN		

Source: Constructed by the author.

A sub-category under international organizations is international financial institutions (IFIs), which are international organizations whose focus is mainly on financial issues and economic development. Yet another sub-category under international financial institutions is regional development banks. These are international financial institutions but focus on specific regions: Africa, America, Asia and Europe; while IFIs such as the World Bank Group have a global focus.

Issues Discussed in Each Chapter, Questions Asked and Propositions

This book will analyze the behavior of small states to see how they act and how they relate to international organizations, especially international financial institutions, as well as other states, including larger states. Small states sometimes need to approach international organizations and other states for assistance, for example during times of crisis. Small states can also assist other states and contribute to international development cooperation. However, that often requires cooperation with the international community, including international organizations. Small states can also be leaders in certain areas such as transition to clean energy but they may need to work with regional or global bodies such as international financial institutions. This will be discussed in the chapters that follow. Usually, small states that are members of international organizations must contribute to them financially and participate in their activities. That requires domestic staff with the knowledge and capacity to work with those institutions. Small states may choose not to be members of all international organizations e.g., Iceland and the Baltic States are not members of the regional development banks focusing on Africa, America and Asia, i.e., the African Development Bank, the Asian Development Bank, and the Inter-American Development Bank.

The first chapter (Small states during a global economic, financial and social crisis – Successes, failures and vulnerabilities. Did they own their reform programs? The case of Latvia and Iceland) examines the interaction between small states and external forces/actors during times of crisis. Those external forces include international organizations, especially the European Union and the IMF; other countries, especially the Scandinavian countries, and major central banks. To what extent were the governments of Iceland and Latvia in control of the situation during the 2008 economic and financial crisis and to what extent did they follow, or did they have to follow, the advice or instructions of outside forces, multilateral and bilateral? This chapter will also examine what role internal forces/actors played in responding to demands from larger nations, namely the Netherlands and the United Kingdom (UK), that were supported by the EU. This included two national referendums in Iceland, unprecedented in its history. This chapter will also critically evaluate the post crisis situation in Latvia and Iceland in terms of both economic outcomes and social progress.

The objective of this chapter is to analyze the challenges faced and action taken by the governments of Iceland and Latvia during the 2008 crisis. To what extent was the response to the crisis the choice of the domestic governments in Iceland and Latvia exercising strong government "ownership"? To what extent were actions taken shaped by external actors, including economic interests, such as bank owners from other countries and international organizations such as the IMF and the EU? Were the policy outcomes favorable for those small states if one considers economic and social performance?

Proposition

It is beneficial for small states to be members of multilateral institutions such as the EU when crisis hits since small states have limited resources and human capacity to deal with crisis situations and are likely to receive support and assistance from international organizations should things go wrong domestically. Small states can also benefit during a crisis from being part of a group such as the Nordic Baltic group since they can receive support from friendly countries in such a group.

The second chapter *(Iceland's cross border banking expansion: dishonesty or incompetence?)* examines the consequences of the privatization of Icelandic banks, followed by aggressive cross border expansion. The chapter will examine action and inaction by the Icelandic government to prevent the collapse of the banks as well as issues of economic integration, namely the EU allowing cross border banking expansion without host country bank supervision. It will also discuss the reactions of major central banks, including the Bank of England, the European Central Bank (ECB) and the Federal Reserve, as well as the Nordic central banks, when the Central Bank of Iceland sought their assistance before the crisis hit. Issues discussed include possible dishonesty and incompetence of the Icelandic government and the international community in reacting to this expansion both pre crisis and when the crisis hit.

The objective of the chapter is to address the following questions: Did the Icelandic government take appropriate action when the Icelandic banks expanded with investments and operations overseas? Was inaction a problem? Can the government be charged with attempting to fake reality? Is it possible that the government was honest but incompetent and therefore not trustworthy? Similarly, did the international community, including the European Union, take appropriate action when the Icelandic banks expanded with investments and operations overseas? Was inaction a problem? Can the international community be charged with attempting to fake reality, i.e., pretend that Iceland had responsibilities that it did not have? Is it possible that the international community was honest but demonstrated incompetence and is therefore not trustworthy? Put differently, during the crisis a failure of European integration was exposed, but larger countries, the UK and the Netherlands, supported by the EU tried to use force to have a small country suffer the consequences.

Proposition

Small countries like Iceland benefit from being members of multilateral arrangements such as the European Economic Area and generally benefit from European integration and open access to markets, including financial markets. When crisis hits, small states such as Iceland also benefit from being part of a group of nations like the Nordic countries and are likely to receive assistance from nations with whom it has friendly political relations.

The third chapter (Small states as contributors to international development cooperation. Can the Baltic States make a difference globally and if so how? What lessons can they learn from the Scandinavian countries?) discusses the international development cooperation of the Baltic States. Theory predicts that small states are more likely to work through international organizations than are larger states. This chapter discusses the bilateral development cooperation in which the Baltic States are engaged with their priority countries, as well as their participation in international development organizations. Reference is made to the Scandinavian countries, which remain very prominent contributors to international development cooperation in spite of their small size and active in shaping the policies of international development organizations.

The objective of this chapter is to assess what role small states can play in assisting their partner countries in implementing economic transition and achieving economic growth and poverty reduction. The countries focused on are mainly the Baltic States as participants in multilateral institutions and providers of bilateral assistance to the partner countries they have selected. How should the Baltic States assist their partner countries in the future? How can the Baltic States best share their transition experience with less advanced transition countries? Should they focus on small bilateral projects or should they work in partnership with other bilateral and multilateral donors? Should they engage in budget support operations and participate in policy dialogue or concentrate on small projects, or some combination of both?

Proposition

Small states can increase their development effectiveness by cooperating with international financial institutions and by engaging in policy dialogue with their priority countries in partnership with IFIs and other countries. Small countries can further increase their development effectiveness by providing technical assistance to support policy actions that they consider important for their priority countries.

The fourth chapter (Small states and the global transition to clean energy. Can Iceland make a difference in developing countries in partnership with the international financial institutions?) discusses Iceland's potential to engage in geothermal energy projects in developing[2] and emerging market economies. Iceland has made the transition to clean energy, electricity production and space heating, which has received international attention. Clean energy projects, including geothermal and hydropower, tend to be large, capital intensive and long term, while Iceland, post crisis, does not have ambulant capital for cross border investments. Given the size and complex nature of cross border energy projects in developing countries, this chapter discusses funding and risk mitigation for cross border energy projects in developing countries in partnership with international financial institutions.

The objective of this chapter is to answer the following questions: How can companies from small countries like Iceland contribute to the transition to clean energy in developing and emerging market economies? How can risks be mitigated when investing in clean energy projects in developing countries? Does the international community offer a comprehensive framework for risk mitigation for investments in developing countries?

---

[2] In this book, the term "developing countries" includes both low and middle income countries, while "emerging countries" are also developing countries but which tend to be in the middle income category.

Proposition

Small states usually have little leverage in solving disputes bilaterally with developing and emerging market countries that are often larger. Developing countries in transition typically have business and investment climates that need improvement and are being developed. Companies from small states can better manage risks in developing countries if they work in partnership with international financial institutions. IFIs have more leverage in developing countries as they often have multiple projects there and engage in policy dialogue, including on regulatory reform. Partnership with IFIs thus improves the risk profile of cross border investments from small states.

The fifth and final chapter (*Small States in a Global Economy. Discussion, lessons learned and conclusions.*) is the concluding chapter and discusses what lessons can be learned from the previous chapters, the challenges small states are faced with in a global economy, and how they can contribute constructively to the development and well being of other countries globally.

Organization of this book

Table 0.2. below shows broadly the organization of the book by chapter, issues discussed, countries analyzed and potential benefits for small states when participating in the activities of international financial institutions.

Table 0.2. Small states and multilateralism. Partnership with IFIs

Chapter 1	Chapter 2	Chapter 3	Chapter 4
Crisis and economic policy response. Austerity vs. growth	Crisis, dishonesty and incompetence. Domestic issues and international issues	Participation in international development cooperation and development effectiveness	Clean energy projects. Technical assistance, advisory service and cross border investments
Countries discussed			
Iceland and Latvia	Iceland	Baltic States and Nordic countries	Iceland
Potential benefits from partnering with IFIs			
Financial assistance, technical assistance and advisory services from IFIs during times of crisis		Increase in development effectiveness by participating in policy dialogue in partnership with IFIs in priority countries	Funding and risk mitigation in developing and emerging markets via partnership with IFIs. Use of IFI funding and risk mitigation instruments

Source: Constructed by the author.

REFERENCES

Crowards, T. (2002). Defining the category of 'small' states. *Journal of International Development*, *14*(2), 143-179, available at: http://onlinelibrary.wiley.com/doi/10.1002/jid.860/abstract (Accessed on April 2, 2014).

East, M.A. (1975). Size and Foreign Policy Behavior: A Test of Two Models. In: C.W. Kegley Jr. et al. (eds) International Events and the Comparative Analysis of Foreign Policy. Columbia, SC: University of South Carolina Press. Evans, G. and Newnham, J. (1998). The Penguin Dictionary of International Relations. London: Penguin Books.

Hoadley, J. S. (1980). Small states as aid donors, *International Organizations* 31, 1, Winter 1980, pp. 121-137, available at: http://www.jstor.org/stable/2706619 (Accessed on April 1, 2014).

Ingebritsen, C. (2006). *Scandinavia in world politics*. Rowman & Littlefield Publishers.

Kahler, M. (1992). Multilateralism with small and large numbers. *International Organizations*, Vol. 46, No. 3 (Summer, 1992), pp. 681-708, available at: http://www.jstor.org/stable/2706992 (Accessed on April 1, 2014).

Keohane, R. O. (1969) Lilliputians' Dilemmas: Small States in International Politics. *International Organizations*, Vol. 23, No. 2 (Spring, 1969), pp. 291-310.

Maass, M. (2009). The elusive definition of the small state. *International politics*, *46*(1), 65-83, available at: http://www.palgrave-journals.com/ip/journal/v46/n1/abs/ip200837a.html (Accessed on April 2, 2014).

Thorhallsson, B. (2005). What features determine small states' activities in the international arena? Iceland's approach to foreign relations until the mid-1990s. *Stjórnmál og stjórnsýsla – Veftímarit, Stofnun stjórnmála og stjórnsýslu*, Háskóli Íslands. 1:1, 107-140, available at: http://www.irpa.is/article/view/861/pdf_4 (Accessed on April 1, 2014).

Thorhallsson, B. (2006). The size of states in the European Union: Theoretical and conceptual perspectives. *European Integration*, *28*(1), 7-31, available at: http://www.tandfonline.com/doi/abs/10.1080/07036330500480490#. UzuCFqJkUm8 (Accessed on April 2, 2014).

Small States during a Global Economic, Financial and Social Crisis - Successes, Failures and Vulnerabilities.
Did They Own Their Reform Programs?
The Case of Latvia and Iceland[1]

Summary

The global economic and financial crisis hit hard in Iceland and Latvia. Economic developments prior to the crisis, as well as responses to the crisis were, however, different in these two countries, yielding different results. Both countries received assistance from the International Monetary Fund (IMF) during the crisis and the IMF has labeled their reform programs as success stories, praising their governments as having had strong "ownership" over their actions during the crisis. Prior to the crisis both countries had privatized their banking systems. In Iceland the banks were sold to local investors. In Latvia the banks were mostly owned by international investors. During the crisis Iceland nationalized its largest banks. In Latvia the foreign owned

---

[1] An earlier version of this chapter was presented by the author at the Baltic and Scandinavian Studies conference at Yale University on March 15, 2014. The author benefited from questions asked and comments made by participants during the conference.

banking system survived. Iceland experienced a large currency depreciation that boosted exports and mitigated GDP decline. In Latvia the national currency, linked to the Euro, did not depreciate but Latvia suffered a large GDP decline with high unemployment. Thus privatization of the banking system prior to the crisis was very different as indeed was the response to the crisis. The post crisis economic situation in Latvia and Iceland is also different with a milder adjustment in Iceland e.g., lower unemployment. It appears that neither Iceland nor Latvia had "ownership" over their reform programs. Iceland was isolated during the crisis and could not assemble assistance to rescue its banking system while in Latvia external actors took control led by the EU and the Nordic owners of the banking system. Both countries adjusted and made sacrifices, implementing painful budget cuts during the crisis so that both countries are enjoying GDP growth well beyond the EU and Euro area. Unemployment has gone down in both countries but high long term unemployment is still a concern in Latvia in spite of large migration from the country. Neither Iceland nor Latvia has yet returned to full economic health, and both face future challenges. By damaging the social fabric in Latvia, a burden has been placed on future generations and many of the youngest and best educated people, potential reformers, have left the country. In Iceland, planned debt forgiveness for households and corporates is a risky strategy that imposes a burden on future generations and encourages free riding in society. This is likely to result in slower economic growth. While this study focuses on Iceland and Latvia the results could be interesting for other small countries. Moreover, the fact that these two countries responded so differently to the crisis makes a comparative case study feasible. Important lessons can be learned about the effects of different policy responses on economic recovery in small countries.

INTRODUCTION

Iceland and Latvia are small countries in Europe hit hard by the 2008 global economic and financial crisis. Both responded, but in different ways. In terms of fiscal adjustment the governments of both countries implemented painful budget cuts although the front loaded fiscal austerity program in Latvia was more radical. In terms of exchange rate policy the response was different. Latvia, an EU member state, maintained a fixed exchange rate, with the Lat pegged to the Euro. In contrast the Icelandic Krona depreciated sharply and the government introduced a policy of capital controls.[2] Latvia received extensive external assistance during the crisis while Iceland was isolated with "friendly" nations hesitating to get involved and some being hostile[3].

In 2011 the incumbent prime minister of Latvia co-authored a book, "How Latvia Came through the Financial Crisis." This book presents Latvia's reform program as a success story, and an example of how a crisis should be resolved (Åslund and Dombrovskis, 2011). The authors even suggested Latvia as a success story for the rest of the world to follow. This chapter will look at that "success story" from the viewpoint of both economic developments and social progress. Iceland on the other hand has not been similarly presented as a success story but it did follow an unconventional path involving massive depreciation and the introduction of capital controls. Practically the whole banking system in Iceland collapsed in a few days while the mostly foreign owned banking system in Latvia was rescued although Parex bank, which was in local ownership, was nationalized.

While Iceland and Latvia are both small European countries hit hard by the global crisis, it is important to keep in mind that in many ways they are very different. They have their own history and culture and they are at different stages of development, economically and socially. Iceland remains outside the EU while Latvia has now been an EU member for about ten years. According to World Bank classifications Iceland is a high income OECD country that has a welfare program similar to other Nordic countries while

---

[2] While Iceland is not a member of the European Union it is part of the European Economic Area where labor, goods, services and capital are to flow freely. Capital controls are inconsistent with this policy, but in the case of Iceland the international community through the IMF, and thus the EU, accepted capital controls in Iceland. The question remains how long this policy will be accepted and when the government of Iceland will be prepared to remove these controls.

[3] The Faroe Islands, Poland and Russia were the only countries that supported Iceland from the beginning. The Scandinavian countries initally hesitated to get involved. The UK was hostile, using anti-terrorism legislation against Iceland. Iceland's dispute with the UK and the Netherlands, because of the so called Icesave accounts, may have influenced the Scandinavian countries. The government of Iceland probably overestimated potential support from the Scandinavian countries, which were more likely to serve their own economic and political interests in the UK and in the Netherlands than to support Iceland during a period of crisis and uncertainty. In fact the Report of the Special Investigation Commission (SIC) chapter 4.5.6.2. documents communications between the Central Bank of Sweden and the Bank of England that show the close relationship between those two institutions when the Central Bank of Iceland was isolated. This shows how naïve the Icelandic authorities were in relying on Scandinavian countries for assistance when they could and should have known that the Scandinavian Central Banks first and foremost would consider their own interests as for them their relationship with the Bank of England was much more important than their relationship with the Central Bank of Iceland.

Latvia remains on the margin of an upper middle income and high income country and is still in transition where poverty, social exclusion and income inequality remain serious concerns.

The fact that Iceland and Latvia are small countries that were severely affected by the crisis, and that they responded differently, makes them an interesting comparator case. Nevertheless, because these countries are different this chapter will also refer to other high and middle income countries in Europe when thought to be relevant and useful.

While the focus here is on Iceland and Latvia the study could also be of relevance for other countries. Important lessons may be learned about the effects of different policy responses during times of crisis, including in the European Union and the Euro area. In fact, among the main reasons for new member states to seek membership in the EU has been its economic success. For the time being this success has disappeared. Both the EU and the Euro area continue to experience slow economic growth and high unemployment especially among its youth. Poverty and social exclusion are increasing concerns within the EU and income inequality is alarming in some countries. High levels of long term unemployment within the EU will without doubt reduce long term growth in the area but little attention has been given to this matter so far.

Iceland recently decided to stop its accession negotiations with the EU and the negotiating team has been dissolved. The benefits of EU membership are in doubt, at least for the time being, and too many people feel that the EU has not adequately dealt with its problems, including a sick banking system where the strategy seems to have been to buy time. There also seems to be a tendency to keep imposing additional burdens on taxpayers to keep the financial sector going.[4] Additionally, social problems are alarming, including dismal prospects for young people to find jobs.

After more than five years since the crisis erupted sufficient time has passed for observers to begin seeing the outcomes from the different policy responses, in terms of both economic and social progress. Perhaps it is time to see what lessons can be learned for Latvia and Iceland; perhaps also for the European Union and the Euro area.

Both countries sought and received assistance from the IMF during the crisis. Iceland also received assistance from the Nordic countries, the Faroe Islands and Poland. Latvia received much broader assistance. As a European Union member it approached the EU, and as an emerging market country it

---

[4] The bailout of the Irish Banks at the cost of taxpayers is particularly alarming.

could approach the World Bank and the European Bank for Reconstruction and Development (EBRD). Iceland as a high income OECD county could not have requested assistance from the World Bank and EBRD. Like Iceland, Latvia also received assistance from the Nordic countries as well as from Estonia, the Czech Republic and Poland.

Iceland received some limited assistance from the Nordic central banks prior to the crisis (1.5 billion Euro). However, that proved insufficient and all its largest banks collapsed during the crisis. In Latvia the rescue of its mostly foreign-owned banking system was a key element in its recovery plan with strong Nordic and EU involvement. Clearly external parties and interests played a key role in determining the fate of the banking system in these two countries as well as in designing their recovery programs. Nevertheless external forces, bilateral and multilateral, including the IMF, claim that the governments of Latvia and Iceland enjoyed strong "ownership" of their reform programs, which they label as successful. EU and Nordic interests were very active in determining in what direction Latvia should go post-crisis but were much less concerned and showed less interest in the fate of Iceland, whose banking system was in local ownership.

The objective of this chapter is to analyze the challenges faced and the action taken by the governments of Iceland and Latvia during the 2008 crisis. To what extent was the response to the crisis the choice of the domestic governments in Iceland and Latvia in exercising strong government "ownership"? To what extent were the actions taken shaped by external actors, including economic interests, such as bank owners from other countries, and international organizations such as the IMF and the EU? Were the policy outcomes favorable for those small states in terms of economic and social performance?

The proposition in this chapter is: It is beneficial for small states to be members of multilateral institutions such as the EU when crisis hits since small states have limited resources and human capacity to deal with crisis situations and are likely to receive support and assistance from international organizations should things go wrong domestically. Small states can also benefit during a crisis from being part of a group such as the Nordic Baltic group since they can receive support from friendly countries in such a group.

What Does Ownership Mean for the IMF? Some Definitions

According to the IMF strong ownership of a program is "when the government is actively engaged in designing the program, publicly communicates its support for the program, and implements it with conviction."[5] A more formal IMF definition of ownership can be found in the 2001 IMF Board paper "Strengthening Country Ownership of Fund-Supported Programs." There, ownership "is a willing assumption of responsibility for an agreed program of policies, by officials in a borrowing country who have the responsibility to formulate and carry out those policies, based on an understanding that the program is achievable and is in the country's own interest" (IMF, 2001, p. 6). In the same report the IMF states that it "generally advocates outward-looking and market-oriented reforms, seeks to minimize adverse social and environmental impacts, and insists upon certain standards of governance on matters pertinent on the use of Fund resources" (IMF, 2001, p. 4).

This is an interesting statement and both Latvia and Iceland can be classified as outward looking and market oriented. Both countries are also very open to external trade but regarding market orientation Latvia is still in transition. The IMF statement on minimizing adverse social impact is notable especially for Latvia given its poor social record and harsh treatment of the most vulnerable members of its society that became even more evident during the crisis. This will be discussed in more detail in later sections of this paper. On governance issues Iceland has for a long time been perceived as a country with a low level of corruption. However, during the crisis serious corruption cases surfaced.[6] In contrast, Latvia has long been associated with corruption and a case of "state capture" according to the World Bank.

A review of the extensive collection of reports on Iceland and Latvia during the crisis that can be found on the IMF website reveals frequent reference to "ownership", often program ownership (referring to reform programs designed and implemented in these countries as a response to the crisis). But whose ownership is the IMF talking about?

In the first definition above, the IMF talks about the government and in a more formal definition talks about officials in a borrowing country. Who are these officials? Are they the cabinet of ministers and the central bank president (who may or may not agree about the reform program)? Does this include e.g.,

---

[5] According to an email from Daria V. Zakharova IMF received on December 16, 2013.
[6] For discussion about government negligence and dishonesty prior to the crisis in Iceland, see chapter 2.

higher political authorities who may take action to overrule the economic authorities, e.g., a president who, under the constitution as in the case of Iceland, can refuse to sign legislation and call for a national referendum? Does this include the parliament or the majority of the parliament? What about regional authorities? What about interest groups or NGOs, and so on?

Often the IMF simply talks about strong program ownership without any clarification of exactly who the owners are. How does the IMF judge whether or not ownership of a program exists? Frequently, lack of clarity and transparency are apparent when the term 'ownership' is used. Thus the concept of ownership can be used to describe commitment, but it can also be abused when it is unclear who is committed. A review of IMF programs, including the recent programs in Latvia and Iceland, shows that ownership of a reform program is frequently mentioned without any attempt at all to explain what ownership is and how the IMF observes ownership. This statement can be used to legitimize actions that in reality have little support in a country. The risk arises, for example, that the authorities in a country may serve narrow interests rather than national interests e.g., political or financial elites.

When the IMF talks about ownership it usually seems to mean some kind of government ownership although it is not clear which players in the government the IMF considers in each case. And even if it is clear which part of the government is taking ownership of a program, what does ownership imply?

On one extreme, the government could be expected to take the responsibility to do what the IMF insists that it does. On the other extreme, ownership could mean that the government takes the lead and designs its own policies and programs so that the IMF only plays a supportive or advisory role. A compromise is also possible where ownership becomes a shared vision of the borrowing government and the IMF. This seems to be the understanding in the formal IMF definition referred to above, which talks about "an agreed program of policies."

In addition to problems in achieving consensus within governments and a shared vision with the IMF, the risk also arises that national authorities are influenced or even captured by strong outside interests. A borrowing government may be dependent on other countries whose private sector has e.g., invested intensively in or has important trade relations with the borrowing country. Another risk relates to interference by other institutions, e.g., international financial institutions such as the World Bank or regional development banks, and supranational institutions such as the European Union of which the borrowing country is a member. The risk is especially high when the borrowing country is in great need of outside assistance from those institutions. The borrowing country may be tempted to serve outside interests when it designs its program at the cost of serving its constituents. This is especially true of situations when the IMF is only providing part of a loan to a borrowing government to support a reform program while third countries or other international organizations provide the bulk of the funding.

Policy Response and "Government Ownership"

When the crisis hit Iceland and Latvia, the response in the two countries was very different. In reality Iceland had no choice but to let its national currency depreciate sharply. The depreciation in nominal terms was about 50 percent. Limited fiscal space and insufficient reserves in the Central Bank of Iceland meant that Iceland did not have the capacity to defend its banks and currency. This is clear and statements that the Icelandic government decided to depreciate its currency do not hold water. Iceland was isolated and sufficient international assistance to defend its local currency could not be assembled.[7]

Latvia on the other hand went for internal devaluation by attempting to cut wages (mainly public wages) and prices sharply. This response was consistent with its goal at the time to adopt the Euro.[8] Latvia's policy response was supported by a large international rescue package worth 7.5 billion Euro, then more than one third of Latvia's GDP. This package was provided by the IMF, the EU, the European Bank for Reconstruction and Development (EBRD), the World Bank, and bilaterally by countries, especially Scandinavian countries, that had made large investments in the banking sector and had a strong interest in Latvia's recovery (see Table 1.1). Even one of the Baltic States, Estonia, offered assistance to Latvia. Latvia's adoption of the Euro required a peg to the Euro and this international effort enabled Latvia to fulfill its commitments.

Iceland, a non EU member state, could not rely on the EU as did Latvia. Moreover, Iceland could not go to the World Bank or the EBRD since Iceland is a high income OECD donor country. Latvia, with its EU membership and middle income status, when the crisis hit, had access to multilateral development banks. In addition, the foreign owners of the banks in Latvia

---

[7] This is well documented in The Special Investigation Commission (SIC) report delivered to the Althingi on April 12 2010. See for example chapter 4.5.6.2.

[8] Latvia adopted the Euro in January 2014.

were not passive bystanders during the crisis: they defended their own interests.

Table 1.1. Latvia Rescue Package – Burden Sharing

	Billion Euro	Percentage of total
EU	3.1	41.3
Nordic countries	1.8	24.0
IMF	1.7	22.7
World Bank and EBRD	0.5	6.7
Czech Republic, Poland and Estonia	0.4	5.3
Total	7.5	100
In Hungary the IMF provided 63 percent of the Rescue Package and in Romania 65 percent.		

Source: IMF, 2013b.

The Latvian government claims to have decided to keep a fixed exchange rate regime in Latvia, while the IMF initially suggested a 15 percent depreciation of the Lat. The policy to keep the exchange rate fixed was, however, clearly favored by external interests, especially Scandinavian banks (mostly Swedish), which owned most of the Latvian banking system, and the European Union. EU interests feared the effects of a large depreciation on the banking sector in the other Baltic States and the Scandinavian countries that then could spill over to other EU member states. Disorderly devaluation would have caused a Swedish Banking crisis (Åslund and Dombrovskis, 2011, p. 116). This is understandable, not only because of Swedish investments in the banking sector in the Baltic States, including Latvia, but also because of inter-linkages between the Nordic banks that made them vulnerable, as will be discussed below. These vulnerabilities still exist post-crisis.

When the banks were privatized in Iceland, they were sold to local interests or more precisely local actors with political interests and connections (see chapter 2). No foreign investment was made in the Icelandic banks and no foreign banks were operating in Iceland when the crisis hit. This was fundamentally different in Latvia where foreign investors became the owners of most of the banking system, except for Parex bank and some other small local banks. Given the size of the banking system in Iceland, with total assets of more than nine times GDP[9] the local government had no choice other than

---

[9] According to the IMF the consolidated assets of the three main Icelandic banks increased from 100 percent of GDP in 2004 to 923 percent at end 2007, reflecting expansion overseas. By

to let the banks fall. In Latvia the mostly foreign owned banking system was rescued via a concerted international effort led by external interests. It is highly questionable whether the Latvian government had any choice other than to rescue the banks if it wanted to keep good standing within the EU. Depreciation of the Lat would clearly not have been in the interests of the Euro area.

As discussed above the IMF likes to talk about strong ownership of the reform program in Iceland and Latvia. In the initial phases of the crisis there was hardly much ownership in Iceland as there was only one way to go: sharp exchange rate depreciation and collapse of the major banks. The government made desperate efforts to save the banks but was isolated (SIC, 2010). Latvian government ownership can also be questioned: as the IMF says, "[t]he European Commission was heavily involved in program design, especially in the fiscal and financial sectors" (IMF, 2013b, p. 7). When discussing the aggressive government cuts in the education and health sectors in Latvia during the crisis, Åslund and Dombrovskis state: "reform starts where the money ends" (Åslund and Dombrovskis, 2011, p. 73). The policy was chosen because the flow of outside money had ended, not necessarily because the government or the people wanted to tread this path. The foreign owned banks also had a strong voice and as the IMF chief economist said in a recent conference paper "if your financial sector is largely composed of foreign subsidiaries, it is a good idea to be friends with the parent banks" (Blanchard, et al., 2013, p. 33). And friends they were.

During the crisis capital controls were introduced in Iceland, but not in Latvia. The decision to introduce capital controls was supported by the IMF, and thus also the EU, whose member states are represented on the IMF board of directors. Those controls were introduced as a temporary measure. Capital controls helped prevent the currency from depreciating further than it did. Nevertheless the sharp depreciation resulted in household and corporate balance sheet problems, which still remain a hotly debated issue in Iceland. Adjustment of corporate and household debt is still debated and the current government has introduced a large package of debt relief for households that it may have a problem to deliver when considering the limited fiscal space available to policymakers. The government plans to implement tax cuts and large write-downs of household debt in the next four years. There is a high risk of free riding here, along with moral hazard. Those who took heavy risks and

---

end-2007, almost 50 percent of the three banks' assets were held abroad (IMF, 2008a, p. 11).

borrowed excessively will be allowed to impose costs on those who were more modest in their investments and borrowed little or nothing. Those who purchased more modest homes or rented a place to live will be punished. This is a dangerous path chosen by the government of Iceland.

The Fortuitous Coordinated Global Disinterest in Iceland's Plight

As argued above there is strong evidence to suggest that neither Iceland nor Latvia had a real choice when the crisis hit. Iceland could not save its banks and had little international support. The Special Investigation Commission's (SIC) report to the Icelandic parliament documents in some detail the desperate attempt by the government of Iceland via the Central Bank of Iceland to assemble outside assistance.

The Nordic central banks were contacted as well as major central banks such as the Bank of England, the European Central Bank (ECB) and the Federal Reserve in the United States. From the SIC report to the Icelandic parliament, it seems clear that a determination not to help strengthen the Central Bank of Iceland's foreign reserves was well coordinated by all these central banks (SIC, 2010).

It was a natural move for the Central Bank of Iceland to turn to the Bank of England for help because of the large expansion of Icelandic banks in the UK. That request was turned down and the SIC report shows that the Bank of England and the Swedish Central Bank were closely cooperating their response to the Central Bank of Iceland. Iceland could not expect much assistance from the ECB given that Iceland is not an EU member state. The large operations of Icelandic banks in the Euro area, e.g., in the Netherlands, must however have been a concern at the ECB.

It was also understandable that the Central Bank of Iceland would turn to the Federal Reserve in the United States for support. During the Cold War years Iceland could count on support from the US during critical times. The US was Iceland's strongest ally. But when the Cold War ended US interest in Iceland sharply diminished. In fact, the US Federal Reserve entered into a currency swaps agreement with Sweden, Norway and Denmark at the end of September 2008, an agreement to which Iceland was not a party. At this point the CBI was isolated and could only assemble limited support from the Nordic central banks. This proved insufficient to defend the local currency from a sharp depreciation and to rescue the local banks. Only after Iceland's banking system had collapsed did sufficient outside support emerge, this time with assistance from the Nordic countries, but under IMF conditions.

The Nordic countries never had a strong interest in saving the locally owned Icelandic banking system although the Icelandic authorities seem to have been naïve enough to think so, at least for some time. There seems to be a tendency among politicians in Iceland to believe that the Nordic countries can be counted upon as allies at all times when crisis hits in Iceland.

What often seems forgotten is that these are also just small countries that have a hard enough time defending their own interest globally. Why would the Nordic countries enter into a serious dispute with the UK to protect Iceland's interest? Their relationship with the UK is far more important than their relationship with Iceland and it is strange to assume that they would not primarily serve their own interests, especially during times of crisis. In addition, the Nordic central banks, especially the Swedish Central Bank/*Riksbank*, did not have much faith in the Central Bank of Iceland's handling of the situation. This became clear in a letter to the SIC from the Governor of the Central Bank of Sweden, Mr. Stefan Ingves, after the collapse of the Icelandic banks. In this letter he states "his opinion that unclear ownership and rapid expansion of the banks' balance sheets had caused a hazard which the Icelandic government had neither seemed to fully grasp, nor fully understand how to deal with by reducing the size of the banks" (SIC, 2010, p. 109).

In retrospect this coordinated global disinterest in Iceland may have been a big blessing for the nation although it may not have appeared so at the time these events were taking place. This meant that the local banks went into bankruptcy and were not saved, all at the cost of taxpayers as so commonly occurred in OECD countries that in many cases may have thrown good money after bad. Ireland is a good example: its banks were saved at taxpayers' cost; also Latvia, where the interests of foreign banks and the Euro area became more important than the interests of the Latvian people, as will be discussed below.

The Icesave[10] Dispute with the UK and the Netherlands

During the expansion of the three largest banks the president of Iceland played a key role in promoting them with high profile speeches overseas (see

---

[10] The Icesave accounts are discussed in more detail in chapter 2.

for example Hilmarsson, 2013). He thus took an active role in fueling their expansion. When the banks fell he played an important role in the international debate over Iceland's sovereign responsibility over the liabilities of these private banks.

When the Icelandic parliament agreed on a repayment scheme for the so called Icesave accounts the president activated a clause in the constitution that allows him to call a public referendum. The overwhelming majority of Icelanders rejected this repayment scheme. Again the parliament passed a new settlement with terms that were widely thought to be more favorable for Iceland. Again the president used his constitutional right to call for a referendum and again the nation rejected the deal.

In a speech after these events took place, the president stated as follows: "And when we faced the (...) Icesave dispute in which the Governments of the United Kingdom and the Netherlands, supported by all EU governments and others, demanded that the ordinary people of Iceland – fishermen, farmers, teachers, nurses – should shoulder through their taxes the debts of a failed private bank – we had to choose between the financial interests as they were presented by the established leadership of Europe and the democratic will of the Icelandic nation and decided to allow democracy to prevail. Following the two referendums, in which the people overwhelmingly voted No, the economy started to recover, becoming healthier with each quarter. The financial doomsayers, whether experts or leaders, who advised strongly against the democratic will of the people turned out to be entirely wrong in their analysis and predictions; a result which certainly should serve as a challenge to many of the policies which are still being advocated and followed in many countries" (Grimsson, 2013, p. 5-6). The president thus saw this not only as a dispute between a small country vs. the UK and the Netherlands, but as a battle of a small nation for democracy against the whole EU establishment. It was clear that the new government, elected after the collapse of the banks, was not able to stand up to the UK and the Netherlands and feared EU pressure even more.

During this crisis the Icelandic constitution served the nation well and fortunately the elected president had the courage to take action against the strong powers that had pushed an unfair and undemocratic deal down the throat of the new government. Later, when the EFTA Court ruled on this case in favor of Iceland, the president commented as follows: "When the EFTA Court last month ruled that there was no legal basis for the case of Britain, the Netherlands and the EU against Iceland, it became clear that in addition to the democratic will of the people, justice and the rule of law was also on our side" (Grimsson, 2013, p. 6). He was right.

EU Desperation and Scandinavian Rush to Latvia's Rescue

In the case of Latvia, it also appears that it had no choice. As soon as the crisis erupted, external actors took control, with a large rescue package (see Table 1.1).Unlike in Iceland, the possibility to let the banking system go under was never an option.

The EU feared the domino effect of a banking collapse in Latvia and acted swiftly, overruling the IMF's initial advice for 15 percent depreciation. There was no need for the Bank of Latvia to make desperate moves in generating interest and assembling assistance from Scandinavia. As the former Latvian PM and his co author document, "the Swedish Riksbank and the Danish central bank offered a bridge loan to keep Latvia going until the IMF-EU-Nordic package was concluded" (Åslund and Dombrovskis, 2011, p. 35). Nor did the Swedish government drag its feet in coming to Latvia's rescue. The "Swedish Minister of Finance Anders Borg called the closest friends of Latvia to an emergency meeting at Arlanda airport in Stockholm on December 10" (Åslund and Dombrovskis, 2011, p 46). There was not only a concern that things could go out of control in Riga: as the incumbent Latvian prime minister documented, "if multiple banks collapsed in all three Baltic Countries, the two Swedish banks, Swedbank and SEB, would be in serious trouble" (Åslund and Dombrovskis, 2011, p. 53).

The Swedish government was not impressed with the early discussion between the government of Latvia and the IMF about possible devaluation of the Lat and the EU was activated to push the IMF into a corner. The "Swedish Prime Minister Fredrik Reinfeldt stated publicly: We think that a clear signal of support from the EU would help them to achieve support from the IMF." (Åslund and Dombrovskis, 2011, p. 86).

Not all observers were impressed with these developments. One author commented: "[i]n Latvia, the neo-liberal insanity continues. The EU and IMF have told the government to borrow foreign currency to stabilize the exchange rate to help real estate debtors pay the foreign-currency mortgages taken out from Swedish and other banks to fuel its property bubble, raise taxes, and sharply cut back public spending on education, health care and other basic needs to "absorb" income. Higher taxes are to lower import demand and also domestic prices, as if this automatically will make output more competitive in export markets" (Auerback, 2009).

The overruled IMF commented as follows: "The unequivocal commitment of the authorities, and of the other stakeholders to the exchange rate peg has determined their choice of program strategy. Though this commitment augurs well for program ownership, the authorities also recognize that their choice brings difficult consequences, including the need for fiscal tightening and the possibility that recession could be protracted" (IMF, 2008b).

Good news for the Euro area. Not such good news for the most vulnerable Latvians.

The Risks of Nordic-Baltic Banking Sector Interconnectedness

As the incumbent Latvian PM and his co author observed after the crisis hit Latvia "[t]he Swedish Riksbank and the Financial Supervisory Authority (Finansinspektionen) should also have paid attention to the excessive exposure of the Swedish commercial banks to the Baltic economies, but they did nothing" (Åslund and Dombrovskis, 2011, p. 29). It seemed that the Swedish authorities had failed in their role in the Baltic States just as their sister institutions had failed in Iceland.

A recent IMF Working Paper has documented the risks and the still obvious vulnerabilities caused by the interconnected Scandinavian and Baltic banks post-crisis. "Over the last 10 years, the Nordic and Baltic financial systems have become increasingly interconnected. The Nordic banks have large cross border operations in the other Nordic countries, which partly explain the large size of the Swedish and Danish banking sectors in relation to the domestic economy. The Nordic banks also dominate the banking sectors in the Baltic countries to a varying extent. This means that risks in one country can easily spread to another" (Grönn and Fredholm, 2013, p. 6).

A common pre-crisis problem both in Iceland and Latvia was that the housing bubble had to a large extent been funded with loans in Euro (or other foreign currencies) taken by people with income in local currency. As Grönn and Fredholm state: "Another characteristic is that many of these banks were exposed to a large share of unhedged borrowers, with income in domestic currency and loans in foreign currency" (Grönn and Fredholm, 2013, p. 6).

This is one key reason why some people in Latvia had a common interest with the foreign banks. They, like the foreign banks, feared the balance sheet effects of devaluation. As Grönn and Fredholm state: "It should be mentioned that there is no risk as long as the fixed exchange rate is maintained, but can potentially imply large credit losses if the currencies were to depreciate. Since investors had underestimated the potential risks in the Baltic countries, the Nordic parent banks were allowed continued access to cheap funding at a price corresponding to the risk of the banking groups. The consequence of the Nordic parent banks not assessing their own risk properly in turn led to the interest rate offered to the Baltic borrowers being too low. This inadequate risk management contributed to large capital flows to these countries as the Nordic banks underestimated the risks of the exposure in the Baltic countries" (Grönn and Fredholm, 2013, p. 7).

When commenting on Iceland they say: "Before the crisis, Iceland's private sector had accumulated a relatively large share of FX-denominated debt as the tightening of monetary policy led to much higher interest rates on loans in Krona than in foreign currency. In addition to the macrofinancial risks posed by the FX-denominated debt, a large part of Icelandic household debt was also indexed to inflation. This exposed the financial sector to similar risks as the household balance sheets could be seriously impaired because of the rapid pass-through to the exchange rate" (Grönn and Fredholm, 2013, p. 7).

In Iceland the government could not defend the currency and a sharp depreciation soon materialized. All three major banks fell and many households faced financial hardship. Some loans were partly forgiven, some were declared illegal and the current government has recently introduced a plan to assist the most vulnerable households e.g., by taxing the banks.

In Latvia external forces kept the Lat at par with the Euro. There was no way that Latvia could have kept the peg on its own account. This was done with harsh austerity measures imposed in a country with an already weak welfare system and the most unequal income distribution in the European Union as will be discussed below. Grönn and Fredholm comment as follows: "However, it was not until after the crisis had materialized that broader austerity measures were implemented and approved by the Latvian government in the general government budget for 2009. The fiscal tightening was a prior action set by the IMF, EU and bilateral lenders" (Grönn and Fredholm, 2013, p. 7).

The former Latvian PM and his co author state that "Latvia also learned from the Swedish and Finnish banking and devaluation crisis in the early 1990s that banking collapses and devaluation should be avoided if possible" (Åslund and Dombrovskis, 2011, p. 117). This is a strange comment given that both Finland and Sweden which, unlike Latvia, have strong welfare systems, both allowed their currency to depreciate sharply during the 1990s crisis, which in both countries was followed by a period of strong export-led growth.

In a report published by the European Union in 2008, Jonung, et al., review the recovery of Finland and Sweden from 1993 to 2000. When commenting on Finland they state that "the biggest macroeconomc change contributing to the recovery was the loosening of monetary policy, including the currency depreciation in the aftermath of the 1992 EMS crisis" (Jonung, et al., 2008, p. 31). The cumulative depreciation of the Markka was more than 30 percent and according to them exports were the first component of GDP to recover. The effects of depreciation turned out to be long lasting. Unemployment in Finland fell from 17 percent in 1994 to 10 percent in 2000 and to 6 percent in 2008. When commenting on Sweden, Jonung, et al., state that "[t]he depreciation of the krona in November 1992 marked the culmination of the crisis and the beginning of the recovery in Sweden" (Jonung, et al., 2008, p. 36). The large depreciation increased Swedish competitiveness. Economic growth turned positive in 1993 and exports were the major driving force behind the Swedish recovery.

It is hard to see what lessons Latvia learned from the crisis in Finland and Sweden since both these countries depreciated their currency sharply followed by export-led growth. This has also been the experience in Iceland. Finland and Sweden did not stick with a fixed exchange rate and implement austerity programs, as Latvia did. However, austerity would not have been as ugly in Finland and Sweden as in Latvia since both countries have strong welfare programs and strong safety nets for the most vulnerable.

Some Economic Outcomes

During the crisis Latvia suffered the greatest fall in GDP of any country in the world: around 23 percent. Iceland was less affected with GDP falling about 10 percent (see Table 1.2). Prior to the crisis Latvia and Iceland had unusually large current account deficits – over 20 percent of GDP (see Table 1.1.; Latvia's current account deficit in 2007 was 22.4 percent of GDP).

Imports declined by about 40 percent in Iceland and Latvia during the crisis and investment collapsed in both countries. Private consumption declined during the crisis but growth has resumed in both countries. Both countries cut their government budget but public consumption adjusted more in Latvia than in Iceland (Darvas, 2011).

**Table 1.2. Real GDP, Consumer Prices, Current Account Balance,
and Unemployment**

Iceland	2008	2009	2010	2011	2012	2013	2014
						Estimate	Projection
Real GDP*	1.2	-6.6	-4.1	2.9	1.6	1.9	2.1
Consumer prices**	12.7	12.0	5.4	4.0	5.2	3.7	3.1
Current account balance***	-28.4	-11.6	-8.4	-5.6	-4.9	-1.2	-1.9
Unemployment****	1.6	8.0	8.1	7.4	5.8	5.1	4.6

Latvia	2008	2009	2010	2011	2012	2013	2014
						Estimate	Projection
Real GDP*	-3.3	-17.7	-0.9	5.5	5.6	4.0	4.2
Consumer prices**	15.3	3.3	-1.2	4.2	2.3	0.7	2.1
Current account balance***	-13.2	8.7	2.9	-2.1	-1.7	-1.1	-1.3
Unemployment****	7.5	16.9	18.6	16.2	15.0	11.9	10.7

Source: IMF, 2013a, IMF, 2013b
*) Annual percentage change
**) Movements in consumer prices are shown as annual averages
***) Percentage of GDP
****) Precent (National definitions of unemployment may differ).

Overall, the economic adjustment involved a larger decrease in output, a larger increase in unemployment, and more emigration in Latvia than in Iceland (see Tables 1.2 and 1.5). The question arises whether an alternative strategy for Latvia could have achieved a better outcome, e.g., by depreciating the Lat by around 15 percent as the IMF suggested. As Blanchard, et al. have stated, nobody can give a definitive answer (Blanchard, et al., 2013, p. 3). However, the experience of Finland and Sweden in the 1990s shows that depreciation in those countries resulted in healthy export-led growth and a reduction in unemployment and that these countries avoided austerity programs with the high human cost that Latvia now has to live with.

After more than five years of adjustment, unemployment in Latvia is about 12 percent and GDP is still about eight percent below the pre-crisis peak. Registered unemployment in Iceland is now about four percent. Both countries enjoy positive GDP growth rates that are much higher than the average EU or Euro area GDP growth rates. Latvia's GDP growth rate was projected by the IMF to be around four percent in 2013 while Iceland's growth was projected around two percent.[11] According to Statistics Iceland, GDP

---

[11] The Statistical Office in Iceland reports higher GDP growth rate for Iceland than does the IMF.

increased by 3.1 percent in the first nine months of 2013 (Statistics Iceland, 2013b). Both countries have dramatically improved their current account balance and the IMF projected only minor current account deficits in Iceland and Latvia[12] in 2013 and 2014 (see Table 1.2).

Social Progress

In terms of unemployment, job losses were much more dramatic in Latvia than in Iceland. As stated above unemployment in Iceland is about four percent but about 12 percent in Latvia, close to the EU average, and about twice the pre-crisis unemployment rate. As the IMF noted in a recent report, the labor market is improving but unemployment, especially long term unemployment, is still high in Latvia (IMF, 2013c, p. 4).[13]

Many economists were critical of Latvia's reform program during the crisis. Nobel Prize winning economist Paul Krugman, for example, stated that "[t]hey have made a desert, and called it adjustment" (Krugman, 2011). The prime minister of Latvia on the other hand stated that "[t]he greatest pleasure in life is doing what people say you cannot do..."[14] (Åslund and Dombrovskis, 2011, p. 118). The question remains: what cost is the government prepared to impose on its people to adjust, and how is this likely to affect the social fabric and long term growth in the country?

Latvia's claim to victory, post-crisis, is to a large extent based on recent GDP[15] growth and reduction in unemployment. It is true that according to this measure Latvia is on a path to recovery, and its GDP growth appears to be

---

[12] For a comprehensive analysis of Latvia's recent export performance, see Vanags (2013).

[13] It remains unclear how far unemployment needs to adjust to reach the natural rate of unemployment in Latvia. According to Blanchard, et al., 2013 output has not yet reached its potential and unemployment is not back to the natural rate. But they may not be very far (Blanchard, et al., 2013, p. 3). The question remains: how can a country with a low minimum wage, weak unions, limited unemployment insurance and employment protection, have such a high natural rate of unemployment?

[14] Here Åslund and Dombrovskis are citing Walter Bagehot, an English economist and journalist.

[15] Gross domestic product, abbreviated as GDP, is the most widely used measure of a country's overall economic health and development. As an aggregate measure of production, GDP is equal to the sum of the gross value added of all resident institutional units (i.e. industries) engaged in production, plus any taxes, and minus any subsidies, on products not included in the value of their outputs. Gross value added is the difference between output and intermediate consumption. See, further, for example, Eurostat:
http://epp.eurostat.ec.europa.eu/statistics_explained/index.php/Glossary:Gross_domestic_product_(GDP)

healthy as compared with other EU11 countries, and strong compared to the EU15 countries, currently with little or no growth.

Recent data on Latvia from the World Bank, for example, show a GDP growth rate of 5.6 percent in 2012, an estimate of 3.6 percent in 2013 and a projection of 4.1 percent growth rate in 2014 (World Bank, 2013b). The two other Baltic States, Estonia and Lithuania, also compare well with other EU11 countries. However, one needs to review these numbers in the context of pre-crisis growth rates where Latvia was the hardest hit country in the world and lost about 23 percent of its GDP (see Table 1.2). After more than five years of adjustment Latvia's GDP remains eight percent below the pre-crisis peak. Nevertheless, the return to a path of healthy growth is a welcome development.

Economic growth in Iceland remains lower. This to a large extent is due to the fact that Iceland is a very open economy with most of its exports going to the EU, which has recently had little or no GDP growth at all. A recent estimate for the third quarter of 2013 from Eurostat shows Euro area GDP growing by 0.1 percent and the EU28 growing by 0.2 percent (Eurostat, 2013). Thus recovery in the EU remains both weak and fragile.

Few would doubt the importance of economic growth, as measured by GDP, as an indicator of economic performance, but the question remains whether this indicator is sufficient to support Latvia's claim to victory and to declare it a success story for other countries to follow.

Measures of Economic Performance and Social Progress

How good is GDP as an indicator of economic and social progress in a country? It may be worth reviewing statements that some Nobel prizewinning economists and policymakers have made about the importance, as well as the limitations, of GDP as an indicator of economic development.

Paul Samuelson, for example, stated that "[w]ithout measures of economic aggregates like GDP, policymakers would be adrift in a sea of unorganized data. The GDP and related data are like beacons that help policymakers steer the economy toward the key economic objectives" (Samuelson and Nordhaus, 1995). It is understandable that economists want to have a common measure of economic progress and development, but the views are diverse. The creator of GDP, Nobel Prizewinning economist Simon Kuznets, once stated that "[t]he welfare of a nation can scarcely be inferred from a measurement of national income" (European Commission, 2013). Thus the creator and promoter of this indicator recognized its obvious limitations. More recently another Nobel Laureate, Joseph Stiglitz, stated that "[n]o one would look just at a firm's revenues to assess how well it was doing. Far more relevant is the balance sheet, which shows assets and liability. That is also true for a country" (Stiglitz, 2005).

So it is clear that there are leading economists in the world who view GDP critically. This includes its creator, who states that is does not measure the welfare of nations adequately. Regarding Stiglitz' comments, additional problems arise. Human capital is normally not included in company balance sheets, yet it is critical, both to a company's profitability, and a country's economic growth.

Policymakers have also commented on GDP as a measure of economic development. Robert McNamara, then the president of the World Bank, for example, commented that "[p]rogress measured by a single measuring rod, the GNP, has contributed significantly to exacerbate the inequalities of income distribution" (European Commission, 2013). Former French president Nicolas Sarkozy once stated that "[n]othing is more destructive than the gap between people's perceptions of their own day-to-day economic well-being and what politicians and statisticians are telling them about the economy" (Sarkozy, 2009). This is an interesting statement coming from someone who has played an important role in policy and decision making in the European Union.

Going "Beyond" GDP When Measuring "Success"

Recently there has been a movement to go "beyond" GDP when measuring progress within the EU. Given the very uneven developments in the EU in terms of economic and social progress it is understandable that the EU wants a more comprehensive picture of status within the union. During the crisis, the EU has also performed poorly according to the GDP measure, especially the EU15. What story would other indicators tell about the EU's economic and social progress?

The Commission on the Measurement of Economic Performance and Social Progress issued a report in 2009.[16] One can argue that the global economic and financial crisis has reinforced the need for additional indicators

---

[16] The commission included Professor Joseph E. Stiglitz, Chair, Columbia University, Professor Amartya Sen, Chair Adviser, Harvard University, and Professor Jean-Paul Fitoussi, Coordinator of the Commission, IEP (Stiglitz, et al., n.d.).

to assess the economic and social situation in the world, in particular poverty and social exclusion, risks and sustainability. GDP per capita and its growth over time also does not tell us how economic benefits are shared within a society. "A 2008 Eurobarometer poll showed that more than two thirds of EU citizens feel that social, environmental and economic indicators should be used equally to evaluate progress. Only just under one sixth prefer evaluation based mostly on economic indicators" (Commission of the European Communities, 2009).

While work based on the Report by the Commission on the Measurement of Economic Performance and Social Progress continues, and new indicators are developed and introduced, one can review some of the indicators that are currently published by Eurostat. Among those indicators is the proportion of people at risk of poverty or social exclusion and the at-risk-of-poverty rate. As to income distribution Eurostat calculates the Gini index and the Income quintile share ratio (see Table 1.3 below for results on Iceland and Latvia).

Table 1.3. Risk of Poverty, Social Exclusion and Income Distribution

Iceland	2007	2008	2009	2010	2011	2012
Proportion of people at risk of poverty or social exclusion	13.0	11.8	11.6	13.7	13.7	12.7
At-risk-of-poverty rate	10.1	10.1	10.2	9.8	9.2	7.9
The Gini index	28.0	27.3	29.6	25.7	23.6	24.0
Income quintile share ratio	3.9	3.8	4.2	3.6	3.3	3.4
Latvia	2007	2008	2009	2010	2011	2012
Proportion of people at risk of poverty or social exclusion	36.0	33.8	37.4	38.1	40.4	36.6
At-risk-of-poverty rate	21.2	25.6	25.7	21.3	19.1	19.4
The Gini index	35.4	37.7	37.4	36.1	35.4	35.9
Income quintile share ratio	6.3	7.3	7.3	6.9	6.6	6.5

Source: Statistics Iceland, 2013a.

Poverty, Social Exclusion and Income Inequality in Latvia and Iceland

Post-crisis Iceland and Latvia have both returned to a positive GDP growth rate, but how are these countries performing according to other indicators currently measured by Eurostat?

In 2012 the proportion of people at risk of poverty or social exclusion in Iceland was the lowest in Europe but in Latvia among the highest (only Bulgaria and Romania had higher ratios than Latvia). The rate in Iceland was 12.7 percent, compared with 36.6 percent in Latvia but 25 percent in the European Union. When focusing on those at risk of poverty the proportion was also lowest in Iceland or 7.9 percent compared to 19.4 percent in Latvia and 17.1 percent within the European Union. The at-risk-of-poverty threshold is defined as 60 percent of median income in each country. Those who fall below that income threshold are considered to be at risk of poverty. Latvia's distribution of prosperity as measured by the Gini coefficient is the most unequal in the EU.

One can argue that Iceland and Latvia should not be compared, using those indicators, because of their different income levels. Latvia is on the margin of an upper middle and high income country (according to World Bank classifications) but Iceland a high income OECD country. However, one needs to keep in mind that the Czech Republic, a country with a similar income level to Latvia, has one of the lowest ratios in the European Union, both in terms of the ratios for the proportion of people at risk of poverty and social exclusion, as well as in terms of the at-risk-of-poverty rate. Slovenia and Slovakia also perform much better than Latvia in terms of those indicators. Moreover, taking income distribution according to the Gini index and the income quintile share ratio, the Czech Republic, Slovenia and Slovakia are among EU countries with the most even income distribution: indeed more even than the average both in the EU(27) and the Euro (17) area.

In a recent IMF report appears the following sentence: "the Latvian authorities do believe that the current degree of inequality is unacceptable and the high level of poverty, tracing back to the collapse of the Soviet Union, should be reduced" (IMF, 2013c, p. 2). Latvia's performance on the four accounts shown in Table 1.3, measuring poverty, social exclusion and income equality, must be considered poor. Latvia has been an independent country for more than 20 years (since 1991) and a member of the European Union for about 10 years (since 2004). Its policymakers must pay more attention to the problems of poverty, social exclusion and income equality, if they want to present Latvia internationally as a success story, and a model for the rest of the world to follow.

According to the EU (in its Europe 2020 report) there is a high level of tax on low income earners in Latvia, high youth unemployment and 40% of the population in Latvia is at risk of poverty or social exclusion – one of the highest rates in the EU (European Commission, 2012). A recent Latvia Competitiveness Report argues that "Latvia's high income inequality is an indicator highlighting the presence of underlying competitiveness weaknesses that not only drive inequality but also negatively affect productivity" (Cunska, et al., 2012, p. 17)

Table 1.4. Poverty, Social Exclusion and Income Distribution in 2012

	GNI per capita (US$)	Proportion of people at risk of poverty or social exclusion	At-risk-of-poverty rate	The Gini index	Income quintile share ratio
Iceland	38.710	12.7	7.9	24.0	3.4
Latvia	14.180	36.6	19.4	35.9	6.5
Bulgaria	6.870	49.3	21.2	33.6	6.1
Romania	8.420	41.7	22.6	33.2	6.3
Czech Republic	18.130	15.4	9.6	24.9	3.5
Slovak Republic	17.170	20.5	13.2	25.3	3.7
Slovenia	22.720	19.6	13.5	23.7	3.4

Source: World Bank 2013a, Statistics Iceland, 2013a.

In terms of the indicators considered by the European Union that measure social progress, Latvia seems to have much more in common with Bulgaria and Romania than the Czech Republic and the Slovak Republic, especially as to income distribution. This is not a favorable outcome for Latvia given that those countries only have about half of Latvia's per capita income and are the poorest countries in the EU. Latvia needs to reform its public policy before presenting itself internationally as a success story.

Why would the EU want to push Latvia even further down on human indicators by insisting on strict fiscal austerity? The social crisis in Latvia is already serious and aggravating it will only further divide the nation. Given this poor record one cannot help wondering where all the social cohesion funds Latvia has received since well before EU accession have gone. This is not only a Latvian failure but also an EU failure. It is also time for Latvia to stop blaming the former Soviet Union for this ugly picture. The Soviet Union collapsed more than 20 years ago and there is a need for Latvians to form some shared vision of how they intend to bring the nation together. There is a need for a society that is more just and where wealth and income are shared, not captured by corrupt elites. Latvia today is no model for other countries to follow.

Emigration

Latvia has claimed victory not only on the basis of GDP growth but also referring to reduction in unemployment. Lower unemployment is a welcome development in Latvia but one needs to keep in mind that emigration explains a part of the reduction in unemployment in both Iceland and Latvia.

According to Darvas (2013) 8.5 percent of Latvians left the country from January 1 2008 to January 1 2012, compared with 2.3 percent in the case of Iceland (see Table 1.5). According to a recent survey only 20 percent of the emigrants who left Latvia during the crisis report an intention of coming back within five years (Blanchard, et al., 2013, p. 30). Those who have left tend to be younger Latvians with a university education, the segment of the population most likely to reform the economy.

Iceland has over the decades lost people but experience shows that a large share of these return when the economy recovers. In Latvia the largely permanent departure of younger and more educated workers may indeed be costly for those who stay, while those who leave may have few incentives to return as Latvia's per capita income remains far below the EU average. In contrast Iceland's per capita income is high in the EU context so that incentives to return during normal times are more obvious than in the case of Latvia.

Table 1.5. Population change from 1 January 2008 to 1 January 2012

	Total population			% change during 2008 – 2011 due to		
	1/1 2008 (millions)	1/1 2012 (millions)	% change	Birth	Death	Other (=migration)
Latvia	2.27	2.04	-10.1	3.7	-5.3	-8.5
Iceland	0.32	0.32	1.3	6.1	-2.5	-2.3

Source: Darvas, 2013.

CONCLUSION

Iceland and Latvia chose very different paths when they responded to the economic and financial crisis that hit in the fall of 2008. The responses of these two small countries have received international attention and continue to be debated.

In terms of GDP growth, both countries are on a growth path. Latvia currently enjoys higher GDP growth than Iceland, but one needs to keep in mind that its GDP fell much more during the crisis and Latvia's GDP remains eight percent below its pre crisis peak. In Iceland unemployment is about four percent, which is only about one third of the unemployment rate in Latvia: about 12 percent. In Latvia unemployment is about the same as average unemployment in the EU, but twice the pre crisis level in Latvia. Neither economy has returned to full pre-crisis health.

Have the reform programs in Iceland and Latvia been successful?

In terms of GDP growth and level of unemployment, Iceland has been successful, but problems related to its large currency depreciation remain, resulting in household and corporate balance sheet problems, and are hotly disputed in a country where the government has limited fiscal space to address these problems. It is also highly questionable whether the government should use its limited fiscal space to implement actions that only favor the part of the population that cannot handle their private debts. One can argue that Iceland has become a society where free riding is becoming popular. Households e.g., demand repeated debt restructuring that eventually will have to be paid by taxpayers and be a burden on the economy and future generations for years to come. The current government has fueled expectations in this area and this behavior may result in much higher public debt and put further economic recovery at risk. As a result Iceland may continue falling behind the Scandinavian countries in terms of per capita income.

Latvia has also achieved healthy economic growth and unemployment has gone down, though it still remains high. The government of Latvia, via its prime minister, has presented the country as a success story for the rest of the world to follow. In terms of the social indicators and measures of income inequality that the EU measures and publishes, Latvia looks bad not only in comparison with Iceland, but also compared with countries at a similar income level (e.g., the Czech Republic and Slovakia). In fact, in terms of social progress Latvia has more in common with Romania and Bulgaria which have a per capita income that is only about half of Latvia's. Under those circumstances one can say that Latvia has shown some success, but the human cost remains high. Latvia can hardly be considered a success in the EU and a model for the rest of the world to follow. Measuring GDP growth only is too narrow. A former Latvian prime minister considers the Latvian program to be a success, and stated that "[t]he greatest pleasure in life is doing what people say you cannot do...". Neither the prime minister nor the government should take pleasure in seeing the dismal status of human development in Latvia and the EU, and the IMF should not declare success when viewing the miserable social progress in Latvia.

Iceland and Latvia were both severely affected by the crisis though the policy response was different, in Latvia's case with a fixed exchange rate, and in Iceland with a flexible exchange rate and large depreciation. Both countries adjusted and made sacrifices, implementing painful budget cuts. Both countries are enjoying GDP growth well beyond the EU and the Euro area and unemployment has gone down although long term unemployment is still a concern in Latvia. As stated above, neither Iceland nor Latvia have yet returned to full economic health and they face future challenges. By damaging the social fabric in Latvia, a burden has been placed on future generations and many of the youngest and best educated have left the country. In Iceland, planned forgiveness of household and corporate debt risks imposing a burden on future generations, encouraging continued free riding, and is likely to result in slower economic growth.

Did Latvia and Iceland own their reform programs?

When the crisis hit Iceland the government tried to assemble external assistance to rescue the three largest banks. That plan was clearly owned by the incumbent government and the financial elite. This was done via the Central Bank of Iceland which contacted the Nordic central banks, as well as major central banks: the Bank of England, the ECB and the US Federal Reserve. The government failed to assemble support and the Icelandic banks fell in just a few days. This was followed by a sharp depreciation of the Krona. Clearly this was not a path chosen by the incumbent government, but in retrospect it can be said that the Icelandic nation was lucky that its sick banking system was not rescued at the cost of taxpayers. Other small countries like Ireland that rescued their banks appear to be paying an extraordinarily high price with a heavy burden placed on future generations. The reforms that took place were implemented under IMF conditions with financial support from the Nordic countries. These reforms have resulted in a mild recovery. Economic growth is satisfactory given the slow growth in the EU which remains Iceland's most important trading partner. Had the incumbent government been able to force taxpayers to bail out the banks the situation in

Iceland would be much worse than it is today. During the Icesave dispute the new government twice agreed to a settlement with the Netherlands and the UK. This settlement was owned by the cabinet and by the majority of parliament. In both cases the president of Iceland called for a referendum and in both cases the nation rejected the government's agreement. The fall of the banks and the depreciation of the Krona soon led to export-led growth and reduced unemployment. Had the previous government succeeded in saving the banks and had the new government succeeded in agreeing on a repayment scheme with the Netherlands and the UK Iceland's overall recovery would at best have been slowed down for years. It was fortunate that the government-owned settlements were rejected. The Banks' rescue was rejected by foreign governments and the Icesave deal was rejected by the nation. Those rejections created fiscal space to defend the welfare system in Iceland.

In Latvia it seems clear that external forces took control to ensure that Latvia could keep the peg with the Euro. Of course there were Latvians who favored a fixed exchange rate, especially those who had borrowed in Euro but had income in Lats. However, when the IMF in cooperation with the government of Latvia worked out a scenario for a modest devaluation, both were pushed aside by the European Union and the Swedish government. The Swedish banks that dominated the banking system in Latvia and throughout the Baltic States feared a domino effect, not only in the Baltic States but also in Scandinavia, which has a banking system that was and still is dangerously interconnected. The Swedish banks were too concerned over the impact of devaluation to let the government of Latvia devalue. The EU, with a serious mess on its hands in the Euro area, was concerned over the potential regional spillover effects of devaluation in Latvia. Thus Latvia implemented an austerity program at the cost of the most vulnerable members of its society. The human costs appear to be high and the ugliness of poverty, social exclusion and income inequality is more visible in Latvia as a consequence of policy choices whose main goal was to serve the Euro area. This reform program may have had the ownership of political cronies but was hardly owned by the majority of the Latvian population, who still remain poor.

REFERENCES

Auerback, M. (2009). In Latvia, the neo-liberal insanity continues. Credit Writedowns, available at: http://www.creditwritedowns.com/2009/10/latvia-the-insanity-continues.html (Accessed on February 8, 2014).

Åslund, A. and Dombrovskis, V. (2011). How Latvia Came Through the Financial Crisis. Peterson Institute for International Economics, Washington, DC, May 2011.

Blanchard, O., Griffiths, M., Gruss, B. (2013). Boom, Bust, Recovery Forensics of the Latvia Crisis. Final Conference Draft to be presented at the Fall 2013 Brookings Panel on Economic Activity September 19-20, 2013, available at: http://www.brookings.edu/~/media/Projects/BPEA/Fall%202013/2013b%20blanchard%20latvia%20crisis.pdf (Accessed on November 11, 2013).

Cunska, Z., Ketels, C., Paalzow, A., Vanags, A. (2013). Latvia Competitiveness Report. Stockholm School of Economics in Riga and the Baltic International Centre for Economic Policy Studies, available at: http://www.sseriga.edu/en/research/lcr/ (Accessed on September 5, 2013)

Commission on the European Communities. (2009). GDP and beyond – Measuring progress in a changing world. Communication from the Commission to the Council and the European Parliament, available at: http://eur-lex.europa.eu/LexUriServ/LexUriServ.do?uri=COM:2009:0433:FIN:EN:PDF (Accessed on December 1, 2013).

Darvas, Z. (2011). A tale of three countries: recovery after banking crises (No. 2011/19). Bruegel Policy Contribution, available at: http://www.bruegel.org/publications/publication-detail/publication/663-a-tale-of-three-countries-recovery-after-banking-crises/ (Accessed on September 7, 2013).

Darvas, Z. (2013). Where does the youth exodus come from? Available at: http://www.bruegel.org/nc/blog/detail/article/1103-where-does-the-youth-exodus-come-from/ (Accessed on November 7, 2013).

Eurostat. (2013). Second estimate for the third quarter of 2013, available at: http://epp.eurostat.ec.europa.eu/cache/ITY_PUBLIC/2-04122013-BP/EN/2-04122013-BP-EN.PDF (Accessed on December 8, 2013)

European Commission. (2012). Europe 2020, available at: http://ec.europa.eu/europe2020/europe-2020-in-your-country/latvija/country-specific-recommendations/index_en.htm (Accessed on December 7, 2013).

European Commission. (2013). Simon Kuznets on GDP and well-being in 1934, available at: http://ec.europa.eu/environment/beyond_gdp/key_quotes_en.html (Accessed on November 7, 2013).

European Commission. (2013). President of the World Bank Mr. Robert McNamara on GDP and social equity in 1973, available at:

http://ec.europa.eu/environment/beyond_gdp/key_quotes_en.html
(Accessed on November 7, 2013).

Grimsson, O. R. (2013). A Clean Energy Economy Lesson From Iceland. A
Speech by the President of Iceland Ólafur Ragnar Grímsson at a meeting
of OECD Ambassadors OECD Paris 27 February 2013, available at:
http://www.forseti.is/media/PDF/2013_02_27_OECD_CleanEnergy.pdf
(Accessed on March 7, 2013).

Grönn, A. and Fredholm, M. W. (2013). Baltic and Icelandic Experiences of
Capital Flow Measures. IMF Working Paper, available at:
http://www.imf.org/external/pubs/cat/longres.aspx?sk=41130.0 (Accessed
on February 7, 2014).

Hilmarsson, H. Þ. (2013). Small states and big banks–the case of Iceland.
Baltic Journal of Economics, (1), 31-48, available at:
http://www.biceps.org/assets/docs/bje/bje2013_no1/Policy_paper_2
(Accessed on September 7, 2013).

IMF. (2001). Strengthening Country Ownership of Fund Supported Programs,
available at: http://www.imf.org/external/np/pdr/cond/2001/eng/strength/
120501.htm (Accessed on February 3, 2014).

IMF. (2008a). Iceland: Financial System Stability Assessment—Update,
available at: http://www.imf.org/external/pubs/ft/scr/2008/cr08368.pdf
(Accessed on August 5, 2013).

IMF. (2008b). IMF Executive Board Approves €1.68 Billion (US$2.35
Billion) Stand-By Arrangement for Latvia, available at:
http://www.imf.org/external/np/sec/pr/2008/pr08345.htm (Accessed on
November 5, 2013).

IMF. (2013a). World Economic and Financial Surveys. World Economic
Outlook (WEO). Transitions and Tensions, October 2013, available
at:http://www.imf.org/external/pubs/ft/weo/2013/02/ (Accessed on
November 7, 2013).

IMF. (2013b). IMF Country Report No. 13/30. Republic of Latvia: Ex Post
Evaluation of Exceptional Access Under the 2008 Stand-By Arrangement;
Public Information Notice on the Executive Board Discussion; and
Statement by the Executive Director for the Republic of Latvia, available
at: http://www.imf.org/external/pubs/ft/scr/2013/cr1330.pdf (Accessed on
March 7, 2014).

IMF. (2013c). IMF Country Report No. 13/28. Republic of Latvia 2012
Article IV Consultation and Second Post-program Monitoring
Discussions, available at: http://www.imf.org/external/pubs/ft/scr/2013/
cr1328.pdf (Accessed on November 11, 2013).

Jonung, L., Kiander, J. and Varita P. (2008). The Great Financial Crisis in
Finland and Sweden. The Dynamics of Boom, Burst and Recovery, 1985-
2000. European Commission, available at: http://ec.europa.eu/
economy_finance/publications/publication13551_en.pdf (Accessed on
February 8, 2014).
Krugman, P. (2011). They Have Made A Desert, And Called It Adjustment.
The New York Times, December 7, 2011, available at:
http://krugman.blogs.nytimes.com/2011/12/07/they-have-made-a-desert-
and-called-it-adjustment/ (Accessed on June 7, 2014)
Samuelson, P. and Nordhaus, W. (1995). *Economics.* Mcgraw-Hill, 15 edition.
Sarkozy, N. (2009). French president Nicolas Sarkozy at the unveiling of the
Stiglitz Report in Paris on 14 September 2009.
Special Investigation Commission (SIC). (2010). Report of the Special
Investigation Commission (SIC) to the Althingi, April 12. 2010, available
at: http://www.rna.is/eldri-nefndir/addragandi-og-orsakir-falls-islensku-
bankanna-2008/skyrsla-nefndarinnar/english/ (Accessed on February 7,
2014).
Statistics Iceland. (2013a). Wages, income and labour market, available at:
http://www.statice.is/?PageID=452&itemid=ef4be73d-87b0-4ccf-ba2e-
b613243dca57 (Accessed on November 11, 2013)
Statistics Iceland. (2013b). Quarterly national accounts, 3rd quarter 2013,
available at:http://www.statice.is/Pages/444?NewsID=9778 (Accessed on
December 7, 2013).
Stiglitz, J.E. (2005). Growth may be everything, but it's not the only thing.
Foreign Affairs. November/December 2005 Issue, available at:
http://www.foreignaffairs.com/articles/61208/joseph-e-stiglitz/the-ethical-
economist (Accessed on December 2, 2013).
Stiglitz, J.E., Sen, A. and Fitoussi, J-P. (n.d.). Report by the Commission on
the Measurement of Economic Performance of Social Progress, available
at: http://www.stiglitz-sen-fitoussi.fr/documents/rapport_anglais.pdf
(Accessed on November 11, 2013).
Vanags, A. (2013). Latvia's Exports: The Real "Success Story", Baltic
International Centre for Economic Policy Studies, Research Report,
available at: http://biceps.org/assets/docs/izpetes-zinojumi/Latvias_
exports (Accessed on October 11, 2013).
World Bank. (2013a). Doing Business 2014. Understanding Regulations for
Small and Medium-Size Enterprises. International Bank for
Reconstruction and Development/The World Bank. Available at:
http://doingbusiness.org/~/media/GIAWB/Doing%20Business/Documents

/Annual-Reports/English/DB14-Full-Report.pdf (Accessed on April 6, 2014).

World Bank. (2013b). E11 Regular Economic Report, Issue 27 June 2013. The World Bank – Europe and Central Asia Region, available at: http://www.worldbank.org/content/dam/Worldbank/document/eca/eu11-rev-report-jun-2013.pdf (Accessed on November 1, 2013).

Chapter 2

ICELAND'S CROSS BORDER BANKING EXPANSION: DISHONESTY OR INCOMPETENCE?[1]

SUMMARY

The 2008 global economic and financial crisis hit hard in Iceland. During the crisis its three largest banks all collapsed in just a few days with severe consequences for the economy and the people. Prior to the crisis, Iceland, a high income OECD country, had experienced strong growth and unprecedented expansion in overseas investments and activities, especially in the financial sector. This chapter focuses on the actions of top government officials in Iceland during this expansion, which ended in the collapse of the Icelandic banks. The chapter also focuses on the actions of the international community when the Icelandic authorities, during a period of great uncertainty, sought assistance to protect the Icelandic economy before the banking system fell. This is important because those actions had consequences not only for Iceland but also for the citizens of other countries, most notably the UK and the Netherlands. The chapter will also review the actions of the

---

[1] Earlier versions of this chapter were presented by the author in seminars at Cornell University on March 3, 2014; University of California Berkeley (UC Berkeley) on May 7, 2014; and University of California Los Angeles (UCLA) on May 3, 2014. The author benefited from questions asked and comments made by participants during the seminars. The seminar at Cornell was sponsored by Cornell's Global Finance Initiative. The seminar at UC Berkeley was co-sponsored by the European Union Center of Excellence; the Institute of European Studies; and the Institute of Slavic, East European, and Eurasian Studies. The seminar at UCLA was sponsored by the UCLA Scandinavian Section.

other Nordic countries which Iceland, as the smallest member of that group, sometimes tends to rely upon for support during difficult times. The United States of America (US) was also an old ally that Iceland could count upon during times of crisis, such as the Cod Wars; therefore, the Icelandic authorities repeatedly sought US support before the crisis hit.

The findings of the chapter are that the government of Iceland made mistakes by not taking credible action to manage risks following a rapid cross border expansion of the Icelandic banking system. The government, including key cabinet ministers responsible for the banking sector, did not take international criticism seriously and focused too much on the image crisis facing the banks rather than the real problem. They acted as if outside international observers and critics needed more information to understand that the Icelandic banks were built on solid ground and on that basis launched a cross border PR campaign. The problem of the banks was considered to be a problem of perception. Maintaining this illusion resulted in inaction, which had severe consequences and resulted in the collapse of the Icelandic economy in October 2008. After its investigation the Special Investigation Commission (SIC) of the Icelandic Parliament, the Althingi, charged key government officials with negligence and one could even argue that they showed dishonesty by pretending that facts from reality were other than they were.

Iceland actively sought assistance from the international community before the banks fell. It first approached the Bank of England and then other institutions such as the Bank for International Settlements, the European Central Bank (ECB), the Nordic central banks and the Federal Reserve in the US. None of these institutions was prepared to provide assistance that might have saved the Icelandic banking system. The Bank of England offered to help in seeking assistance from the international community to reduce the size of the Icelandic banking system and was in contact with the Swedish Riksbank when considering the situation in Iceland. The Nordic countries provided some limited financial assistance under conditions agreed upon with the government of Iceland, but this was insufficient to rescue the banks. The Bank for International Settlements and the ECB were rather passive, while the US Federal Reserve refused point blank to assist Iceland.

In retrospect Iceland was lucky that its banking system was not rescued by the major central banks as this could have brought the debt level of the country to an unsustainable level. Iceland was fortunate not to have to serve the interest of the Euro area and that the so called Icesave dispute was resolved in national referendums and eventually in the EFTA Court. It could be argued that the international community showed dishonesty by deliberately and falsely claiming that Iceland had a responsibility to provide a sovereign guarantee for the debts of its private banks, a responsibility which the EFTA Court later ruled that Iceland did not have.

INTRODUCTION

The global economic and financial crisis that started in the fall of 2008 hit the Icelandic economy hard. During this crisis its three largest banks (Glitnir, Kaupthing, and Landsbanki)[2] all collapsed with dire consequences for the economy and the people. Prior to the crisis Iceland had experienced strong economic growth and unprecedented expansion in cross border investments and activities, especially in the financial sector.

During a crisis of this magnitude the government has an important role to play, including action to intervene in developments that may endanger economic stability and pose an imminent threat to the welfare of the nation. This includes taking action if developments in a particular sector, such as the financial sector, make the economy extremely vulnerable.

The international community also has a role to play in assisting a small country during a crisis, especially since this was a crisis on a global scale, and because the Icelandic banking expansion was at least partly the result of a flaw in European integration. Other countries also need to behave responsibly, as failure to do so not only affects the country where the banking system falls, but also their own citizens. The international community should also refrain from using strong-arm tactics against small states and trying to impose unjust and illegal actions.

This chapter will focus on the behavior of top government officials in Iceland during an aggressive ongoing cross border banking expansion. Did the Icelandic government take appropriate action when the banks expanded with cross border investments and operations overseas? Was inaction a problem? Can the government be charged with attempting to fake reality? Is it possible that the government was honest but incompetent and therefore not trustworthy? Similarly, did the international community, including the European Union, take appropriate action when the Icelandic banks expanded with investments and operations overseas? Was inaction a problem? Can the international community be charged with attempting to fake reality, i.e., pretend that Iceland had responsibilities that it did not have? Is it possible that

---

[2]These three banks accounted for about 85% of Iceland's financial system.

the international community was honest but demonstrated incompetence and is therefore not trustworthy? Put differently, during the crisis a failure of European integration was exposed, but larger countries, the UK and the Netherlands, supported by the EU tried to use force to have a small country suffer the consequences.

The proposition in this chapter is that small countries like Iceland benefit from being members of multilateral arrangements such as the European Economic Area (EEA) and generally benefit from European integration and open access to markets, including financial markets. When crisis hits, small states such as Iceland also benefit from being part of a group of nations like the Nordic countries and are likely to receive assistance from nations with whom it has friendly political relations.

The primary focus falls on certain government officials in Iceland in the shape of the cabinet ministers responsible for the banking system. These include the prime minister, the minister of finance, and the minister of business affairs. The role of the president of Iceland, who has traditionally been a symbolic and ceremonial figure in the government, is also discussed. Other officials also mentioned include the governors of the Central Bank of Iceland (CBI) as well as the director of the Icelandic financial supervisory authority (FME).

The foreign officials discussed are primarily central bank officials (as well as representatives of international organizations, including the European Union and international financial institutions). All these officials are mentioned in the report of the Special Investigation Commission of the Parliament of Iceland published in April 2010.

The methodology used in this chapter is the case study method. Compared to other research methods, a case study enables the researcher to examine the issues involved in greater depth. According to Yin (Yin, 2009, p. 101-102) six sources of evidence are most commonly used in case studies. These are: documentation, archival records, interviews, direct observations, participant-observation, and physical artifacts. Each of these sources has advantages and disadvantages and according to Yin one should "note that no single source has a complete advantage over all the others. In fact, the various sources are highly complementary, and a good case study will therefore want to use as many sources as possible" (Yin, 2009, p. 101). Among the sources of evidence used for the analysis in this chapter are documentation/secondary data, including reports and scholarly literature, articles and books. The author also exchanged emails with scholars in the field of economics, political science, public administration and philosophy/ethics. These communications when referred to are documented in footnotes. Direct observation also plays a role in this chapter as the author draws on his experience and observations while living in Iceland prior to and during the crisis. However, preference was given to using well documented evidence that is publicly available and listed in the references. In addition to scholarly articles the study refers to reports prepared by recognized Icelandic and international scholars. It is likely that more scholarly journal articles than are currently available will appear on this topic in the future, though that remains to be seen. This case study does not present results that can be evaluated on the basis of statistical significance and one should be careful about generalizing or projecting the findings of one case study onto another case or situation. However, some lessons from the study could have wider relevance than for Iceland only. This is especially true for small countries with a large banking sector, using their own currency, and with limited fiscal space to support the banks during a crisis.

Definitions, Some Theoretical Considerations and Issues for Discussion

The word honesty is sometimes mentioned in the economics, political science and public administration literature, but the author has so far not found a definition of what exactly is meant by honesty in these fields. Contact was made with economists, public administration specialists, political scientists and lawyers without finding a definition of what honesty means in those professions. A literature review in these fields also did not yield a definition. Several reports and scholarly articles reviewed mention honesty, but without providing a definition. A key report on the sources of sustained economic growth, i.e., the "Growth Report – Strategies for Sustained Growth and Inclusive Development" for example mentions honesty as important in the public sector and one can find statements like: "A culture of honest public service must be fostered and maintained", and: "But stable, honest, and effective government is critical in the long run" (Growth Report, 2008, p. 4-5). However, there is no definition of what honesty is, and in fact, a commission that included two Nobel Prize winning economists, as well as many other internationally recognized scholars and policy makers, never defined what honesty is.[3] This seems to be a common and troubling problem in that the word honesty is used without specifying its exact meaning.

The report of the Special Investigation Commission (SIC), established by the Icelandic parliament, the Althingi, to investigate and analyze the processes leading to the collapse of the three main banks in Iceland, mentions honesty. One can, for example, find a quote such as "honesty is the best policy." But honesty is never defined. Furthermore the working group on ethics under the SIC did not make any judgement as to whether or not government officials showed dishonesty in their work prior to the banking crisis. [4]

In this chapter honesty[5] is defined with Ayn Rand's discussion of honesty in mind. Rand's honesty is a refusal to pretend that facts from reality are other than they are. According to Rand one should not fake reality for others or oneself. Rand states that the virtue of honesty is that "one must never attempt to fake reality in any manner." (Rand, 1961, p. n.p). Honesty "is the recognition of the fact that you cannot fake existence" and "is the recognition of the fact that the unreal is unreal and can have no value." (Rand, n.d, p. n.p). In other words what is not so is not so. Things must be understood for what they are.

Tara Smith devotes a chapter to honesty in her outstanding book "Ayn Rand's Normative Ethics – The Virtuous Egoist." According to Professor Smith, faking "refers to familiar forms of pretending that things are other than they are, such as deliberately omitting pertinent information about a subject, covering something up, or twisting one's account of a situation to foster misleading impressions"[6] (Smith, 2006, p. 76). And she goes on to note that "[m]isrepresenting facts does not change them. However successfully one might fool another person, faking is ultimately futile" (Smith, 2006, p. 105). Pretending that things are other than they are does not make them other than they are. As Tara Smith notes, "[d]ishonesty can sometimes fool other people,

---

[3] According to an email from Professor Danny Lepziger, Commission Vice Chair to the author, received on August 13, 2012.

[4] According to an email from Professor Vilhjálmur Árnasson to the author received on July 27, 2012. Professor Árnason was the leader of a special three-person working group on ethics that was mandated in the Special Investigation Commission legislation by the Alþingi.

[5] When searching for a definition of honesty the author was in contact with Professor Tara A. Smith who recommended Ayn Rand's discussion of honesty in Galt's speech, as well as in her essay "The Objectivist Ethics," which is in *The Virtue of Selfishness*. For fuller elaboration, see Leonard Peikoff's discussion of honesty in *Objectivism: The Philosophy of Ayn Rand*, pages 267-276. Professor Smith also devotes a chapter to honesty in her book *Ayn Rand's Normative Ethics: The Virtuous Egoist*. Email received from Professor Smith September 17, 2012.

[6] Tara Smith also refers to Peikoff's Objectivism, p. 267-268 where he explains that honesty is its obverse: the rejection of unreality, the recognition that only existence exists.

but it cannot fool reality" (Smith, 2006, p. 81). "Facing reality is in a person's interest, even when certain aspects of reality are threatening, because it allows him to proceed rationally – realistically – and thus with the chance of overcoming threats...." (Smith, 2006, p.105).

In addition to Rand's definition, and Smith's discussion, of honesty, the following statement from Susan Rose-Ackerman is also used in this chapter: "Honesty is an important substantive value with a close connection to trust. Honesty implies both truth-telling and responsible behavior that seeks to abide by the rules. One may trust another person to behave honestly, but honesty is not identical to trustworthiness. A person may be honest but incompetent and so not worthy of trust" (Rose-Ackerman, 2001, p. 526).

Ayn Rand's definition and Rose-Ackerman's observation triggered the following issues that need to be kept in mind when answering the research questions stated in the introduction above:

(i)   Was the behavior of top government officials prior to the crisis in Iceland dishonest in the sense that they pretended that facts from reality were other than they were? Did they try to convince the nation and the international community that the Icelandic economy was not facing imminent danger even if they knew that a collapse of the banking system was likely?

(ii) If they were honest and thought that the banking system would survive was it because they were incompetent and did not see the danger? Were they honest but incompetent and thus not trustworthy?

(iii) Was the international community (governments including central banks as well as international organizations) dishonest in its response to the Icelandic authorities when they requested assistance to rescue the banking system? This question needs to be addressed since attempts were made to have the Icelandic government give a sovereign guarantee for foreign deposits in failed private banks beyond the amount the accounts had been insured for. Did the international community seek to fake reality by deliberately and falsely claiming that Iceland had a responsibility that it did not have? Such actions could have serious consequences, not only for Iceland, but also for citizens of other countries involved. Dishonesty here could include deliberately omitting pertinent information or twisting one's account of a situation to foster a misleading impression.

(iv) Was the international community incompetent in the sense that it did not understand that flaws in European banking regulations had resulted in excessive cross border banking expansion in Europe that could contribute to, or even cause, a global banking crisis?

The Extraordinary Expansion of the Icelandic Banking Sector Prior to the Crisis

Prior to the global economic and financial crisis that started in October 2008, the Icelandic banks had grown extraordinarily. According to the IMF the consolidated assets of the three main Icelandic banks increased from 100 percent of GDP in 2004 to 923 percent by end 2007, reflecting expansion overseas. By end 2007, almost 50 percent of the three banks' assets were held abroad (IMF, 2008, p. 11)

Access to global debt finance markets was a key driving force behind this growth. The big three banks also enjoyed high credit ratings inherited from Iceland's sovereign debt rating at the time. According to the Special Investigation Commission (SIC) the three banks issued around 14 billion Euro in foreign debt securities markets during 2005, which represented just over 100 percent of Iceland's GDP that year. Most of the funding matured in only three to five years. Refinancing risk was thus imminent (SIC, 2010a).

In early 2006, during the so-called mini crisis, international debt funding dried up temporarily. Once the liquidity crisis started in 2007, foreign deposits and short term securitized funding became the main source of funding for the three banks. This short term funding was sensitive to market conditions and thus risky (SIC, 2010a).

According to the SIC, other countries with relatively large financial systems managed to avoid disastrous banking outcomes; unlike Iceland, those nations have long experience and proven ability in supervising large, international banks. Their accumulated reputation for careful prudential supervision therefore offsets their inability to provide fully reliable lender of last resort protection, at least to some extent. But in Iceland the financial supervisory authority (FME)[7] was in general understaffed and lacked experience, while the foreign currency reserve of the Central Bank of Iceland (CBI) was low, and the deposit insurance fund was underfunded (SIC, 2010a).

---

[7] The financial supervisory authority in Iceland (Fjármálaeftirlitið/FME) is a regulatory organisation charged with the task of supervising financial enterprises, referred to as regulated entities (see further http://en.fme.is/).

How could this happen in a high income developed country like Iceland? How could Iceland move from privatization of state owned banks to an exploding banking sector and then to collapse in just a few years?

What Did the Experts Say About the Viability of the Icelandic Banking Sector Before and After the Collapse?

A number of experts, local and international, commented on the viability of the Icelandic banking system as well as on the soundness of the government's macroeconomic policies both prior to the banks' collapse (including after the so called mini crisis in 2006) as well as after their collapse in October 2008 (see, for example: Aliber, 2008; Buiter and Sibert, 2008a and 2008b; Danílsson and Zoega, 2009; Danske Bank, 2006; Eggertsson and Herbertsson, 2009; Flannery, 2009; Herbertsson and Mishkin, 2006; Jännäri, 2009; Portes, 2008; Portes and Baldursson, 2007). It is especially interesting to recall the remarks made prior to the collapse as they may have influenced government action, or inaction. It is also interesting to review some comments made after the collapse to see what lessons may have been learned from this catastrophic event. The next two sections will focus on some of the analysis carried out and statements made.

Expert Opinions Prior to the Collapse of the Banks in October 2008

Danske Bank issued a critical report in 2006 highlighting some of the macroeconomic imbalances in Iceland. "Based on the macro data alone, we think the economy is heading for a recession in 2006-7. GDP could probably dip 5-10% in the next 2 years, and inflation is likely to spike above 10% as the ISK depreciates markedly" and "we see a substantial risk of a financial crisis developing as an integral part of an Icelandic recession in 2006-7." (Danske Bank, 2006).

Iceland is a former colony of Denmark, where large investments had recently been made by Icelandic companies and any negative comments from Copenhagen were likely to be taken with some suspicion in Reykjavík. Talking about a possible financial crisis during a period that many people experienced as a boom was not likely to be taken too seriously in Iceland. Nevertheless Icelandic business interests and cabinet ministers responded with assistance from individuals in academia. An international PR campaign was launched to present a favorable view of the Icelandic banks and point to a strong government that balanced its fiscal budget and carried only small debts on its books. The Iceland Chamber of Commerce commissioned well known and respected Icelandic economists who, joining forces with distinguished and internationally known foreign colleagues, together painted a favorable picture of Iceland's banking system and its economy. In 2006 Herbertsson and Mishkin issued a report entitled: "Financial Stability in Iceland" (Herbertsson and Mishkin, 2006) and in 2007 Baldursson and Portes issued a report entitled: "The internationalization of Iceland's financial sector" (Baldursson and Portes, 2007). The title of the Herbertsson and Mishkin report is especially ironic given what happened in 2008; indeed, Mishkin was accused in the well known movie "Inside Job"[8] of having changed the title of the paper on his CV to "Financial Instability in Iceland", a label more in line with what subsequently happened. The Herbertsson and Mishkin report painted a picture of a stable, strong financial system in Iceland. According to the report Iceland was "an advanced country with excellent institutions (low corruption, rule of law, high education, and freedom of the press). In addition, its financial regulation and supervision is considered to be of high quality. Iceland also has a strong fiscal position that is far superior to what is seen in the United States, Japan and Europe" (Herbertsson and Mishkin, 2006, p. 8). According to the report, three traditional routes to financial instability have manifested themselves in recent financial crises: 1) financial liberalization with weak prudential regulation and supervision, 2) severe fiscal imbalances, and 3) imprudent monetary policy. None of these routes were said to describe the prevailing situation in Iceland (Herbertsson and Mishkin, 2006, p. 8). So politicians and business leaders in Iceland did not have much to worry about according to the report so that the government could well use these results to justify inaction during a time when it should have been taking drastic measures such as insisting on downsizing the banking sector and stabilizing the economy, including a very large current account deficit.

The Baldursson and Portes report came out in 2007 and again a pretty picture was painted of the state of banking affairs in Iceland. According to the report: "On the criteria of deposit ratios, the characteristics of market funding, and others, Icelandic banks come out well in a comparison with their Nordic peers – and their overall and core profitability is higher" (Portes and

---

[8] In the movie "Inside job" Mishkin is said to have received US$124,000 for his contribution to the report http://www.youtube.com/watch?v=5msVl3oZl4U .

Baldursson, 2007, p. 3). Furthermore, according to the report "[o]verall, the internationalisation of the Icelandic financial sector is a remarkable success story that the markets should better acknowledge" (Portes and Baldursson, 2007, p. 3). Here Icelandic banks are said to outperform other Nordic banks and Icelanders have every reason to be proud of their large banking system while the markets should do a better job in appreciating a "remarkable success story." At the time, this idea seemed to occupy the minds of many politicians, who seemed to think that foreign critiques were insufficiently informed about the Icelandic way and needed more education to understand the realities in Iceland. In fact, according to Portes and Baldursson "[t]he 'mini-crisis' of 2006 was an informational crisis, arising from external criticisms of the banks' reliance on market funding with short maturities, questions of earnings quality, cross-ownership, and lack of transparency, as well as perceived macroeconomic imbalances in the Icelandic economy" (Portes and Baldursson, 2007, p. 1). Danske bank and other critiques were thus misinformed and unappreciative of Icelandic success.

Not every report was positive: well known economists pointed to weaknesses in the financial system and the Icelandic economy. Warnings thus came not only from Danske Bank in 2006. Among scholars who expressed concern was Robert Z. Aliber of the University of Chicago Business School, who presented a paper at the University of Iceland in May 2008 (Aliber, 2008). Anne Sibert of Birkbeck College and Willem Buiter of the London School of Economics, who were commissioned by Landsbanki to write a report about the Icelandic banking system in early 2008 (Buiter and Sibert, 2008b), also expressed concern about the situation in Iceland.

Aliber was deeply critical of the banks' expansion as well as the overall economic situation in Iceland. At the time of Aliber's visit, Icelandic bankers were still seen there as national heroes, often linked to the Vikings and their golden age. Aliber could not help joking in his lecture "[a]nd the Icelandic banks may have a compensating advantage in the form of the "Viking spirit", although it is not clear how this plays out in … Norway and Denmark and Sweden" (Aliber, 2008, p. 22).

According to Aliber, "[t]he increase in asset prices and household wealth in Iceland between 2002 and 2007 was larger in percentage terms than … comparable increases in most other countries. The likelihood that Iceland is likely to remain immune from the market forces that are leading to declines in the price of real estate and increases in the costs of capital in the United States, Britain, and other countries seems low" (Aliber, 2008, p. 23).

In a meeting with the then incumbent prime minister, Aliber urged the government to split each of the Icelandic banks into separate domestic retail banks and foreign investment banks (Rannsóknarnefnd Alþingis, 2010, p. 226). After the meeting the prime minister commented: "He (Aliber) did not talk the whole thing down as he did in his lecture, he was just a nice old man on a visit."[9] The prime minister did not take an international expert like Aliber seriously and preferred to chat about common friends at Brandeis University where Aliber had taught and where the prime minister had graduated.

In early 2008 Buiter and Sibert were asked by Landsbanki, one of the three big banks, to write a paper on the causes of the financial problems faced by Iceland and its banks, and on the available policy options for the banks and the Icelandic authorities (Buiter and Sibert, 2008a). In April 2008 they submitted a paper entitled: "The Icelandic banking crisis and what to do about it: The lender of last resort theory of optimal currency areas." In July 2008, they presented a slightly updated version of the paper in Reykjavík before an audience of economists from the CBI, the Ministry of Finance, the private sector and the academic community. In April and July 2008, the "Icelandic interlocutors considered our paper to be too market-sensitive to be put in the public domain and we agreed to keep it confidential" (Buiter and Sibert, 2008a, p. n.p). This paper was made public only after the collapse of the three large banks in Iceland (Buiter and Sibert, 2008b).

Buiter and Sibert's 2008 analysis focused on the banks' liquidity problems caused by the absence of a credible lender of last resort. As they stated, "[t]he main message of our paper is, however, that it was not the drama and mismanagement of the last three months that brought down Iceland's banks. Instead it was absolutely obvious, as soon as we began, during January 2008, to study Iceland's problems, that its banking model was not viable. The fundamental reason was that Iceland was the most extreme example in the world of a very small country, with its own currency, and with an internationally active and internationally exposed financial sector that is very large relative to its GDP and relative to its fiscal capacity" (Buiter and Sibert, 2008a, p. n.p). Furthermore according to Buiter and Sibert, "[t]he only way for a small country like Iceland to have a large internationally active banking sector that is immune to the risk of insolvency triggered by illiquidity caused

---

[9] "[H]ann var ekkert að tala þetta allt niður eins og hann gerði svo í ræðu sinni, hann var bara huggulegur, gamall kall sem var að koma þarna." (Rannsóknarskýrsla Alþingis, 2010, bindi 8, p. 226). http://www.rannsoknarnefnd.is/html/vidauki1.html see also http://www.economicdisasterarea.com/index.php/features/aliber-in-iceland-2008-just-a-nice-old-man-on-a-visit/

by either traditional or modern bank runs, is for Iceland to join the EU and become a full member of the euro area. If Iceland had a global reserve currency as its national currency, and with the full liquidity facilities of the Eurosystem at its disposal, no Icelandic bank could be brought down by illiquidity alone. If Iceland was unwilling to take than [sic] step, it should not have grown a massive on-shore internationally exposed banking sector" (Buiter and Sibert, 2008a, p. n.p). According to Buiter and Sibert it ought to have been clear to everyone (presumably including Icelandic politicians) that the banks' business model was not viable long before the global economic and financial crisis hit in the fall of 2008. "This was clear in July 2008, as it was in April 2008 and in January 2008 when we first considered these issues. We are pretty sure this ought to have been clear in 2006, 2004 or 2000. The Icelandic banks' business model and Iceland's global banking ambitions were incompatible with its tiny size and minor-league currency, even if the banks did not have any fundamental insolvency problems" (Buiter and Sibert, 2008a, p. n.p).

The Collapse of the Icelandic Banks in October 2008

The collapse of the Icelandic banks in October 2008 was a shock to the Icelandic nation as well as to many internationally. In fact, it can be said that this was the first time that financial events in a tiny country like Iceland could send shockwaves through the international financial markets. As before the collapse, experts continued to express their views. One of these was Portes, who had painted a favorable picture of the situation in Iceland in a report in November 2007. In his *Financial Times* column of 13 October, 2008 Portes argued that "[l]ike fellow Icelandic banks Landsbanki and Kaupthing, Glitnir was solvent. All posted good first-half results, all had healthy capital adequacy ratios, and their dependence on market funding was no greater than their peers'. None held any toxic securities. These banks had been managed well since their "mini-crisis" in early 2006" (Portes, 2008, p. n.p). Thus after the collapse Portes still maintained that the banks were solvent, but how could he know the quality and value of the banks' assets with any certainty? Buiter and Sibert pointed out that the "only parties likely to have substantive knowledge of the quality of a bank's assets are its management, for whom truth telling may not be a dominant strategy and, possibly, the regulator/supervisor. In this recent crisis, however, regulators and supervisors have tended to be uninformed and out of their depth. We doubt Iceland is an exception to this rule. The quality of the balance sheet of the three Icelandic banks has to be viewed by outsiders as unknown" (Buiter and Sibert, 2008a, p. n.p). We now know that the FME in Iceland in charge of the task of supervising financial enterprises was understaffed and lacked experience.

Kaarlo Jännäri, [10] a retired director general of the Finnish financial supervision authority, who prepared a report on banking regulation and supervision in Iceland after the collapse of the banks, concluded that: "There might – just might – have been a possibility for the Icelandic banks to survive if the almost total freezing of the international financial markets had not taken place and confidence in Iceland had not been lost. Even in that case, they probably would have needed government support to maintain their solvency, as credit losses would have risen due to the deterioration of their loan portfolios" (Jännäri, 2009, p. 37). Mark J. Flennery[11] who prepared a report for the Icelandic Special Investigation Commission just after the banks' collapse stated that "[i]n the end, we cannot establish definitively whether one or all of the banks was in fact insolvent during that first week of October. However, their increasing loan delinquencies after March 2008 and the low recovery values implied by the FME's ultimate settlement with the Old (receivership) banks imply that insolvency was a good possibility even before the banks encountered their terminal funding crises. One is left with the strong suspicion that some or all of the banks were insolvent – and hence that the market's unwillingness to lend was rational" (Flannery, 2009, p. 106).

Weaknesses in EU banking regulations, insufficient supervision and inappropriate policy responses in Iceland as well as the global financial crisis all contributed to the storm in October 2008. As risk aversion replaced financial mania in the international financial markets community, the Icelandic banks were doomed. Only a concerted international rescue effort could have saved the banks in October 2008. At this point the government of Iceland was isolated and could not assemble assistance. The outrageous bullying behavior

---

[10] In November 2008, as part of its stand-by arrangement with the IMF, the Icelandic Government undertook to invite an experienced bank supervisor to assess the regulatory framework and supervisory practices in Iceland and to propose necessary changes. Kaarlo Jännäri, the retired Director General of the Finnish Financial Supervision Authority, was invited to carry out the assessment and prepared a report entitled: "Report on Banking Regulation and Supervision in Iceland: past, present and future." http://eng.forsaetisraduneyti.is/media/frettir/KaarloJannari__2009.pdf

[11] Mark J. Flennery, Professor of Finance at the University of Florida, prepared a report for the Icelandic Special Investigation Commission just after the banks collapse entitled; "Iceland's Failed Banks: A Post-Mortem." http://sic.althingi.is/pdf/RNAvefVidauki3Enska.pdf

of the British government also did not help.[12] After the collapse of the three largest banks the only way forward seemed to be to try to regain some international credibility by entering into negotiations with the IMF and agree on a program to stabilize the troubled economy. In October 2008 the government of Iceland was left with no other choice.

How Did the Government of Iceland React to Concerns and Criticism?

Prior to the crisis and the collapse of the Icelandic banks the government had great ambitions regarding the potential for growth of the banking sector, even proposing that Iceland should become an international financial centre (Invest in Iceland, 2006). In fact, a report was published on the issue by a committee appointed by the prime minister (Nefnd forsætisráðherra um alþjóðlega fjármálastarfsemi, 2006). The chairman of the committee was Sigurður Einarsson, then the chairman of the board of directors of Kaupthing Bank, one of the three big banks. According to the Invest in Iceland Agency, "Iceland´s positive business environment, low tax rates and efficient infrastructure make the country an ideal candidate for an international finance center according to a new report compiled for the Prime Minister by a team of experts" (Invest in Iceland, 2006, p. n.p). Furthermore, although "Iceland does not have a long history as a financial center and is much better known for competitively priced sustainable energy and quality seafood (...) extensive reforms, including liberalisation and privatisation, [have] changed the business environment dramatically during the last decade and Iceland is now recognized as one of Europe's most competitive economies" (Invest in Iceland, 2006, p. n.p). The government thus saw in the banks a great growth opportunity.

Liberalization of the financial markets and privatization of the state owned banks was good music internationally at this time. Indeed, these efforts were supported globally by institutions such as the IMF and the World Bank. As it turned out, supervision of the banks in Iceland was weak and many people still question how privatization of the state owned banks was implemented with few politically influential groups taking control and involving managers with

---

[12] The UK authorities invoked the 2001 Anti-Terrorism, Crime and Security Act, passed after the September 11, 2001 terrorist attacks in the USA, to justify freezing the UK assets of Landsbanki and Kaupthing.

little experience in international banking. As Jännäri pointed out, "[f]or the most part, the new owners and the people behind them were not traditional commercial bankers; instead, they had the rather innovative and somewhat adventurous mindset of investment bankers, which favoured a strategy of rapid growth and highly leveraged, aggressive deals" (Jännäri, 2009, p. 14).

How could this happen in a developed OECD country like Iceland? How could Iceland move from privatization of its state owned banks, to ideas for creating a financial centre, to an exploding banking sector, and then to collapse? As Eggertsson and Herbertsson point out in a paper entitled "System Failure in Iceland and the 2008 Global Financial Crisis", "the prime minister talked about turning Iceland into a full-scale center of international finance. Scholars have documented how communities that are caught in extreme price bubbles become virtually manic and throw caution [to] the wind. Iceland is no exception, although, as always, there were early critics and skeptics." (Eggertsson and Herbertsson, 2009, p. 28 to 29). And further: "Modern capitalism has had its fair share of financial manias, panics and crises, but the global financial exuberance and the subsequent crash in the first decade of the 21st century stands out as exceptional and has been compared to the events leading to [the] Great Depression" (Eggertsson and Herbertsson, 2009, p. 11).

As discussed above, respected international experts issued warnings to the government about the expansion of the Icelandic financial sector well before the collapse in 2008. This included, for example, the Danske Bank report in 2006, Aliber´s lecture in 2008, as well as the Buiter and Sibert report in 2008. Lower credit ratings issued by rating agencies were yet another warning signal. Refusal by the Bank of England, the European Central Bank, and the Federal Reserve to increase the CBI's foreign exchange reserves (discussed below) should also have been a warning to the government and triggered an immediate response from the key ministers involved. [13] However, in Iceland the response to negative reports and lower credit ratings was generally one of shock and anger over what was seen as unfair and unsubstantiated criticism. Business interests and cabinet ministers, aided by experts from some Icelandic universities, initiated a public relations campaign and painted a positive picture of the situation; for example, by emphasizing the excellent standing of the government, which was virtually debt free and balanced its budget. Given the numerous warnings mentioned above, this could be interpreted as an

---

[13] The responsibility for money, banking and finance in Iceland is divided between three ministries, those of the prime minister, the minister of finance, and the minister of business affairs.

attempt to convince others that facts from reality were other than they were, and thus dishonest behavior.

Kaarlo Jännäri claims that foreign supervisors and central banks, with which he was in contact when he was preparing his report on banking regulation and supervision in Iceland, generally commented favorably on the cooperative and friendly attitude of the Icelandic authorities. However, he also comments that "[s]ome disappointment has also been expressed about the willingness of the CBI and the FME to share the concerns they had about the Icelandic banks with their EU counterparts before the crisis exploded. There are feelings that the Icelandic authorities were protective of the banks and tried to tone down the worries expressed by their foreign counterparts. This has undermined the credibility of the FME and the CBI in the eyes of their colleagues. The FME and the CBI consider these criticisms to be unfair and unjustified" (Jännäri, 2009, p. 12). This again could be taken as an attempt by the government to fake the facts, to deny reality. Furthermore he comments that "[t]he supervisors were too timid and lacked legal authority in their efforts to intervene in these developments, but the overall national pride in the success of the banks would probably have made it futile even to try while the going was good and success followed success. By the time the tide turned, it was too late, and there was too little that could be done to avoid catastrophe" (Jännäri, 2009, p. 37).

The same may have applied to the Icelandic Cabinet of Ministers. They may have lacked the courage to intervene and simply decided on a hands-off policy and were hoping for the best rather than preparing for the worst. As Daníelsson and Zoega observe, "[b]y not addressing the pending failure of the banking system, perhaps in the hope that the instability would disappear, we cannot escape the feeling that the Icelandic authorities gambled for resurrection, and failed" (Zoega and Daníelsson, 2009, p. 14). But could the banks have been saved even if the cabinet had interfered in full force? Eggertsson and Herbertsson have expressed their opinion as to whether it was still possible to restructure the banking system in 2006, following the early warning signs and criticisms from abroad. They "believe that even then, had they desired, the banks could have either downsized or split and moved their headquarters for foreign operations abroad" (Eggertsson and Herbertsson, 2009, p. 28). But in their view "only the prime minister and the cabinet could have made the critical political decision to reverse the spectacular growth of the country's banking system or relocate most of it overseas" (Eggertsson and Herbertsson, 2009, p. 28). But the cabinet did not take action after the 2006 mini crisis and decided to defend the banks instead of downsizing or moving their HQ overseas. The cabinet chose to be inactive during a critical time in Iceland's history. Their hopes for resurrection did not materialize. They seem to have refused to face reality. The consequences were dire.

The Special Investigation Commission and Its Report to the Althingi

A Special Investigation Commission (SIC) delivered its report to the Icelandic parliament, the Althingi, on April 12, 2010. The Commission was established by the Althingi in December 2008[14] to investigate and analyze the processes leading to the collapse of the three main banks (Glitnir, Kaupthing and Landsbanki) in Iceland. The following section gives a flavor of the failure of leadership and coordination at top government level in Iceland before the crisis hit, with disastrous consequences. In fact, in its report the SIC named ministers and high level government officials who were thought to have shown negligence. The report, which totals nine volumes, is quite extensive but only a few points can be highlighted in this section.

According to the SIC, the balance sheets and lending portfolios of the Icelandic banks expanded beyond the capacity of their own infrastructure. Growth had been especially rapid during the latter part of 2007. The banks' rapid lending growth had the effect, according to the SIC, that their asset portfolios became fraught with high risk. In the view of the SIC this kind of large scale, high risk growth was not compatible with the long term interests of solid banks (SIC, 2010b, p. 1). For the banks, access to international financial markets was the principal premise for their extensive growth. According to the SIC "[t]here were mainly two reasons why international financial markets opened their doors to the banks, firstly, because of their good credit rating. This was to some extent inherited from the Treasury. Secondly, they had access to European markets, on the basis of the EEA Agreement" (SIC, 2010b, p. 1). The banks that had operated as state owned banks for decades before their privatization had earned a reputation for being rather conservative and reliable so that economic integration in Europe via the EEA agreement opened doors for the Icelandic banks to European financial markets.

The SIC made strong comments on the lack of government response during the critical time prior to the crisis: "When the banking system had become far too big, relative to the size of the Icelandic economy, the

---

[14] By Act No. 142/2008.

governmental authorities needed to respond. No later than in 2006 it would have been necessary to take action, if there was to be any chance of preventing the collapse of the banks, without severely impacting upon the value of their assets. Neither that year nor the next did the authorities try, in a decisive way, to have the banks reduce the size of their balance sheets" (SIC, 2010b, p. 2). In addition, government policy that the bank's headquarters should remain in Iceland meant that Iceland was responsible for their supervision.

The SIC was also heavily critical of the government's macroeconomic policies during the period when the banks expanded: "The authorities decided to lower taxes during an economic expansion period. This was done despite expert advice and even against the better judgement of policy makers who made the decision. This decision was highly reproachable. The changes made to the lending guidelines at the Housing Financing Fund in 2004 also fuelled expansion. The changes in the lending guidelines were one of the biggest mistakes in monetary and fiscal management made in the period leading up to the banks' collapse. That mistake was made with full knowledge of the likely consequences. The repercussions were quick to emerge and the consequences were even greater under the global low interest rate environment at the time. These decisions in fiscal and monetary management and others named in the report exacerbated the imbalance in the economy. They were a factor in forcing an adjustment of the imbalances, which ended with a very hard landing" (SIC, 2010b, p. 5). According to the SIC, it was mostly left to the Central Bank of Iceland (CBI), to counteract the effects of expansion by raising interest rates.

According to the SIC, "[f]rom November 2007 onwards the Board of Governors of the CBI became increasingly concerned about the situation that was developing in the operational environment of the banks. The Board of Governors described these concerns either directly to the Prime Minister and a small group of ministers, or within the platform of the government consultative group. In spite of these concerns there is no evidence that the Board of Governors of the CBI made available to the government formal propositions for necessary measures." (SIC, 2010b, p. 8).

And key cabinet ministers failed to report these problems to others in the government as the SIC states "[n]othing suggests, either from the government's minutes or the accounts of those who reported to the SIC, that the ministers of the Icelandic government responsible for economic affairs (the Prime Minister), banking affairs (the Minister of Business Affairs) or the state's finances (the Minister of Finance) submitted to the government a specific report on the problems of the banks or its possible impact on the state's economy and finance when the banks started to face constraints in their operations and until the banking system collapsed in October 2008" (SIC, 2010b, p. 10). Again this shows a failure of coordination and the cabinet as a whole seemed not to have been informed formally. Nor was the cabinet activated to share responsibility or discuss possible governmental actions.

According to the SIC, "[i]n 2008 the Prime Minister had quite a few meetings with the Chairman of the CBI Board of Governors and the CEOs of the banks. During the period from February until May 2008 [the] Board of Governors had at least five meetings with the Prime Minister, [the] Minister of Finance and the Minister for Foreign Affairs. Banking affairs came under the domain of the ministry of Mr. Björgvin G. Sigurðsson, Minister for Business Affairs. He was not summoned to attend any of these meetings, in spite of the fact that the problems the banks were facing and the liquidity crisis were being discussed there" (SIC, 2010b, p. 10). This shows a grave coordination failure within the government and as the SIC emphasizes, "[a]s the leader of the government, the Prime Minister had the responsibility to inform the Minister of Business Affairs of the aforementioned meetings so that he could attend to his duties" (SIC, 2010b, p. 10).

As stated earlier in this chapter, the ministers considered outside criticism of the banks unjustified, unfair and due to lack of information. Foreign critiques needed education and efforts were mostly spent on improving the image of the banks. As the SIC states, "[i]t is the assessment of the SIC that the government's actions concerning matters relating to the banks were unfocused when the situation became more dire [at] the beginning of 2008. The ministers focused too much on the image crisis facing the financial institutions rather than the obvious problem, that the Icelandic financial system was far too large in relation to the Icelandic economy. When the ministers intended to improve the image of the banking system by partaking in public discussions, mainly abroad, it was done without any assessment of the financial capability of the state to come to the banks' assistance and without information being available on the cost of a possible financial shock" (SIC, 2010b, p. 10). From the above it seems that the SIC was of the opinion that the government was faking reality by focusing on an image crisis instead of the obvious problem.

On examining the analysis presented by the SIC, the powerlessness of the government and the authorities, in terms of reducing the size of the financial system in time before a financial shock hit, becomes evident. As the SIC states, "[i]t appears that both the parliament and the government lacked both the power and the courage to set reasonable limits to the financial system. All the energy seems to have been directed at keeping the financial system going. It had grown so large, that it was impossible to risk that even one part of it would collapse" (SIC, 2010b, p. 17). Thus the government hoped for the best but did not prepare for the worst. Unfortunately the worst case scenario materialized when the government was finally forced to face reality.

In its conclusions, the SIC names ministers and high level officials and accuses them of negligence: "The SIC's assessment, pursuant to Article 1(1) of Act no. 142/2008, was mainly aimed at the activities of public bodies and those who might be responsible for mistakes or negligence within the meaning of those terms, as defined in the Act. Although the SIC was entrusted with investigating whether weaknesses in the operations of the banks and their policies had played a part in their collapse, the Commission was not expected to address possible criminal conduct of the directors of the banks in their operations. On the basis of events and viewpoints that are described in more detail in individual chapters of this report, the SIC is of the opinion that Mr. Geir H. Haarde, then Prime Minister, Mr. Árni M. Mathiesen, then Minister of Finance, and Mr. Björgvin G. Sigurðsson, then Minister of Business Affairs, showed negligence, within the meaning of Article 1(1) of Act No 142/2008, during the time leading up to the collapse of the Icelandic banks, by omitting to respond in an appropriate fashion to the impending danger for the Icelandic economy that was caused by the deteriorating situation of the banks. The SIC is also of the opinion that Mr. Jónas Fr. Jónsson, then Director General of the FME, and Mr. Davíð Oddsson, Mr. Eiríkur Guðnason and Mr. Ingimundur Friðriksson, then Governors of the CBI, showed negligence, within the meaning of Article 1(1) of Act No 142/2008, in the course of particular work during the administration of laws and rules on financial activities, and monitoring thereof" (SIC, 2010b, p. 18).

In April 2012 the former prime minister, Geir H. Haarde, was found guilty before a special court, the Landsdómur, for not holding cabinet meetings when things turned critical in the period leading up to the crisis in 2008.[15] His

---

[15] The trial and the verdict drew attention in the international media, see examples below:
CNN World: http://articles.cnn.com/2012-04-23/world/world_europe_iceland-haarde-verdict_1_
    landsbanki-icesave-haarde?_s=PM:EUROPE
Financial Times: http://www.ft.com/intl/cms/s/0/13c2552a-6eb3-11e1-acf0-00144feab49a.html#
    axzz1zrlEtSUi
Bloomberg: http://www.businessweek.com/printer/articles/51940?type=bloomberg
The Guardian: http://www.guardian.co.uk/world/2012/mar/05/iceland-pm-charged-crisis
The Telegraph: http://www.telegraph.co.uk/finance/financialcrisis/9221480/Ex-Iceland-PM-Geir-
    Haarde-to-escape-punishment-despite-guilty-verdict-over-banking-collapse.html
BBC: http://www.bbc.co.uk/news/world-europe-17817174.

response to the media was: "I always found that charge to be even more ridiculous than the others. I still hold that view. It is therefore my opinion that the Court has made a grave error in reaching this conclusion and I therefore plan to take this case to the European Court of Human Rights as soon as I can" (x-D, 2012).

The President of Iceland Prior to the Crisis

In the Icelandic political system the president remains a largely ceremonial figure. However, he is influential both locally and internationally and has been very active in promoting Icelandic business interests abroad. His role in this crisis is therefore worth examining. As stated above, according to the Special Investigation Commission "[n]o later tha[n] 2006 it would have been necessary to take action, if there was to be any chance of preventing the collapse of the banks, without severely impacting upon the value of their assets. Neither that year nor the next did the authorities try, in a decisive way, to have the banks reduce the size of their balance sheets" (SIC, 2010b, p. 2).

What did the president of Iceland say about the Icelandic banking sector in 2006? In a speech at "The Kaupthing Seminar" in Helsinki in May 2006 the president said: "Yes, the future does indeed offer fascinating opportunities – and the growing strength of the Icelandic banking sector will, as before, play a crucial role, both in itself and by providing valuable connections to the international banking community. The three leading Icelandic banks – Kaupthing, Landsbanki and Glitnir – are amongst the fastest growing banks in the world. And the largest of the three, Kaupthing, has already established a pivotal position in Northern European banking. It has been both a privilege and an education for me to follow the growth of their activities and witness the praise that the Icelandic banks have received from their foreign clients – to confirm how the Icelandic banks have become key players in international financing for prominent European and American companies" (Grímsson, 2006, p. 5).

Like the government, the president is concerned about the image of the banks: the outside world needs to be informed and educated about the Icelandic banking sector. At "the Kaupthing Seminar" the president makes his view on this very clear when he says "[w]e have, however, been reminded of valuable lessons. One is that if you are a player in the global financial system, it is of paramount importance to keep foreign confidence in your financial institutions. Another is that reporting or misreporting by others can play a role.

It is worth noting that in the avalanche of reporting and evaluation to which we have been submitted in recent weeks, there is a prevailing characteristic: - The greater the knowledge of Iceland and the longer the experts have followed the Icelandic voyage, the more positive, informed and optimistic the conclusions have been. We have to admit, however, that we could be more active in explaining our case; but then you have to remember that we Icelanders make up the nation that discovered America 1000 years ago but did not tell anyone about it. We only wrote the story down in books for ourselves, in texts we alone could understand. Consequently, Christopher Columbus got all the glory when he stumbled upon America 500 years later.

Now we have to do better: to build on the tradition of storytelling, aimed currently not only at ourselves but also at others. It is important to further the extensive knowledge and detailed understanding of the Icelandic experience; to be both transparent and open – willing to engage in dialogue with others" (Grímsson, 2006, p. 7). At the Walbrook Club in London on May 3, 2005 the president offered a list of a dozen or so elements that he believed had been crucial to Iceland's "success story." One was that "Icelanders are risk takers. They are daring and aggressive" (Grímsson, 2005, p. 4).

The president of Iceland can hardly be blamed for the collapse of the banks in the fall of 2008. But he also did not urge the bankers to show caution during a time when it was most critical. On the contrary he encouraged further risk taking and expansion. Currently he also encourages cross border expansion of Iceland's energy sector, which would involve large, long term investments, with long repayment periods. Such investments in emerging markets could be risky, especially for companies from small countries (see e.g., Hilmarsson, 2008, 2010 and 2012). The president is a highly educated man with extensive experience. He should have known what dangers the banks could face with further expansion, risk taking and aggressiveness. He should not have fueled excessive risk seeking behavior and he should have listened more to critics. He should also know the risks that energy companies may face when investing in emerging market economies or in a submarine cable to Europe which is currently under discussion with the UK government.

The Roles of the Central Bank of Iceland and Financial Supervisory Authority

So far this chapter has mostly focused on the action of key ministers and the president with less discussion of the role of the Central Bank of Iceland

(CBI) and the Icelandic financial supervisory authority (FME). Clearly both those institutions should have played a key role in monitoring and supervising the banking system in Iceland prior to the crisis.

The fact that the banks' headquarters remained in Iceland also meant that Iceland was responsible for their supervision. The FME, the institution that bore the main responsibility for monitoring the activities of the banks, was understaffed and its staff was inexperienced (SIC, 2010a). The FME obviously did not have the institutional capacity to do its job properly and it ought to have known that. It should have had information about the health of the banks' balance sheets, but as Buiter and Sibert point out, regulators and supervisors tend to be uninformed and out of their depth. Unfortunately Iceland was no exception to this rule (Buiter and Sibert, 2008a, p. n.p). Moreover, as Jännäri, the former director general of the Finnish financial supervision authority, noted "[t]he supervisors were too timid and lacked legal authority in their efforts to intervene in these developments" (Jännäri, 2009, p. 37). It was also difficult to intervene forcefully when the banks were expanding and success followed success. Moreover, according to the SIC, "the FME did not sufficiently concern itself with some basic questions, such as the size of the banking system, and the Authority's necessary reactions in regard to its much too rapid growth" and in addition "[i]n its supervisory duties the FME was lacking in firmness and assertiveness, as regards the resolution of and the follow-up of cases" (SIC, 2010b, p. 16-17). In this situation the FME was in effect powerless and did not act effectively as it should have done.

The CBI foreign reserves were low, and the deposit insurance fund was underfunded (SIC, 2010a). The CBI must have known prior to the crisis that it could not act as a credible lender of last resort. According to the SIC it was mostly left to the CBI to counteract the effects of expansion by raising interest rates. And "[f]rom November 2007 onwards the Board of Governors of the CBI became increasingly concerned about the situation that was developing in the operational environment of the banks. The Board of Governors described these concerns either directly to the prime minister and a small group of ministers, or within the platform of the government consultative group" (SIC, 2010b, p. 8). In spite of these concerns, according to the SIC no evidence exists that the board of governors of the CBI made available to the government formal propositions for necessary measures to be taken. This is unfortunate as it could have helped the government in its response and in policy making. Given the severity of the situation the CBI should have formally notified the government with a recommended course of action based on its assessment.

As for the CBI and the FME, they were both seen as unwilling to "share the concerns they had about the Icelandic banks with their EU counterparts before the crisis exploded" (Jännäri, 2009, p. 12). The Icelandic authorities were thus seen as being protective of the banks and trying to tone down worries expressed by their foreign counterparts. As Jännäri points out, this undermined the credibility of the FME and the CBI in the eyes of their colleagues among foreign supervisors and central banks (Jännäri, 2009, p. 12). This lack of credibility obviously made it even more difficult to get advice and support from institutions in other countries when it was much needed.

Government Negligence and Dishonesty?

According to the Special Investigation Commission (SIC), particular government officials showed negligence and made mistakes by not taking credible action to manage risks following a rapid cross border expansion of Iceland's largest banks. This had severe consequences and resulted in the collapse of these banks in October 2008. Instead of addressing problems in the economy the government launched a PR campaign and according to the SIC the ministers over-focused on the image crisis facing the financial institutions rather than addressing the obvious problem. In speeches overseas, the president of Iceland aggressively supported the ministers in their efforts. With that in mind the ministers and the president could be charged with attempting to fake reality, thus showing dishonesty according to Rand's definition of the term. Moreover, as some scholars put it, the authorities gambled for resurrection, and failed (Daníelsson and Zoega, 2009). Nevertheless, one needs to keep in mind that the analysis carried out by scholars who downplayed the problem may have confused the government, which may claim that it was honest in its inaction (Herbertsson and Mishkin, 2006: Portes and Baldursson, 2007). In that situation one can speculate whether the government was honest but incompetent and therefore not trustworthy. Some scholars presenting a favorable assessment of the Icelandic banks were paid for their analysis, as was definitely the case with Mishkin. This undermines the credibility of the Herbertsson and Mishkin report. Other scholars warned the government strongly prior to the crisis but were ignored. These include: Danske Bank, 2006; Aliber, 2008; Buiter and Sibert, 2008a. Indeed, Buiter and Sibert claim that the end of a non-viable business model was obvious from the beginning, years before the crisis. Additionally, the fact that the Icelandic government had prepared an Emergency Act[16] prior to the collapse of the Icelandic banks shows that the government was aware that things could go seriously wrong, with severe consequences.

Could the Collapse of the Icelandic Banking System Have Been Prevented?

The Icelandic government should have encouraged and if necessary enforced more risk mitigation via regulations, monitoring and supervision of the banks' cross border activities long before the crisis. It is clear that credible action to mitigate those risks was not taken. The financial supervisory authority did not have institutional capacity to supervise the banks and the CBI reserves were too low for it to act as a lender of last resort.

It is possible that the collapse of the banks could have been prevented had the government (the prime minister and the cabinet) taken a drastic measure and insisted on downsizing the banking sector or relocating most of the banks' cross border operations. As Buiter and Sibert forcefully argue, it ought to have been clear to everyone long before the global economic and financial crisis hit in the fall of 2008 that the banks' business model was not viable: "This was clear in July 2008, as it was in April 2008 and in January 2008 when we first considered these issues. We are pretty sure this ought to have been clear in 2006, 2004 or 2000" (Buiter and Sibert, 2008a, p. n.p). The government effort to try to improve the image of the banks in this situation was absurd.

According to the SIC, "[i]n replies made by administrators of governmental institutions who reported to the SIC, the statement was frequently encountered that it did not fall under the functional area of the person concerned, or his institution, to address or take responsibility for the project in question. It was also repeatedly stated, that other institutions or officials were responsible for such issues or tasks" (SIC, 2010b, p. 18). On that basis, the government of Iceland needs to look carefully at how the obligations of individual institutions and officials may be better defined and the division of labor clarified and made sharper. This lack of clarity only made things worse when the crisis hit and added to the confusion, exactly when the government needed to act swiftly and forcefully.

---

[16] (No. 125/2008).

The Central Bank of Iceland and Its Pre Crisis Attempt
to Increase Its Foreign Exchange Reserves

From March to early October 2008 the Central Bank of Iceland (CBI) made desperate attempts to increase its foreign exchange reserves. The communications, including emails, between the CBI and other central banks approached were documented and made public by the Special Investigation Commission (SIC) that delivered its report to the Althingi on April 12, 2010.

According to the SIC report, the Bank of England was first approached in March 2008 because of large Icelandic cross border bank operations in the UK. The CBI requested a bilateral currency swap arrangement with the Bank of England. The Bank of England appeared to be suspicious about the intentions of the CBI and wanted clarification of what the funds would be used for. In late March 2008 a formal letter was written and sent from the CBI to the European Central Bank (ECB). The response to that letter was to ask if the CBI had approached the IMF, the Bank of International Settlements, and other central banks, in addition to the Bank of England. It is notable that in March 2008 the ECB thought that the IMF should be contacted.

During the IMF Spring Meetings in Washington DC in April 2008, CBI representatives met with Nordic central bank officials, including central bank governors. According to the SIC report it appears that the governor of the Swedish central bank, the Swedish Riksbank, Stefan Ingves, had been given the responsibility of coordinating reactions to the CBI request on behalf of the Nordic central bank governors.

It is clear that Mr. Ingves did not have much confidence in the CBI representatives. In a letter to the SIC on January 22, 2010 he commented that "[M]y own impression was that the Icelandic representatives were stressed, not particularly well prepared, and not fully appreciated [sic] the risks at hand" (Rannsóknarnefnd Alþingis, 2010, p. 170). Discussion also arose about conditions in the event of financial assistance from the Nordic countries to Iceland, showing that at this stage not much trust existed between the CBI and the other Nordic central banks and not much trust in the government of Iceland either.

During the 2008 IMF Spring Meetings the governor of the Bank of England, Mervyn King, stated that it was necessary for the CIB to clarify how the swap arrangements would be used. He also asked what the government would do if a run on the banks occurred the next day. This shows that the Bank of England thought that the Icelandic banking system could be at risk of collapsing at any time. Finally, Timothy F. Geithner, president of the Federal

Reserve Bank of New York, was approached. He had already been in contact with other central bank governors and is reported to have "had doubts" explaining that assistance to Iceland would need to be large to have the intended effects, more than US$10 billion.

On April 23, 2008 Mr. King sent a letter to Davíð Oddsson, governor of the CBI, in which he said that in his "judgement, the only solution to this problem is a programme to be implemented speedily to reduce significantly the size of the Icelandic banking system" (Rannsóknarnefnd Althingis, 2010, p. 172). Furthermore he stated that he "would very much like to discuss how the international community could offer help to Iceland in respect of designing such a solution by raising the matter at the dinner of G10 Central Bank Governors to be held in Basel on 4 May. I have spoken about this with Stefan Ingves, Governor of the Riksbank in Sweden, and we shall both be requesting a discussion at the dinner" (Rannsóknarnefnd Althingis, 2010, p. 173). In his letter in response, Mr. Oddsson asked Mr. King to reconsider and stated that "[t]he Icelandic banks are well capitalised but they are dealing with a problem of perception" (Rannsóknarnefnd Althingis, 2010, p. 174). Mervyn King did not respond to that letter.

On May 16, 2008 a currency swap arrangement between the CBI and the Nordic central banks was signed under conditions agreed to by the CBI governors and key Icelandic ministers (the prime minister, the foreign minister and the finance minister). None of the major central banks were involved and the amount was a modest 1.5 billion Euro. On June 6, 2008 Mr. Oddsson wrote a letter to Timothy F. Geithner informing him that in his opinion the currency swap agreements with the Nordic countries had been successful and "[a]lso, as demonstrated by the Nordic facility, the size of the arrangement is not necessarily a decisive issue at this juncture. In my view the perception of strong allies is more important. An arrangement with the Fed would therefore be of monumental significance. I would very much appreciate it if you would give the matter some further thought and be in touch. We would be happy to provide any further information that you would deem helpful." [...]"The perception of strong and far reaching alliances is more important than size. The perception of a lack of allies may have [the] opposite effect" (Rannsóknarnefnd Alþingis, 2010, p. 179).

At the end of September 2008, currency swap agreements between the United States and the Nordic countries (Denmark, Norway and Sweden) were announced – Iceland was not included. The same day Mr. Oddsson wrote to Mr. Geithner that "[t]he announcement this morning of the new currency swaps appears to have enhanced confidence for the participating countries.

However, given the perception that the Nordics are one, including Iceland, the new agreement may appear to the markets as having left us in the lurch" (Rannsóknarnefnd Althingis, 2010, p. 179). The Federal Reserve was asked to reconsider, but in early October the final answer was no.

At this point in time Iceland was completely isolated. The three largest Icelandic Banks collapsed in early October 2008 and Iceland had no other option but to approach the IMF. An agreement between the government of Iceland and the IMF was signed on October 24, 2008.

The Response of the International Community: (Dis)Honesty or Incompetence?

As discussed above, considerable research has been done regarding the pre-crisis actions and inactions of the government of Iceland. Less attention has been given to the actions and the inactions of the foreign governments and officials approached by the Icelandic government for assistance before its banking sector collapsed. Were they honest in their actions *vis-à-vis* their own citizens or the citizens of Iceland? This is a question that merits research and would, in fact, merit a separate investigation. Is it possible that they acted honestly but were incompetent and therefore not trustworthy e.g., not understanding or recognizing flaws in European integration and the possible consequences?

Before the crisis hit, the Icelandic banks had, as discussed above, expanded their operations into the UK and the Netherlands. This included the so called "Icesave" accounts, which were offering interest rates that were considered favorable by many. As Joseph E. Stiglitz states in his book *Freefall*, "[t]he depositors foolishly thought there was a 'free lunch': they could get higher returns without risk" (Stiglitz, 2010, p 23). They may also have thought that their own governments in the UK and the Netherlands were doing their regulatory job. When these privately owned Icelandic banks could no longer honor their commitments during the 2008 crisis the UK used strong-arm tactics, including invoking an anti-terrorist law against Iceland and insisting that Icelandic taxpayers bail out depositors from the UK and the Netherlands beyond the amounts the accounts had been insured for. As Stiglitz asks: "Why should Iceland's taxpayers be made to pay for the failure of a private bank, especially when the foreign regulators had failed to do their job of protecting their own citizens?" (Stiglitz, 2010, p. 23). Many Icelanders asked the same question.

As Stiglitz argues, the banking expansion in Iceland "exposed a fundamental flaw in European integration" (Stiglitz, 2010, p. 23). In "the single market" any European bank could operate in any EU country and the responsibility for regulation was put on the home country (in this case Iceland). If the home country failed to do its job the citizens of other countries could lose large sums of money: "Europe didn't want to think about this and its profound implications; better simply make little Iceland pick up the tab, an amount some put as much as 100 percent of the country's GDP" (Stiglitz, 2010, p. 23). This is a sharp criticism of the EU and coming from a Nobel Prizewinning economist. An investigation into the actions and inactions of foreign government and international officials, including EU officials, would be justified and those individuals and the institutions involved should be held accountable.

After the crisis hit, the Icelandic government twice reached a settlement on the Icesave accounts that were approved by the majority of the Icelandic parliament, the Althingi. The president of Iceland twice refused to sign the legislation approved by the Althingi. This triggered two national referendums in which the people overwhelmingly voted no. Finally the EFTA Court ruled that there was no legal basis for the case of Britain, the Netherlands and the EU against Iceland.

The president of Iceland described these events well in a speech at a meeting of OECD ambassadors in Paris on 27 February 2013: "And, when we faced the (...) Icesave dispute in which the Governments of the United Kingdom and the Netherlands, supported by all EU governments and others, demanded that the ordinary people of Iceland – fishermen, farmers, teachers, nurses – should shoulder through their taxes the debts of a failed private bank – we had to choose between the financial interests as they were presented by the established leadership of Europe and the democratic will of the Icelandic nation and decided to allow democracy to prevail.

Following the two referendums, in which the people overwhelmingly voted No, the economy started to recover, becoming healthier with each quarter. The financial doomsayers, whether experts or leaders, who advised strongly against the democratic will of the people turned out to be entirely wrong in their analysis and predictions; a result which certainly should serve as a challenge to many of the policies which are still being advocated and followed in many countries.

When the EFTA Court last month ruled that there was no legal basis for the case of Britain, the Netherlands and the EU against Iceland, it became clear that in addition to the democratic will of the people, justice and the rule of law was also on our side" (Grímsson, 2013, p. 5-6).

Trade relations between Iceland and the UK have been important for both nations for decades. Political relations have, however, sometimes been tense. When Iceland expanded its fisheries territory to 200 miles, the UK government sent its navy into Icelandic territory, an unprecedented act given that both Iceland and the UK are NATO member states. The dispute over fisheries territories, the so-called Cod Wars, was long with dangerous friction between the Icelandic Coast Guard and the British Royal Navy. Again, in this case too the UK used strong-arm tactics, in essence behaving like colonizers against a colony.

Recently the UK government has expressed strong interest in purchasing electricity from Iceland via a submarine cable to the UK. This would help the UK meet its growing energy needs and be part of its transition to clean energy. A submarine cable would be a large and long term investment. Moreover, if successful it could benefit both nations. But several issues need to be settled, including energy prices, energy quantity, contract duration, as well as funding and ownership of the cable. Given past tensions the question remains whether these two nations can cooperate on such a large project so as to be mutually beneficial.

The experience that Iceland underwent during the crisis means that Iceland needs to rethink its foreign policy and how it relates to other nations that have often been considered friendly. The UK has been hostile towards Iceland before, so its refusal to assist followed by aggressive action, poorly disguised as being under an anti-terrorist act, should not come as a surprise. Iceland also perhaps naïvely tends to consider the other Nordic countries as big brothers who would help their little brother if things went wrong. History shows that the Nordic countries think primarily of their own interests when crisis hits and their own interest would often be to protect their relations with larger nations like the UK rather than help the smallest "Nordic brother." This was also the case during the Cod Wars. Relations with the US have also fundamentally changed. Had the financial crisis hit during the Cold War the response from the US would probably have been far different from what it turned out to be post Cold War.

Given the verdict of the EFTA Court it is now clear that Iceland did not have the responsibility to provide a sovereign guarantee for the failed private banks. Considering the demands from the UK and the Netherlands, supported by the EU, one could argue that they behaved dishonestly in deliberately and falsely claiming that Iceland had responsibilities that it did not have. The possibility also arises that these parties failed to understand pre-crisis weaknesses in EU regulation and their reaction should rather be labeled as incompetence than dishonesty. In that case more international efforts should have been made to assist Iceland when weaknesses in the EU financial system materialized.

CONCLUSION

Clearly, by promoting the idea that Iceland should become an international financial centre, the government did express strong faith in the banking sector and did encourage its expansion. The president of Iceland was also a strong supporter of expansion by the three largest banks as can be seen from the speeches he made overseas. The government generally welcomed the expansion of the banks but did not take credible measures to protect the economy in the event of a banking crisis. Private interests via the Iceland Chamber of Commerce aided by academics, including internationally recognized scholars, also published reports that could be used to justify government inaction. This was done by arguing that the size of the banks did not call for drastic measures.

Possibly, the collapse of the banks could have been prevented had the government (the prime minister and the cabinet) taken a drastic measure in the shape of insistence on downsizing the banking sector or relocating most of its cross border operations.

The government, including key cabinet ministers responsible for the banking sector in Iceland, did not take international critics seriously. Moreover, according to the SIC, ministers over-focused on the image crisis facing the banks rather than on the obvious problem.

They seem to have thought that foreigners needed more information to understand that the Icelandic banks were built on solid ground and therefore launched a cross border PR campaign. The president also supported this campaign in his speeches overseas. If the ministers knew that the economy was facing imminent danger but decided to fake reality and pretended that facts from reality were other than they were, this behavior could be classified as dishonesty according to Rand's definition. However, the possibility remains that they honestly thought a PR campaign could stabilize the situation and decided to take that risk, in a gamble for resurrection. If so, and in the light of the SIC conclusions, one can ask whether they were then honest but incompetent and thus not trustworthy. However, if they thought all was well, why then would they have prepared the Emergency Act prior to the collapse of the Icelandic banks?

It is difficult to reach a final judgment as to whether or not the ministers responsible for the banking sector in Iceland can be charged with dishonesty in the sense that they sought to fake reality. However, the SIC states that the problem was obvious and the fact that the ministers had prepared an emergency law prior to the crisis confirms that they knew that things could go wrong but only took action at the last minute. Furthermore, in its conclusions the SIC was of the opinion that the prime minister, the minister of finance, and the minister of business affairs showed negligence during the time leading up to the collapse of the Icelandic banks by omitting to respond in an appropriate fashion to the impending danger for the Icelandic economy that was caused by the deteriorating situation of the banks. Additionally, the SIC was of the opinion that the director general of the financial supervisory authority, along with the three governors of the CBI, showed negligence in the course of particular work during the administration of laws and rules on financial activities and monitoring thereof. It is imperative that the government of Iceland look carefully at how the obligations of individual institutions and officials may be better defined and the division of labor clarified and made sharper.

The Icelandic government should in the future encourage and enforce more risk mitigation via regulations, monitoring and supervision of private sector cross border activities. This applies not only to the banking sector but also to other sectors such as the energy sector, e.g., a possible submarine electricity cable to Europe. More research needs to be done to see if the government has taken sufficient steps in its legislative, regulatory and institutional reforms to reduce the probability of another catastrophic collapse occurring in the future.

When the Central Bank of Iceland made attempts to increase its foreign exchange reserves in March 2008, there was little trust between the CBI and other central banks. It was logical that the CBI would first contact the Bank of England given the large operations of Icelandic banks in the UK. Both institutions had an interest in finding a solution if possible. The Bank of England offered its assistance to approach the "international community" to help reduce the size of the Icelandic banks, but it was unclear how this could be done and Iceland had few reasons to trust the Bank of England. As discussed above, mistakes were made in Iceland, but it is also clear that the UK has a long history of hostility towards Iceland, for example during the "Cod Wars."

When the banking system fell in Iceland the UK again used strong-arm tactics: invoking an anti-terrorist law against Iceland. Given this history pre- and post-crisis, Iceland needs to be careful in its relations with the UK. The government of Iceland twice reached a settlement on the Icesave accounts, settlements rejected in two national referendums.

Arguably, the governments of the Netherlands and the UK tried to fake reality by suggesting that the Icelandic government, i.e., Icelandic taxpayers, should be made responsible for paying the debts of private banks. The EFTA Court ruling confirms that Iceland did not have this responsibility. In retrospect one can argue that the EU showed dishonesty by supporting the Netherlands and the UK in demanding a sovereign guarantee for failed private banks. The Icelandic banking expansion exposed weaknesses in EU integration and may also confirm a certain incompetence within the EU in designing an EU-wide banking system.

The Nordic countries were hesitant to support Iceland during the crisis. Their relationship with the Netherlands and the UK is much more important, politically and economically, than their relationship with Iceland. The close coordination between the Riksbank of Sweden and the Bank of England on how to respond to Iceland's problems shows that the Nordic countries first and foremost take care of their own interests during times of crisis. This can hardly be considered dishonesty but it shows that they are not trustworthy protectors of Iceland's interests.

Additionally, the Nordic countries had enough problems on their own hands: being by far the largest owner of the banking systems in the Baltic States made them vulnerable and the Scandinavian banking systems were closely interlinked. A Baltic banking crisis could have triggered a Scandinavian banking crisis that could then have destabilized the fragile European Banking system as discussed in chapter 1 of this book. The Baltic and Scandinavian banking systems still remain heavily interconnected and vulnerable post-crisis.

The US could be counted on as Iceland's strong ally during the Cold War but weaker political ties after the Cold War meant that they no longer want to get involved. Following its own interest can hardly be considered dishonest but also shows that Iceland cannot rely on the US for assistance during times of crisis.

In retrospect Iceland was lucky that its banking system was not rescued by major central banks as this could have brought the debt level of the country to an unsustainable level. Iceland was fortunate not to have to serve the interest of the Euro area and the Icesave dispute was resolved in two national referendums and eventually in the EFTA Court. However dishonest and incompetent the Icelandic and foreign officials may have been, democracy found a way to ameliorate what could have been a truly catastrophic situation for Iceland.

REFERENCES

Aliber, R.Z. (2008). Monetary Turbulence and the Icelandic Economy. Lecture at the University of Iceland, May 5, 2008, available at: http://www.hi.is/files/skjol/icelandlecutre-May-2008.pdf (Accessed on June 20, 2014).

Buiter, W., and Sibert, A. (2008a). The collapse of Iceland's banks: the predictable end of a non-viable business model, available at: http://voxeu.org/article/iceland-s-banking-collapse-predicable-end-and-lessons-other-vulnerable-nations (Accessed on June 19, 2014).

Buiter, W., and Sibert, A. (2008b). The Icelandic banking crisis and what to do about it: The lender of last resort theory of optimal currency areas. *CEPR Policy Insight No. 26*, available at: http://www.willembuiter.com/iceland.pdf (Accessed on June 5, 2014).

Daníelsson, J., and Zoega, G. (2009). Collapse of a Country. Second edition, available at: http://www.riskresearch.org/files/e.pdf (Accessed on June 16, 2014).

Danske Bank (2006). Research. Iceland: Geyser crisis, available at: http://www.mbl.is/media/98/398.pdf (Accessed on May 20, 2014).

Eggertsson, T., and Herbertsson, T. T. (2009). System Failure in Iceland and the 2008 Global Financial Crisis. *Paper presented at the 13th Annual Conference of ISNIE,* Walter A. Haas School of Business, University of California at Berkeley, June 18-20, 2009, available at: http://papers.isnie.org/paper/373.html (Accessed on May 12, 2014).

Flannery, M. J. (2009). Iceland's Failed Banks: A Post-Mortem. Prepared for the Icelandic Special Investigation Commission, available at: http://sic.althingi.is/pdf/RNAvefVidauki3Enska.pdf (Accessed on May 16, 2014).

Grímsson, Ó. R. (2005). How to succeed in modern business: Lessons from the Icelandic voyage. A speech at the Walbrook Club London May 3, 2005, available at: http://www.forseti.is/media/files/05.05.03.Walbrook.Club.pdf (Accessed on June 1, 2014).

Grímsson, Ó. R. (2006). Icelandic ventures: Can the success continue? A speech at the Kaupthing Seminar in Helsinki on May 24, 2010, available at: http://forseti.is/media/files/06.05.24.Helsinki.Conference.pdf (Accessed on June 3, 2014).

Grímsson, Ó. R. (2013). A clean energy economy lessons from Iceland A Speech by the President of Iceland Ólafur Ragnar Grímsson at a meeting of OECD Ambassadors, OECD Paris 27 February 2013, available at: http://www.forseti.is/media/PDF/2013_02_27_OECD_CleanEnergy.pdf (Accessed on June 3, 2014).

Growth Report - Strategies for Sustained Growth and Inclusive Development. (2008). International Bank for Reconstruction and Development/The World Bank 2008, available at: http://cgd.s3.amazonaws.com/ GrowthReportComplete.pdf (Accessed on April 20, 2014).

Herbertsson, T. Þ., and Mishkin, F. S. (2006). Financial stability in Iceland. Iceland Chamber of Commerce, available at: http://www.vi.is/files/ 555877819Financial%20Stability%20in%20Iceland%20Screen%20Versio n.pdf (Accessed on May 10, 2014).

Hilmarsson, H. Þ. (2008). Private Sector Investments from Small States in Emerging Markets: Can International Financial Institutions Help Handle the Risks? *Stjórnmál og stjórnsýsla*, veftímarit Stofnunar stjórnsýslufræða og stjórnmála, fræðigreinar 4. árgangur 2. tbl., bls. 113-132, available at: http://skemman.is/is/stream/get/1946/8972/23944/1/a.2008.4.2.1.pdf (Accessed on April 10, 2014)

Hilmarsson, H. Þ. (2010). Public-Private Partnerships and Energy Sector Investments in Emerging Market Economies: Can the Risk Mitigation Instruments Offered by International Financial Institutions Help Private Investors From Small States? *Bridges Scientific Journal*, 2010, 2 (51), p. 33 - 43.

Hilmarsson, H. Þ. (2012). Small States and Large Private Sector Investments in Emerging Market Economies in Partnership with International Financial Institutions. In Innovation Systems in Small Catching-Up Economies: New Perspectives on Practice and Policy. *Springer Book Series on Innovation, Technology and Knowledge Management*, Volume 15, Part 2, 139-158, ISBN-10: 1461415470, ISBN-13: 978-1461415473. DOI: 10.1007/978-1-4614-1548-0_8.

IMF. (2008). Iceland: Financial System Stability Assessment—Update, available at: http://www.imf.org/external/pubs/ft/scr/2008/cr08368.pdf (Accessed on June 1, 2014).

Invest in Iceland. (2006, November). Iceland to become an international financial centre.

Jännäri, K. (2009). Report on Banking Regulation and Supervision in Iceland: past, present and future, available at: http://eng.forsaetisraduneyti.is/media/frettir/KaarloJannari__2009.pdf (Accessed on June 1, 2014).

Nefnd forsætisráðherra um alþjóðlega fjármálastarfsemi. (2006). Alþjóðleg fjármálastarfsemi á Íslandi, available at: http://www.forsaetisraduneyti.is/media/frettir/Skyrsla.pdf (Accessed on May 23, 2014).

Portes, R. (2008). The shocking errors of Iceland's meltdown. *Finanical Times,* available at: http://www.ft.com/intl/cms/s/0/80f767e4-9882-11dd-ace3-000077b07658.html#axzz1yd3SisEB (Accessed on May 2, 2014).

Portes, R., Baldursson, F. M. and Ólafsson, F. (2007). The Internationalisation of Iceland's Financial Sector. Iceland Chamber of Commerce, available at: http://www.vi.is/files/15921776Vid4WEB.pdf (Accessed on April 20, 2014).

Peikoff, L. (1991). Objectivism: The Philosophy of Ayn Rand. New York: Penguin, 1991.

Rand, Ayn. (n.d.). John Galt Speech, available at: http://www.amberandchaos.net/?page_id=73 (Accessed on June 26, 2014)

Rand, A. (1961). The Objectivist Ethics. *Paper delivered by Ayn Rand at the University of Wisconsin Symposium on "Ethics in Our Time" in Madison, Wisconsin, on February 9, 1961, available at:* http://www.nscp.org/uploaded_files/1/files/IA-Lab-3-Supplemental.pdf (Accessed on April 5, 2014).

Rannsóknarnefnd Alþingis. (2010). Aðdragandi og orsakir falls íslensku bankanna 2008 og tengdir atburðir. Bindi 1 og 8, available at: http://www.rannsoknarnefnd.is/ (Accessed on May 3, 2014).

Rose-Ackerman, S. (2001). Trust, honesty and corruption: reflection on the state-building process. *European Journal of Sociology*, Vol. 42., Issue 3, December 2001, pp. 526-570.

SIC (Special Investigation Commission). (2010a). Press Conference 12. April 2012, available at: http://sic.althingi.is/ (Accessed on April 2, 2014).

SIC (Special Investigation Commission). (2010b). Report of the Special Investigation Commission (SIC). Volume 1, Chapter 2, available at: http://sic.althingi.is/pdf/RNAvefKafli2Enska.pdf (Accessed of June 4, 2014).

Smith, T. (2006). Ayn Rand´s Normative Ethics. The Virtuous Egoist. Cambridge University Press.

Stiglitz, J. E. (2010). *Freefall: America, free markets, and the sinking of the world economy.* WW Norton & Company.

Yin, R. K. (2009). *Case Study Research. Design and Methods* (4th ed., Vol. 5). California:SAGE Inc.

X-D. (2012). Mr. Geir H. Haarde former Prime Minister. His statement on the verdict delivered by Landsdómur, available at: http://www.xd.is/i-brennidepli/frettir/nr/1768 (Accessed on April 4, 2014).

Chapter 3

SMALL STATES AS CONTRIBUTORS TO INTERNATIONAL DEVELOPMENT COOPERATION. CAN THE BALTIC STATES MAKE A DIFFERENCE GLOBALLY AND IF SO HOW? WHAT LESSONS CAN THEY LEARN FROM THE SCANDINAVIAN COUNTRIES?[1]

SUMMARY

In spite of many challenges faced by the Baltic States during the recent economic and financial crisis, their progress since independence in 1991 has been impressive. In little more than two decades these countries have transformed themselves from being centrally planned economies and provinces in the former Soviet Union into modern countries that are now firmly integrated in the global economy. Since independence they have, for example, become members of the EU, NATO and the WTO. They are also members of international financial institutions such as the World Bank Group (WBG) and the European Bank for Reconstruction and Development (EBRD). According to World Bank classifications all the Baltic States have now achieved high income status.

---

[1] An earlier version of this chapter was discussed at the 23rd Conference on Baltic Studies at the University of Illinois at Chicago on April 26, 2012. The author benefited from questions asked and comments made by participants during the conference.

All the Baltic States have established their international development programs and are contributing bilaterally, as well as taking part in the operations of multilateral organizations. The Baltic States are challenged by small budgets and limited institutional capacity. They need to decide which countries to support, in what sectors, which policy reforms, and so on. They also need to decide what type of engagement is suitable given their own comparative advantages as contributors globally. Given the complexity of international development cooperation the selection of partners, sectors, and aid modalities must be under constant review. Donor countries always need to think of new ways to increase the effectiveness of use of their limited resources.

When reconsidering and developing their foreign aid programs it can be useful for the Baltic States to review the experience of their neighbouring countries to see what lessons can be learned. In the Bretton Woods institutions the Nordic Countries[2] and the Baltic States already cooperate extensively. Among the Nordic countries the Scandinavian countries, Denmark, Norway and Sweden, all small states, are leaders in international development cooperation and can, as a group, have an impact on development policy and development approaches worldwide. When cooperating with the Baltic States the Nordic countries could also benefit from the experience of the Baltic States, which have recently implemented successful economic transitions often under challenging conditions.

Among the conclusions of this chapter is that when small countries such as the Baltic States act alone as donor their influence is likely to be rather limited. For small donor countries projects can certainly allow them to plant their flag and to better control use of their money. But in the big picture of things, the impact of small projects can be quite marginal. Policy lending under instruments such as Poverty Reduction Support Credits and Development Policy Loans/ Development Policy Operations gives small donors a seat at the table for policy dialogue. However a small country would probably be more effective if it focuses only on a few key policy actions. A small donor country may also increase its impact by combining involvement in budget support operations with technical assistance for the ministries or agencies in charge of those key policy actions. The partner country receiving technical assistance can then rely on the products of that technical assistance

---

[2] In this book reference is made to the Nordic countries which are: Denmark, Finland, Iceland, Norway and Sweden. Reference is also made to the Scandinavian countries which are: Denmark, Norway and Sweden.

as an input to policy dialogue, and on the technical assistance program itself to deliver on policy actions.

Participation in budget support operations should not be seen as a panacea and does not guarantee success. Budget support instruments can however be very useful for dialogue on government wide policy issues and economic reforms in the recipient country. Provision of technical assistance, including in financial management, is necessary for developing and transition economies receiving budget support and can enable them to use government systems more effectively. Using the project approach and budget support should not be seen as an either/or choice. Both types of assistance can be used simultaneously and budget support could be introduced gradually, especially for recipient countries with the weakest country systems. To achieve poverty reduction in the long term, sustainable economic growth is necessary. Budget support operations can support economic policies that are conducive to economic growth.

INTRODUCTION

In spite of many challenges faced by the Baltic States during the recent economic and financial crisis, their progress since independence in 1991 has been impressive. In roughly two decades these countries have been transformed from centrally planned provinces in the former Soviet Union to modern countries that are firmly integrated into the global economy. Since independence they have become members of the EU, NATO and the WTO.[3] They are also members of international financial institutions such as the World Bank Group (WBG) and the European Bank for Reconstruction and Development (EBRD).

According to the World Bank all the Baltic States perform well globally and are now classified as high income countries (World Bank, 2013a). In its "Doing Business" report, which evaluates the business and investment climates in 189 countries, the bank ranks all three Baltic States among the 24 top performers in the world (see Table 3.1.). This is a clear indication that their reform programs have been successful in creating a favourable climate for private sector business and investment. This is not to suggest that there is no

---

[3] Estonia and Latvia are members of the Euro area and Lithuania plans to become a member in 2015.

room for improvement. Compared to the Nordic countries the Baltic States still have far to go in terms of per capita income and living standards.

**Table 3.1. Population, income and business environment
of the Baltic States**

	Population	Income level	GNI Per capita (US$) 2013	Ease of doing business rank
Estonia	1.3	High income	15,830	22
Latvia	2.0	High income	14,180	24
Lithuania	3.0	High income	13,850	17

Source: World Bank, 2013a.

As countries become more prosperous, expectations are raised globally, including in the EU and at the UN, that they will play a more active role in assisting other countries that have been less successful in their economic development. The Baltic States have all initiated their own development programs but are challenged by their small development budgets. These small budget allocations can be viewed as a low commitment to contributing internationally.

The current contribution levels of the Baltic States suggest that they still tend to give priority to their own narrow self interest, not fully considering how active participation in international development cooperation can both be beneficial for their partner countries and can also help strengthen the image of the Baltic States as independent countries and make them more prestigious players in the global arena. Arguably, their approach internationally is to continue free riding on other wealthier countries, especially richer EU members.

In addition to reconsidering their low contribution to international development cooperation, the Baltic States must, like all other donor countries, constantly review and revise their development programs, policy, and instruments used when assisting partner countries. When reconsidering and developing their foreign aid programs it can also be useful for the Baltic States to review the experience of other countries to see what lessons can be learned. The Scandinavian countries, Denmark, Norway and Sweden have, in spite of being relatively small countries, remained among donor countries that could be classified as leaders in development cooperation and are among the few countries in the world that contribute more than 0.7 percent of their GNI to international development cooperation[4] (see Table 3.5.). In addition to large bilateral development programs they are members and active participants in international financial institutions such as the WBG, the EBRD as well as in all the regional development banks.[5] This participation includes efforts to influence the policy agendas of those institutions.

Multilaterally the Nordic Countries and the Baltic States already cooperate extensively, including in the Bretton Woods institutions. At the World Bank Group the Baltic States share an executive director's Office with the Nordic Countries. A similar arrangement is used at the IMF. Nordic-Baltic cooperation also extends to the EBRD, where Iceland shares an office with Estonia and Sweden, Latvia works with Norway and Finland, and Lithuania works with Denmark[6] (European Bank for Reconstruction and Development, n.d.).

The Scandinavian countries, Denmark, Norway and Sweden, are leaders in international development cooperation and as a group can have a greater impact on development policy and development approaches worldwide than one might expect small states to be able to do. The per capita income of the Nordic countries is still much higher than that of the Baltic States, but when cooperating with the Baltic States the Nordic countries can benefit from the experience of the Baltic States in the shape of recently having implemented successful economic transitions.

The objective of this chapter is to assess what role small states can play in assisting their partner countries in implementing economic transition and achieving economic growth and poverty reduction. The countries focused on are mainly the Baltic States as participants in multilateral institutions and providers of bilateral assistance to the partner countries they have selected. How should the Baltic States assist their partner countries in the future? How can the Baltic States best share their transition experience with less advanced transition countries? Should they focus on small bilateral projects or should they work in partnership with other bilateral and multilateral donors? Should they engage in budget support operations and participate in policy dialogue or concentrate on small projects, or some combination of both?

The proposition considered is that small states can increase their development effectiveness by cooperating with international financial

---

[4] The two other countries that have achieved this status are the Netherlands and Luxembourg, both small states.

[5] The regional development banks are the Asian Development Bank, the African Development Bank and the Inter-American Development Bank.

[6] That group of countries also includes Ireland and FYR Macedonia.

institutions and by engaging in policy dialogue with their priority countries in partnership with IFIs and other countries. Small countries can further increase their development effectiveness by providing technical assistance to support policy actions that they consider important for their priority countries.

Asking the above questions now is highly relevant since the Baltic States are recovering from the 2008 economic and financial crisis and are likely to increase their contribution to international development cooperation in the coming years. All the Baltic States have their ongoing development cooperation programs and like larger countries need to think about the effectiveness of the programs they support with their limited resources. In addition, the Baltic States, as EU member states, are currently challenged by their obligations as EU members to increase their contributions to international development cooperation. They are all far from fulfilling their EU commitments, but post crisis they can be expected to give more attention to international development cooperation. The target was to increase their official development assistance to 0.17 percent of GNI by 2010 and 0.33 percent of GNI by 2015. It seems likely that in the coming years the contributions of the Baltic States to international development cooperation will increase substantially, especially when their economies return to pre-crisis income levels. In fact, a recent World Bank EU11Regular Economic Report projects healthy economic growth rates for all the Baltic States in the near future (World Bank, 2013b), higher than average among EU11 countries[7] and much higher than average economic growth in the Euro area[8] (see Table 3.2.)

Table 3.2. The Baltic States, the EU11 and the Euro Area: Economic growth prospects

	2012	2013p	2014f
Estonia	3.9	1.3	3.0
Latvia	5.5	3.9	4.2
Lithuania	3.7	3.0	3.5
EU11	0.8	1.0	2.3
Euro Area	-0.6	-0.5	1.1

Source: World Bank, 2013b.
p: projection, f: forecast.

---

[7] The EU11 countries are: Bulgaria, Croatia, the Czech Republic, Estonia, Hungary, Latvia, Lithuania, Poland, Romania, Slovenia, the Slovak Republic,

[8] The Euro area countries are: Austria, Belgium, Cyprus, Estonia, Finland, France, Germany, Greece, Ireland, Italy, Latvia, Luxembourg, Malta, the Netherlands, Portugal, Slovakia, Slovenia, and Spain.

Among the aims of this chapter is to draw the attention of policy makers in the Baltic States, who are in the process of formulating their development programs, to recent trends in international development cooperation. Studying these trends and the way other small states, including the Nordic countries, have implemented their development programs, can help the Baltic States increase the effectiveness of their own programs. The other aim of the chapter is to contribute to the academic literature on Baltic international development cooperation. Very little has been written so far in this area and more research and discussion in schools in the Baltic States could both increase awareness about international development cooperation in these countries and help policy makers shape these programs in the future.

Methodology

The methodology used in the chapter is the case study method. Compared to other research methods, a case study enables the researcher to examine the issues addressed in greater depth. According to R. K. Yin (2009, p. 101-102) six sources of evidence are most commonly used in case studies. These are: documentation, archival records, interviews, direct observations, participant observation, and physical artifacts. Each of these sources has advantages and disadvantages and according to R. K. Yin (2009, p. 101-102) one should "note that no single source has a complete advantage over all the others. In fact, the various sources are highly complementary, and a good case study will therefore want to use as many sources as possible" (Yin, 2009, p. 101).

The sources of evidence used for the analysis in this chapter include documentation and secondary data, such as reports and scholarly literature. The author also exchanged emails with and interviewed various experts in the field, including in the ministries responsible for international development cooperation in the Baltic States. These communications when referred to are documented in footnotes. Direct observation also plays a role in this chapter as the author draws on his own experience and observations having worked in the Baltic States for the World Bank Group for four years, from 1999 to 2003, while they were implementing transition just before EU accession. Preference was given to using well documented evidence that is publicly available and listed in the references. However one needs to keep in mind that hardly any scholarly literature is available on this subject.

This comparative case study does not present results that can be evaluated on the basis of statistical significance, so that care is needed in generalizing the findings of one case study on another case or situation. However, some lessons from the study may have wider relevance than just for the Baltic States. This is especially true of small countries that have implemented economic transition, successfully and sometimes unsuccessfully, and wish to share their experience with other less advanced transition countries but have limited financial sources to do so.

Partner Country Selection

The Baltic States have all selected priority partner countries (see Table 3.3.). As the table shows most of the priority partner countries are lower or upper middle income countries in Europe and Central Asia. The only exceptions are three low income countries: Afghanistan, which is supported by Estonia and Lithuania; and Kyrgyzstan and Tajikistan, which are supported by Latvia.

Currently Estonia supports: Afghanistan, Armenia, Azerbaijan, Georgia, Moldova and Ukraine, as priority partner countries. Latvia selected Belarus, Georgia, Moldova and Ukraine as its development cooperation priority countries and recently also added Kyrgyzstan, Tajikistan and Uzbekistan. Finally, Lithuania supports Afghanistan, Belarus, Georgia, Moldova and Ukraine as priority partner countries.

Table 3.3. The Baltic States and their priority partner countries

	Country	Population Millions	Income level	GNI per capita, US$	Ease of doing business
Estonia: Development cooperation - priority partner countries[9]	Afghanistan	29.8	Low income	622	164
	Armenia	3.0	Lower middle income	3.720	37
	Azerbaijan	9.3	Upper middle income	6.050	70
	Belarus	9.5	Upper middle income	6.530	63
	Georgia	4.5	Lower middle income	3.280	8
	Moldova	3.6	Lower middle income	2.070	78

---

[9] See list of Estonia's priority partner countries: http://www.vm.ee/?q=en/taxonomy/term/55

	Country	Population Millions	Income level	GNI per capita, US$	Ease of doing business
	Ukraine	45.6	Lower middle income	3.500	112
Latvia: Development cooperation priority countries[10]	Belarus	9.5	Upper middle income	6.530	63
	Georgia	4.5	Lower middle income	3.280	8
	Kyrgyzstan	5.6	Low income	990	68
	Moldova	3.6	Lower middle income	2.070	78
	Tajikistan	8.0	Low income	860	143
	Ukraine	45.6	Lower middle income	3.500	112
	Uzbekistan	29.8	Lower middle income	1.720	146
Lithuania: Priority partner countries[11]	Afghanistan	29.8	Low income	622	164
	Armenia	3.0	Lower middle income	3.720	37
	Azerbaijan	9.3	Upper middle income	6.050	70
	Belarus	9.5	Upper middle income	6.530	63
	Georgia	4.5	Lower middle income	3.280	8
	Moldova	3.6	Lower middle income	2.070	78
	Ukraine	45.6	Lower middle income	3.500	112

Sources: World Bank, 2013a; Ministry of Foreign Affairs, Latvia, 2014; Government of the Republic of Lithuania, 2014; Ministry of Foreign Affairs, Estonia, 2014a.

The Baltic States have thus chosen to share their experience with less advanced transition countries further to the south and the east in Europe and Central Asia. With this country selection the Baltic States can contribute to economic development and promotion of peace and stability in the region they live in and are part of. What is unique with the selection of these priority countries is that they are mainly middle income, not the poorest low income countries in the world. This is common for country selection in the EU11

---

[10] List of priority countries provided via email from the Ministry of Foreign Affairs, Latvia, on April 16, 2014. See also http://www.mfa.gov.lv/en/news/press-releases/2014/march/11-5.
[11] List of countries provided according to Development Policy Guidelines of the Republic of Lithuania for 2014-2016 approved on January 15, 2014.

countries, but is very different from the EU15[12] countries that emphasize assistance to low income countries, particularly in Sub-Saharan Africa, where the Baltic States are not yet active. Support for Afghanistan, a low income country, is probably related to the Baltic States' NATO membership. Lithuania, for example, has given priority to its program in Afghanistan and reports its program there as the biggest since becoming a member of the international donor community (Ministry of Foreign Affairs, Lithuania, 2014). Estonia also contributes to the Afghanistan Reconstruction Trust Fund which is supported by 33 other donors and administered by the World Bank (World Bank, 2014). Estonia's contribution to the Afghanistan Reconstruction Trust Fund is generous considering the size of its development budget.

In contrast, the Nordic countries spend most of their international development budget to support low income countries, with Sub-Saharan Africa receiving more assistance than any other region (see Table 3.4. listing their top ten recipient countries). The only country in the top ten recipient group for the Nordic countries that also appears among the priority partner countries of the Baltic States is Afghanistan. All the Nordic countries except Iceland include general budget support and policy dialogue as part of their development assistance program.

Table 3.4. Top ten recipients of the Nordic Countries

	Denmark	Finland	Norway	Sweden	Iceland
1	*Tanzania*	*Tanzania*	Afghanistan	*Congo, Dem. Rep.*	*Uganda*
2	*Mozambique*	*Mozambique*	*Tanzania*	*Tanzania*	*Malawi*
3	*Ghana*	Afghanistan	West Bank and Gaza Strip	Afghanistan	*Mozambique*
4	Afghanistan	*Ethiopia*	*Sudan*	*Mozambique*	Afghanistan
5	*Uganda*	Nepal	*Mozambique*	*Sudan*	*Namibia*
6	Bangladesh	Vietnam	*Uganda*	*Kenya*	West Bank/ Gaza Strip
7	*Kenya*	Kenya	*Zambia*	West Bank and Gaza Strip	Nicaragua
8	Vietnam	*Zambia*	*Malawi*	Somalia	Haiti
9	Bolivia	Nicaragua	Pakistan	*Uganda*	*Guinea-Bissau*
10	Nepal	*Sudan*	Somalia	*Ethiopia*	Bosnia and Herzegovina

Source: OECD, 2013a. *Italics: Sub-Saharan Africa.*

---

[12] The EU 15 countries are: Austria, Belgium, Denmark, Finland, France, Germany, Greece, Ireland, Italy, Luxembourg, the Netherlands, Portugal, Spain, Sweden and the United Kingdom

Contributions to International Development Cooperation and EU and UN Commitments

The Baltic States, which joined the EU in 2004, are currently challenged by their obligations as EU members to increase their contributions to international development cooperation. The EU target for new member states was that they increase their official development assistance to 0.17 percent of GNI by 2010 and to 0.33 percent of GNI by 2015. According to numbers provided by the OECD, in 2012 none of the Baltic States had reached the target of 0.17 percent of GNI that they were supposed to have reached in 2010. In 2012 Lithuania contributed 0.13 percent of GNI, Estonia 0.11 percent of GNI, and Latvia 0.07 percent of GNI, (see Table 3.5.).

In contrast the Scandinavian countries, Denmark, Norway and Sweden, contribute well above the UN target for the high income donor group which is 0.7 percent of GNI. Finland is not far from meeting this target but Iceland, which made pre crisis efforts to increase its contributions, lags embarrassingly behind (see Table 3.5.).

Table 3.5. Overseas Development Assistance/Gross National Income Ratio

	2008	2009	2010	2011	2012
Baltic States					
Estonia	0.10	0.10	0.10	0.11	0.11
Latvia	0.07	0.07	0.06	0.07	0.07
Lithuania	0.11	0.11	0.10	0.13	0.13
Nordic Countries					
Denmark	0.82	0.88	0.91	0.85	0.83
Finland	0.44	0.54	0.55	0.53	0.53
Iceland	0.47	0.35	0.29	0.21	0.22
Norway	0.89	1.06	1.05	0.96	0.93
Sweden	0.98	1.12	0.97	1.02	0.97

Source OECD, 2014a.

Multilateral versus Bilateral Contributions and Development Cooperation

Any country participating in international development cooperation needs to decide how large a share it allocates to its bilateral assistance program and how much it allocates to multilateral institutions. As Tables 3.6.1 and 3.6.2 show, the small budget of the Baltic States goes mostly to pay for their participation in multilateral institutions. This is especially the case for Latvia. In contrast the Scandinavian countries spend most of their international development fund on bilateral programs (see Tables 3.6.1. and 3.6.2.). This is in spite of the fact that the Scandinavian countries have a wider membership in multilateral institutions than the Baltic States. The Scandinavian Countries are, for example, members of the regional development banks, i.e., the African Development Bank, the Asian Development Bank and the Inter-American Development Bank and need to contribute to those institutions, whereas the Baltic States are still not members.

Does this mean that the Baltic States place a higher priority on multilateral development cooperation than other small states such as the Scandinavian countries? This is unlikely to be the explanation. A more likely reason for the relatively large portion contributed to multilateral development cooperation in the Baltic States is that their total development budgets are so small that when they have paid their share in the multilateral institutions they are members of, there is not much left for bilateral activities. This is especially true of Latvia. The international development budgets of the Scandinavian countries, Denmark, Norway and Sweden, are so large that when they have paid their multilateral contributions according to internationally agreed formulas about two thirds of their contributions usually remain unallocated. And this is in spite of the fact that they have paid supplementary contributions (i.e., contribute more than the agreed international formula says they should) to institutions such as the International Development Association (IDA), the arm of the World Bank that lends to the poorest developing countries on concessional terms.

Table 3.6.1. Multilateral Development Assistance/Total Development Assistance ratio

	2008	2009	2010	2011	2012
Baltic States					
Estonia	73.4	80.4	73.8	67.0	63.0
Latvia	80.4	90.5	89.7	93.7	94.5
Lithuania	68.9	78.1	55.4	60.2	57.5
Nordic Countries					
Denmark	34.8	32.2	26,8	26.9	28.6
Finland	40.6	38.7	37.1	40.3	39.5
Norway	23.2	22.5	23.3	25.1	25.9
Sweden	33.6	33.8	35.7	35.0	30.6

Sources: OECD, 2014a; OECD, 2014b; OECD, 2013b, p. 105; OECD, 2012, p. 105; OECD 2011, p. 81.

Table 3.6.2. Bilateral Development Assistance/Total Development Assistance ratio

	2008	2009	2010	2011	2012
Baltic States					
Estonia	26.7	19.6	26.2	30.0	37.0
Latvia	19.6	9.5	10.3	6.3	5.5
Lithuania	31.1	21.9	44.6	39.8	42.5
Nordic Countries					
Denmark	65.2	67.8	73.4	73.1	71.4
Finland	59.4	61.3	62.9	59.7	60.5
Norway	76.8	77.5	76.7	74.9	74.1
Sweden	66.4	66.2	64.3	65.0	69.4

Sources: OECD, 2014a; OECD, 2014b; OECD, 2013b, p. 105; OECD, 2012, p. 105; OECD, 2011, p. 81.

Medium and Long Term Trends

While the contributions of the Baltic States to international development cooperation can be expected to grow until 2015, it seems impossible that any of them will be able to reach the 0.33 percent of GNI target by 2015. In fact, Estonia, the only Baltic State that has a multiannual plan for its contributions to development cooperation, plans to reach 0.176 percent of GNI by 2015 (see Table 3.7.). Estonia was supposed to reach 0.17 percent of GNI in 2010 and has so far not been able to live up to that less ambitious multiyear plan.

Table 3.7. Funds allocated for development cooperation and humanitarian aid in the state budget of Estonia through 2010-2015 (million Euro per annum)

	2010	2011	2012	2013	2014	2015
GNI	13,502	14,147	14,850	15,613	16,442	17,026
% of GNI (government proposal 13.05.2010)	0.104	0.119	0.143	0.149	0.162	0.176
Total official development cooperation and humanitarian aid funds	14.00	16.97	21.31	23.28	26.76	30.06

Source: Estonian Government (n.d.).

Given their income level and economic growth, the Baltic States need seriously to consider how they can move closer to the EU target. Not only do the new EU member states[13] fall short of fulfilling their international commitments, but most of the EU15 countries also fall short of their 0.7 percent of GNI target while in fact only Sweden, Luxembourg, Denmark, and the Netherlands, all small states, actually fulfill this commitment (Council of the European Union, 2012). In the Nordic-Baltic group the contributions of Denmark, Norway and Sweden are particularly impressive.

Priority Sectors/Areas in Partner Countries

Like all donor countries the Baltic States need to prioritize the spending of their development budgets. Currently the Baltic States are struggling to link their small budgets to the Millennium Development Goals and other international development agreements. In fact, in its "Strategy for Estonian Development Cooperation and Humanitarian Aid 2011 and 2015" Estonia states that its development cooperation is built on twenty international agreements for which meetings took place in places such as: Beijing, Cairo, Copenhagen, Doha, Johannesburg, Monterrey, Rio de Janeiro, Rome, and elsewhere. Most of those meetings are related to the United Nations and some to the European Union. This is not to suggest that representatives from the Baltic States attended all these meetings, but in spite of the dismal results in eradicating world poverty, travel has truly flourished for representatives of aid agencies.

It is also a major effort for anyone to become familiar with all the declarations, plans, consensuses, decisions, programs, codes, strategies, action plans, joint statements, principles, rules, guidelines, conclusions, and so on, that the international community has come up with. This is especially true of small countries with very small development budgets.

Latvia with its tiny development budget states that "[t]aking into account that Latvia's presidency of the EU coincides with the year of assessing the UN [Millennium Development Goals] (2015) it is important for Latvia to participate actively and responsibly in international discussions and in planning and implementation of ... EU development cooperation policy" (Ministry of Foreign Affairs, Latvia n.d.). This must be a difficult task for

---

[13] i.e. the new member states joining the EU in 2004 and 2007.

Latvia, which has the EU Commissioner for Development, but recently practically eliminated its bilateral development budget.[14]

In spite of all these challenges the Baltic States have made their decisions as to what sectors and areas they want to give priority to in their partner countries (see Table 3.8.). As the table shows the Baltic States have decided to focus on transition issues relevant to middle income countries. This makes sense for the Baltic States, as they have recent and relevant transition experience to share.

Table 3.8. Priority sectors/areas of the Baltic States in their partner countries

Estonia[15]	Latvia[16]	Lithuania[17]
(i) Education and health (human development); (ii) Good governance and democratization; (iii) Sustainable economic development (including environment); (iv) Horizontal field: Information and communications technology.	(i) Fostering market economy (international trade and Deep and Comprehensive Free Trade Area standards and requirements); (ii) Promoting good governance (civil society, local governments, state administration reforms); (iii) Environment; (iv) Education.	(i) Promotion of democracy; (ii) Rule of law and human rights; (iii) Economic development; (iv) Euro-integration processes; (v) Administrative capacity building.

Is There Support for International Development Cooperation in the Baltic States?

As discussed above the economies of the Baltic States are growing and expectations within the EU are that as member states they will increase their

---

[14] Andris Piebalgs is the EC Commissioner for Development, see http://ec.europa.eu/commission_2010-2014/piebalgs/index_en.htm

[15] According to an email to the author from the Estonian Ministry of Foreign Affairs dated April 25, 2011.

[16] These are the overall priorities of the Latvian government but priority sectors/areas may differ from country to country according to an email from the Latvian Ministry of Foreign Affairs on April 16. 2014. See also http://www.am.gov.lv/en/policy/DevelopmentCo-operation/info/

[17] According to the website of the Lithuanian Ministry of Foreign Affairs accessed on April 27, 2011. For detail on priority sectors/areas in each partner country see Development Cooperation Policy Guidelines of the Republic of Lithuania for 2014-2016 (Government of Lithuania 2014).

contributions to international development cooperation. But is there public support in the Baltic States for international development cooperation?

According to the Eurobarometer 2012 survey public support for development cooperation is rather strong in the Baltic States. The 2012 survey shows that 85 percent of Lithuanians, 80 percent of Latvians and 73 percent of Estonians consider it important "to help people in developing countries." Moreover, as many as 35 percent of Lithuanians, 29 percent of Latvians and 23 percent of Estonians considered it very important "to help people in developing countries" (European Commission, 2012, p.8). This support for development cooperation is notable because the Baltic States were hard hit by the 2008 global economic and financial crisis, especially Latvia. However, support is lower than it was in 2010 according to the 2010 Eurobarometer survey (European Commission, 2010).[18]

Do the Baltic States see added value in having EU Member States working together on helping developing countries? According to the Eurobarometer 2010 survey a notable difference exists in terms of the level of importance the Baltic States attach to having the EU countries working together. Estonia shows the strongest support for EU cooperation or 84 percent, Latvia 78 percent and Lithuania 54 percent. In spite of this difference the majority of people feel that there is value added in having EU Member States working together on helping developing countries by responding to the question either with a "yes, definitely" or "yes, to some extent" (European Commission, 2010, p.14)

In the 2010 Eurobarometer survey 49 percent of Estonians, 57 percent of Latvians and 65 percent of Lithuanians felt that the EU should either increase aid to developing countries beyond what has already been promised or keep their promise to increase aid (European Commission, 2010, p. 17). However, the citizens of the Baltic States do not seem to know much about where aid goes. In Latvia, for example, 63 percent say they know nothing about where their national aid goes, while 54 percent say they know nothing regarding EU aid. The pattern is similar for Estonia (national: 60 percent, EU: 57 percent), Lithuania (national: 61 percent, EU: 52 percent) (European Commission, 2010, p. 53). Thus little awareness exists about development cooperation programs in general in spite of support for development cooperation.

---

[18] According to the 2010 survey 89 percent of Lithuanians, 86 percent of Latvians and 84 percent of Estonians considered it important "to help people in developing countries." However, 38 percent of Lithuanians, 33 percent of Latvians and 32 percent of Estonians considered it very important "to help people in developing countries" (European Commission, 2010, p. 9).

Project Approach, Budget Support and Policy Dialogue.
Definitions and Some Theoretical Considerations

What approach should the Baltic States choose for their international development cooperation: the project approach or budget support, or a combination of both? The answer to this question depends in part on what strengths they have and what they want to offer to their partner countries. Where do they have comparative advantages over other donors?

The so called project approach means that the donor country, in this case the Baltic States, defines sector specific projects, with an agreed timetable, in cooperation with the receiving country, but the financial administration of the project is maintained within the donor country. This level of donor involvement is out of line with the mainstream approach in international development cooperation as conducted today, which increasingly emphasizes country ownership using the planning, budgetary and procurement systems of the receiving/partner country.[19] Internationally there has been discussion and emphasis on budget support to recipient countries, and on assisting them in creating an overall policy environment conducive to long term economic growth. The European Union has supported this effort and is a large budget support provider.

Estonia recently developed country assistance strategy papers for two of its partner countries, Georgia and Moldova, which do have discussion about donor coordination, although, as the country strategy papers state: "The Estonian Ministry of Foreign Affairs is responsible for the strategic planning, implementation, monitoring, and coordination of the activities of ... Estonian

---

[19] In 1980 the World Bank introduced its first structural adjustment loan. This marked a shift from project aid to a program based approach, where policy conditionality played an important role. Since then there has been a substantial shift in the international institutional environment for development cooperation and a number of important donor meetings have taken place, and declarations issued on aid effectiveness. Among these are: the Copenhagen Summit in 1995, the Millennium Development Goals of 2000, the Monterrey Consensus 2002, the Rome and Paris Declarations on Aid Efficiency of 2003 and 2005, and the Roundtables on Managing for Development Results (These were organized by the World Bank and took place in Washington DC 2002, in Marrakesh in 2004, and in Hanoi 2007). The Global Partnership for Effective Development Cooperation was also created in Busan, Korea in 2011. The World Bank Comprehensive Development framework launched in 1999 is a notable change in the World Bank's development approach and the OECD Development Assistance Committee guidelines are also important. As a result, the key words in the current development paradigm are: ownership, alignment, harmonization, and results orientation. This has also resulted in increased emphasis on budget support to recipient countries and in creating an overall policy environment conducive to long-term growth.

development cooperation. Practical implementation of development cooperation activities is undertaken by other ministries and their agencies, other constitutional institutions, local authorities, the non-profit and business sectors. Progress monitoring and reporting, auditing and controlling will be undertaken in accordance with the related legislation and additional guidance issued by the Ministry of Foreign Affairs. Each year the Ministry of Foreign Affairs shall submit a report on the implementation of the development cooperation programme to the Government of the Republic of Estonia" (Ministry of Foreign Affairs, Estonia, 2014b). It is a good sign that the Estonian government has a country strategy and is aware of the activities of other donors. However, questions remain about the role of the recipient country. For example, can there be true recipient government ownership of a program that is managed by the donor? And again, what is the role of the recipient country in program or project evaluation?

One way for the Baltic States to share their transition experience is to become active in policy dialogue with their partner countries. This could be done by shifting some of the resources from projects in their bilateral aid programs to provision of budget support in partnership with other donors. As S. Koeberle and Z. Stavreski (2006, p. 3) note: "Budget support has become an increasingly important mode of development assistance, receiving growing attention from bilateral donors and international financial institutions in the context of a partnership-based approach to aid. This form of aid promises benefits for both donors and recipient countries: increasing scope for scaling up development assistance, reducing transaction costs, strengthening country ownership, and achieving greater development effectiveness than traditional modes of aid delivery" (Koberle and Stavreski, 2006, p. 3). This is especially noteworthy for the Baltic States as their comparative advantages may lie in sharing their recent transition experience with less advanced transition countries. Policy advice cannot only be prescriptive and based on standardized development models but should assist countries in developing their own solutions for applying principles that have been recognized as valid development approaches. Consultations with successful transition countries like the Baltic States, which have recently implemented similar reforms, can aid in the process that needs to be undertaken by less advanced transition countries.

But what exactly is budget support? A variety of definitions can be found. In a World Bank publication S. Koeberle and Z. Stavreski (2006) define budget support as "financial assistance that supports a medium-term program and is provided directly to a recipient country's budget on a regular basis, using the country's own financial management systems and budget procedures" (Koberle and Stavreski, 2006, p. 5). According to the OECD Development Assistance Committee Guidelines and Reference Series, budget support is defined as "a method of financing a partner country's budget through a transfer of resources from an external financing agency to the partner government's national treasury. The funds thus transferred are managed in accordance with the recipient's budgetary procedures" (OECD, 2006a, p. 26). According to the European Commission, "[b]udget support is a way of implementing development aid which consists in giving financial aid to the treasuries of the recipient countries. This aid increases the resources available to the recipient country to implement its own budget according to its own procedures. What generally characterises budget support is that it goes directly to the partner governments and is integrated into their own systems of appropriation, procurement and accounts, and is not connected to specific projects" (European Commission, 2008, p. 15).

Common to all these definitions is the notion of direct financial support to the partner country's budget. Given the current size of the Baltic development budget these transfers cannot be large in absolute terms, but they would allow the Baltic States to participate in a broad based dialogue and share their transition experience. In fact, many donors consider an opportunity for open dialogue on broad policy reforms to be one of the most important elements of budget support arrangements. As Koberle and Stavresky emphasize: "Smaller bilateral donors, in particular, value the opportunity to contribute effectively to the dialogue on government policies" (Koberle and Stavreski, 2006, p. 20). It is important that policy dialogue between donors and the partner country is well informed and supported by well targeted analytical work and technical assistance. Here some of the small technical assistance and capacity building projects provided by the Baltic States could become more effective if they supported specific policy actions.

Given trends internationally, one may ask whether the time has come for small countries like the Baltic States to engage in policy dialogue with developing countries and provide direct budget support in partnership with other donors, including small states, as well as international financial institutions. Many donors, including Nordic Countries, are involved in budget support, using it as a means to engage in policy dialogue with developing countries and to help the government of the receiving country to take the lead as well as ownership of overall policy reform in the country. In fact according to a World Bank Independent Evaluation Group Poverty Reduction Support Credit evaluation the Scandinavian countries were among the biggest bilateral budget support providers in several African countries. In 2007 Sweden was, for example, among the top three bilaterals providing budget support to countries such as Tanzania, Mozambique, Burkina Faso, Rwanda and Mali. The same year Norway was among the top three bilaterals providing budget support to Uganda and Malawi while Denmark was among the three top bilaterals in budget support to Benin (World Bank, 2010a).

An example of a recent budget support operation to Africa is the ninth Poverty Reduction Support Credit of the World Bank, providing budget support to the Government of Mozambique. This operation supports broad based policy reform in Mozambique based on policy dialogue with the government.

According to the World Bank, Poverty Reduction Support Credit 9 will assist the Government of Mozambique in its efforts to (i) improve the business climate by simplifying business licenses and registration; (ii) improve transparency in the management of extractive industries; (iii) expand the scope of social protection programs while enhancing their targeting, design and impact on beneficiaries and (iv) improve public financial management in auditing, public investment management and debt management (World Bank, 2013d).

This Poverty Reduction Support Credit is a good example of harmonization with other donors. It is based on a Memorandum of Understanding signed between the government of Mozambique and 19 donors, including small states such as Denmark, Finland, Norway and Sweden, supporting the state budget. The principles of this operation are as follows: (i) predictability and alignment with domestic systems; (ii) joint monitoring, and policy actions or expected outcomes of the program are to be based on the common Performance Assessment Framework; (iii) no separate reporting to donors is required; and (iv) mutual accountability (World Bank, 2013d).

Although the Baltic States may initially use the project approach when they assist other countries they may soon also want to consider budget support and engage in policy dialogue. This may be important for them since, as new EU member states, they are committed to increasing their overseas development assistance to 0.33 percent of GNI by 2015. As aid volumes increase the project approach may become too time consuming and out of line with practice of other donors. This assumes that the Baltic States will make an effort to increase their contributions which, unfortunately, they have been slow to do so far.

The Baltic States and Development Policy Operations

Among the characteristics that distinguish the Baltic States from the Nordic countries in their development cooperation is that their priority countries are mainly middle income countries whereas the Nordic countries focus mainly on low income countries. In fact, as noted above, the EU11 countries tend to support middle income countries whereas the EU15 countries focus on low income countries. Budget support operations, like the Poverty Reduction Support Credits that Nordic countries have participated in, support low income IDA countries as classified by the World Bank.

Another World Bank Institution, the International Bank for Reconstruction and Development (IBRD), which supports middle income countries, provides budget support via Development Policy Loans. Donor harmonization is needed for both instruments, Poverty Reduction Support Credits and Development Policy Loans. According to the World Bank, Development Policy Operations emphasize country ownership and alignment, government consultation with stakeholders in design of the reform program, donor coordination, and results and requires systematic treatment of fiduciary risks (World Bank, 2009b).

Funds are made available to the recipient based upon "(a) maintenance of an adequate macroeconomic policy framework, as determined by the Bank with inputs from IMF assessments; (b) satisfactory implementation of the overall reform program; and (c) completion of a set of critical mutually agreed prior policy and institutional actions (prior actions) between the Bank and the client" (World Bank, 2009b). Prior actions are a set of mutually agreed policy and institutional actions that are deemed critical to achieving the objectives of the program supported by a development policy operation and that a country agrees to take before the World Bank Board approves a loan (World Bank, 2009b).

The Baltic States have been recipients of similar operations and have experience in working with the international community on those operations, including the World Bank, bilateral donors and the EU. They could therefore play a useful role here and would, given their recent experience, have comparative advantages over the Nordic Countries in helping their partner countries in implementing reforms under Development Policy Loans or Development Policy Operations.

Partner Countries, Policy Dialogue and Donor Coordination

Some of the partner countries of the Baltic States have recently been receiving budget support via Development Policy Loans or Development Policy Operations from the World Bank, in partnership with other bilateral donors, and other multilateral institutions (see Table 3.9.).

Table 3.9. Priority partner countries of the Baltic States receiving. Development Policy Loans (DPL)/ Development Policy Operations (DPO). In million US$

Country	Project ID	Name	Board Date	IBRD	IDA
Afghanistan	P107921	Strengthening Institutions DPO	06/04/09	0.0	35.0
Armenia	P115626	DPO 1	07/02/09	0.0	60.0
Armenia	P116451	DPO 2	01/11/11	4.0	21.0
Armenia	P122195	DPO 3	02/14/12	30.0	50.0
Belarus	P115626	DPL	07/02/09	200.0	0.0
Georgia	P112700	DPO 1	07/02/09	0.0	85.0
Georgia	P117698	DPO 2	07/29/10	10.0	40.0
Georgia	P122202	DPO 3	07/21/11	0.0	40.0
Moldova	P112625	Economic Recovery DPO	06/24/10	0.0	25.0
Ukraine	P115143	Financial Rehabilitation DPL1	09/17/09	400.0	0.0

Source: World Bank, 2013c.

The World Bank Country Partnership Strategy for Georgia for the financial years 2010-2013 (FY10-FY13) reported a series of three annual Development Policy Operations, within a programmatic framework that provide both immediate budget support to the government while supporting reforms in selected areas – improving public finances, strengthening social safety nets, and building external competitiveness. According to the World Bank the cross-sectorial content of the Development Policy Operations and their leveraging of budget support operations from other partners, such as the Netherlands, the Asian Development Bank or the European Commission gives them high prominence. The World Bank also highlights the benefits of the programmatic approach, not just for budget support operations but also on the analytic side, to deliver just-in-time advice, and this practice will, according to the bank, continue throughout the program (World Bank, 2009a).

According to the World Bank's Economic Recovery Development Policy Credit 2010, Moldova received development funding from several multilateral and bilateral donors in collaboration with the World Bank. The policy notes that supported the Development Policy Operation dialogue with the Moldovan government were developed jointly with the UN, the IMF, the EU, the UK Department for International Development, and the Swedish International Development Cooperation Agency. Complementing the IMF and Bank operations, the EU provided budget support of 50 million Euro to contribute to the sustainable economic development of rural areas, as envisaged under the EU-Moldova Action Plan (World Bank, 2010b). Thus the DPL operation's dialogue with Moldova is developed jointly with multilateral institutions and bilateral donors, i.e.: the UN, IMF, EU, and the UK and Swedish aid agencies noted above. In addition to this the EU provided budget support to a joint EU-Moldova Action Plan.

Georgia and Moldova are both priority countries of all the Baltic States and are undertaking reforms that are often similar to the reforms that the Baltic States implemented in the recent past. Why are the Baltic States not active in supporting those reform efforts? Countries such as the Netherlands, Sweden and the UK are involved, but they have never implemented the transition from communist central planning to market economy; while their contributions could be, and possibly are, very important; nevertheless the Baltic transition experience is undoubtedly more relevant for Georgia and Moldova.

It is important to note that budget support is not always appropriate. In the World Bank Country Partnership Strategy for Ukraine for the financial years 2012-2016 (FY12-FY16) the World Bank states that "inconsistent implementation of past reforms and significant governance problems create unacceptable risks for the Bank to provide direct budget support" (World Bank, 2012, p. 17). According to the World Bank the authorities in Ukraine are aware of the need for more consistency and have committed themselves to a program of addressing some of the most prominent governance concerns, including: public procurement, VAT refunds, transparency in the energy sector, business regulation and red tape, and government investment in failed financial institutions. The government and the World Bank will jointly evaluate progress in these areas to determine whether Development Policy lending can be resumed (World Bank, 2012, p. 17).

The Baltic States could, like the Netherlands, the UK, and Sweden, participate in some budget support operations such as those described above in countries like Georgia and Moldova, or in other European and Central Asian partner countries. They are already participating in budget support operations multilaterally as members of the World Bank, including with their contributions to the World Bank's International Development Association and the European Union's European Development Fund.

However, some government officials in the Baltic States that were contacted when this chapter was being prepared seemed rather discouraged. One government official, for example, stated that Estonia only had 1 vote out of 720 in the European Development Fund and thus did not "have much weight in the decision making process."[20] Estonia also contributes 500,000 Euro to the Afghanistan Reconstruction Trust Fund, of which 50 percent is earmarked for education and 50 percent for budget support. Estonia, however, considers itself too small to participate in policy dialogue with the Afghan Government via the donor group.[21] Thus Estonia does not use its budget support to share its transition experience. An official from Lithuania, though, stated that: "We do participate in the [European Development Fund] coordination process."[22] A Lithuanian official reported "cases of sectorial budget support in Afghanistan" as well as policy dialogue in Belarus in partnership with the Swedish International Development Agency.[23]

Unfortunately it seems that lack of funding discourages the governments of these three small countries and in spite of relevant transition experience they hesitate to participate. In its new "Law on Development Cooperation and Humanitarian Aid", the Lithuanian Government opens up the possibility for "budget assistance." The new law defines budget assistance as "financial assistance transferred to the budget of the partner country engaged in the poverty reduction programme, which depends on the partnership and mutual responsibility based dialogue, the assessment of activities and the strengthening of capacities" (Government of Lithuania, 2013). Opening up the possibility to provide budget support and engage in policy dialogue is the first step. Increased funding and implementation must follow.

In a recent article E. Andrespok and A. I. Kasekamp (2012) refer to a conference paper (Hilmarsson, 2011) as follows: "Former World Bank official Hilmar Þór Hilmarsson (2011) argues that the Baltic States should follow the Nordic states and switch from their small projects based approach in bilateral assistance to budget support and policy dialogue with the recipient countries, through which, he believes, they can maximize their impact. While this approach might indeed bring the Baltic States in line with the general trend

---

[20] According to an email to the author from the Ministry of Foreign Affairs in Estonia dated March 26, 2012.

[21] According an to email from the Ministry of Foreign Affairs in Estonia dated April 19, 2014 and May 5, 2014.

[22] According to an email to the author from the Ministry of Foreign Affairs in Lithuania dated March 29, 2012.

[23] According to an email to the author from the Ministry of Foreign Affairs in Lithuania dated April 27, 2011.

among international donors, it undervalues the significance of new donor countries being able to show their flags and thereby build up public support for development cooperation expenditure" (Andrespok and Kasekamp, 2012, p. 122). This statement is partially based on a misunderstanding of budget support. If the Baltic States participate in budget support their primary goal would be to increase their development effectiveness by sharing their recent experience via policy dialogue. This could indeed increase their visibility and international prestige. At the same time they could support policy actions they favor with some of their smaller technical assistance or capacity building projects. Also if they engage in policy dialogue, for example, on education reform or health reform, this could be complemented with support in building a school or a hospital. Thus the world is not black or white here, i.e., only budget support or only the project approach. Each can support the other. The key question, however, is what combination of aid instruments is most effective for the Baltic States given their valuable experience in reform and limited budget resources. As the World Bank stated when discussing a recent series of Development Policy Operations to Armenia, one of the priority countries of the Baltic States: "A well-designed development policy operation can be effectively used to garner additional donor resources. In the wake of the crisis, Armenia's engagement with the Bank in 2009 under the [Development Policy Operations] series helped it to get additional funding and technical assistance from other donors...." (World Bank, 2013e, p. 23–24). The Baltic States can help here.

Should Small Donors Engage in Policy Dialogue with Partner Countries? Some Cases

Does it make sense for small donors to shift from projects and provide broad based support to their partner countries in cooperation with other larger donors? When analyzing the cases of Austria and Ireland, both small states, and their participation in Programme-Based Approaches (PBAs) L. Leyser (2008) "finds that a shift towards PBAs actually seems to be more important for small bilateral donors than for large ones" (Leyser, 2008, p. 2). According to Leyser (2008) "PBAs enable small donors to 'punch above their weight' in terms of influence and to realise endeavors that would be impossible alone" (Leyser, 2008, p. 34). Commenting on the Irish experience Leyser (2008) argues that "[t]he most remarkable effect of Irish PBA engagement has been its lead position in most of the PBAs it participates. PBAs make Irish Aid "bigger" relative to its share of funding" (Leyser, 2008, p. 3) The case of Ireland can be looked at as an example of small country influence when working in partnership with other larger donors.

Small donors like the Baltic States may still be uncertain whether or not to shift toward budget support due to their relatively small aid budgets and low capacity compared with larger donors. Small donors may be concerned that their voice will not be heard if they provide assistance in partnership with larger donors. They may fear possible loss of identity and visibility. But small donors can also have an advantage due to their comparatively neutral and non-threatening nature. This may even enhance their leadership credentials because other larger donors and governments are willing to support them. Small donors like the Baltic States have no colonial ties. They may have important expertise. The Baltic States, for example, have recently implemented successful transition in many policy areas. Small donors can also have an important role as brokers between larger donors and the partner country and facilitate harmonization. Leadership in a donor group by countries like the Baltic States would hardly ever be considered threatening to any other donor country or the partner country receiving assistance.

For small donors projects can certainly allow them to plant their flag and to better control use of their money. But in the big picture of things, the impact of small projects may be quite marginal. Policy lending under a Poverty Reduction Support Credit-like or Development Policy Loan/Development Policy Operation umbrella gives small donors a seat at the table for policy dialogue. However, a small country would probably be most effective if it focuses only on a few key policy actions. A small donor country may also increase its impact by combining involvement in budget support with technical assistance for the ministries or agencies in charge of those key policy actions. The partner country receiving technical assistance can then rely on the products of that technical assistance as an input in policy dialogue, and on the technical assistance program itself to deliver on the policy actions (e.g., drafting a decree).

In a recent Independent Evaluation Group[24] evaluation of World Bank Poverty Reduction Support Credits the bank even complains that "[i]ndividual

---

[24] The Independent Evaluation Group is charged with evaluating the activities of the IBRD and the IDA (the World Bank), the work of the International Finance Corporation in private sector development, and Multilateral Investment Guarantee Agency guarantee projects and services. The director-general of the Independent Evaluation Group reports directly to the World Bank Group Board of Directors. The goals of evaluation are to provide an objective assessment of the results of the Bank Group's work and to identify and disseminate lessons learned from experience.

small donors can sometimes unduly influence the agenda" (World Bank, 2010a, p. 43). This study also notes that "[b]udget support groups often have uneven membership with a few large core donors and a large number of smaller donors, as well as nonfinancing members, which find it desirable to have a seat at the table" (World Bank, 2010a, p. 48) and "in the case of Vietnam, donors complain that the Bank sometimes appears too demanding for small donors and suggests a more effective division of labor toward donors who have expertise in a sector" (World Bank, 2010a, p. 56). When participating in budget support operations small donors may thus want to be selective in the actions they propose and support those actions with technical assistance to increase their impact. Small donors, like the Baltic States, can thus exercise influence beyond their monetary contribution if they are technically competent and well prepared. The World Bank and other international financial institutions should welcome such engagement.

Budget Support and Policy Dialogue. Are the Fiduciary Risks Higher?

Some donors, such as the Baltic States, may be hesitant to engage in budget support because of the perceived fiduciary risks involved. But the question remains whether there is reason to believe that budget support is necessarily more prone to corruption than investment projects. There seems to be no research that settles this issue unambiguously. To begin with, fiduciary risk seems hard to measure in any rigorous way. "An Evaluation of General Budget Support (1994-2004)" is the title of an independent study carried out by the University of Birmingham on behalf of more than thirty donor and partner countries. It was initiated and supported by the OECD Development Assistance Committee's Evaluation Network. According to the OECD: "The team of evaluators found no clear evidence that budget support funds were, in practice, more affected by corruption than other forms of aid" (OECD, 2006b, p. 1). Furthermore when discussing fiduciary risk Ritva Rainikka at the World Bank says "there is no clear evidence that the risk is greater for budget support than project aid" (Reinikka, 2008).

Countries receiving budget support also often receive assistance to improve their financial management systems. Indeed, according to the World Bank: "To reduce fiduciary risks associated with budget support, [Poverty Reduction Support Credits] were intended to strengthen domestic budget processes" (World Bank, 2010a, p. xiii). According to the World Bank,

Development Policy Operations aim to help the borrower achieve sustainable poverty reduction through a program of policy and institutional actions, for example, strengthening public financial management, improving the investment climate, addressing bottlenecks to improve service delivery, and diversifying the economy. This represents a shift away from the short term macroeconomic stabilization and trade liberalization reforms of the 1980s-90s towards more medium term institutional reforms (World Bank, 2009b).

Economic Policy and Growth

If a donor country that is using the project approach decides also to get involved in budget support operations, there needs to be some certainty, or at least a reasonable likelihood, that good economic policy and good governance leads to stronger and shared economic growth. If engaged in policy dialogue with partner countries the Baltic States would also want to see results and increased effectiveness of their aid programs in partner countries.

The so called Washington Consensus attempted to summarize the outcome of the debate on what policy stances are conducive to economic development[25] (Williamson, 2000; Center for International Development, Harvard University, 2003). Although empirical evidence is available to support many of the policies in the Washington Consensus the international financial institutions were heavily criticized during the 1980s and the early 1990s for interpreting the policy prescription too literally, without country specific circumstances, institutional conditions, or effects on poverty.

The debate continues about the relationship between a good policy environment and economic growth. C. Burnside and D. Dollar (2000) published a famous article more than a decade ago making the case that aid had a positive impact on economic growth in countries with good economic policies (Burnside and Dollar, 2000). They concluded that making aid more systematically conditional on the quality of policies would likely increase its impact on developing countries' growth. Other authors have been more

---

[25] In its original formulation, the Washington Consensus prescribed a policy that could be summarized in ten propositions as follows: (i) fiscal discipline, (ii) a redirection of public expenditure priorities toward fields offering both high economic returns and the potential to improve income distribution, such as primary health care, primary education, and infrastructure, (iii) tax reform (to lower marginal rates and broaden the tax base), (iv) interest rate liberalization, (v) a competitive exchange rate, (vi) trade liberalization, (vii) liberalization of FDI inflows, (viii) privatization, (ix) deregulation (in the sense of abolishing barriers to entry and exit), (x) secure property rights.

cautious in concluding that aid promotes growth in countries with sound policies (see for example Easterly, Levine and Roodman, 2004) and emphasize that the seminal paper of C. Burnside and D. Dollar (2000) does not provide the final answer on this critical issue.

The debate on the relationship between economic policies and growth is likely to be ongoing for a very long time, and it is safe to say that we do not know with any certainty which policies are most conducive to economic growth and poverty alleviation. However, while no one has found a "magic bullet" for growth, some things do seem important, including sensible macroeconomic management[26]; laws and policies that create an environment conducive to private sector activity with low transaction costs; and an economy open for international trade (see, for example, Rajan, 2005). Investment in health and education also ought to be encouraged. Emphasis in the Washington Consensus on macroeconomic stability and outward orientation has been and remains an important component of sustainable development strategies.

In 2008 the so called Commission on Growth and Development issued a report entitled "The Growth Report - Strategies for Sustained Growth and Inclusive Development". The report identified some of the distinctive characteristics of high growth and asked how other countries can emulate them. This report drew inspiration from economies that had been able to sustain growth at an average of 7 percent or more for 25 years or longer. Those successful economies shared five common features that were summarized in a report which followed in 2010: (i) they fully exploited the world economy, (ii) they maintained macroeconomic stability, (iii) they mustered high rates of investment, (iv) in allocating resources, these economies paid due respect to market signals, and (v) as a complement to these functioning markets, the successful economies also had committed, credible and capable governments. As the commission stated, these characteristics are easy to identify but harder to know how to replicate in new places and new circumstances. In fact the commission stated that it "does not provide a formula for policy makers to apply – no generic formula exists" (Commission on Growth and Development, 2008, p. 2). According to the report, governments should be pragmatic in their pursuit of high growth and the Commission stated that "[i]f there were just one valid growth doctrine, we are confident we would have found it" (Commission on Growth and Development, 2008, p. 4).

---

[26] This would for example include: Fiscal discipline, moderate inflation, and a reasonable competitive exchange rate.

The report encourages governments to pursue experimental growth to implementation of economic policy and cites Deng Xiaoping "crossing the river by feeling the stones." In its 2008 report the commission stated that growth can be explained and expressed the hope that it can be repeated. The report was written just before the crisis and in a follow up report in 2010 the commission acknowledged that the two ingredients that needed most rethinking were financial reform and export promotion. However the commission was of the view that the growth model in the original report still remained the best strategy to follow (Commission on Growth and Development, 2010).

According to the Commission on Growth and Development some guidelines exist on what constitutes good economic policy. Those guidelines summarized by the commission can presumably be used both by governments implementing reforms as well as by donors supporting reforms and engaging in policy dialogue with partner governments. In addition, the Baltic States had periods of strong growth after EU accession and are now back on a growth track. They can share this experience, both failures as well as successes.

CONCLUSION

The Baltic States have implemented major economic transitions during the last two decades. They are now firmly integrated in the global economy and are members of key international organizations including the EU, NATO, WTO, WBG, EBRD, amongst others. They have also initiated their own bilateral development programs and selected partner countries as well as priority areas or sectors.

In spite of the recent economic and financial crisis, public support for international development cooperation is rather strong in the Baltic States, although public awareness about the projects and partner countries selected and development projects remains low. All the Baltic States fall short of fulfilling EU targets for EU11 countries as a percentage of GNI. It is time for them to take international development cooperation more seriously. During their transition they received support from the international community in terms of both funding and advice. They have grown sufficiently to play a more active role globally in assisting other less advanced transition countries. Here they can learn from the Nordic countries, especially Denmark, Norway and Sweden.

Small countries such as the Baltic States cannot currently contribute large amounts of funds to international development cooperation. However, their transition experience, successes and failures can be valuable for other less advanced transition countries. All three Baltic States, Latvia, Lithuania and Estonia, have achieved high income status. These countries can become important contributors to policy dialogue in their partner countries where they can share their experience. In doing so, their influence and effectiveness could be enhanced by working in partnership with international financial institutions and other bilateral donors, including the Nordic countries. Currently the Baltic States mainly assist middle income countries further to the south and east, in Europe and Central Asia. The Baltic States can, for example, advise transition countries on public administration reform, institution building, European integration, and so on. The Baltic States already contribute to budget support operations multilaterally through their EU membership and contributions to the World Bank but keep a low profile in policy dialogue.

Due to EU commitments to increase their contributions to development cooperation and projected economic growth in the next few years, the aid volumes of the Baltic States are likely to increase substantially. Shifting some of their assistance from the project approach to budget support to open up the possibility for policy dialogue is an option they need to consider.

When small countries such as the Baltic States act alone their influence is likely to be rather limited. For small donors projects can certainly allow them to plant their flag and to better control use of their money. But in the big picture of things, the impact of small projects can be quite marginal. Policy lending under a Poverty Reduction Support Credit-like umbrella or Development Policy Loans/ Operations gives small donors a seat at the table for policy dialogue. However a small country would probably be more effective if it focuses only on a few key policy actions. A small donor country may also increase its impact by combining involvement in budget support with technical assistance for the ministries or agencies in charge of those key policy actions. The partner country receiving technical assistance can then rely on the products of that technical assistance as an input to policy dialogue, and on the technical assistance program itself to deliver on policy actions.

Some of the partner countries of the Baltic States are receiving budget support and are engaged in policy dialogue with the World Bank, in partnership and with support from the European Union, other multilateral development institutions as well as bilateral donors. This is done via Development Policy Loans/Operations. The Baltic States have so far not participated in such partnerships.

Participation in budget support operations should not be seen as a panacea and does not guarantee success. However, budget support instruments can be very useful for dialogue on government wide policy issues and economic reforms in the recipient country. Provision of technical assistance, including in financial management, is necessary for developing and transition economies receiving budget support and can enable them to use government systems more effectively. Using the project approach and budget support should not be seen as an either/or choice. Both types of assistance can be used simultaneously and budget support could be introduced gradually especially for recipient countries with the weakest country systems. To achieve poverty reduction in the long term, sustainable economic growth is necessary. Budget support operations can support economic policies that are conducive to economic growth.

REFERENCES

Andrespok, E. and Kasekamp, A. I. (2012). Development Cooperation of the Baltic States: A Comparison of the Trajectories of Three New Donor Countries. Perspectives on European Politics and Society. Vol. 13, No. 1, pp. 117-130. doi: 10.1080/15705854.2011.649166.

Burnside, C. and Dollar, D. (2000). Aid, Policies, and Growth. *American Economic Review*. Vol. 90, No. 4, pp. 847-68. doi: 10.1257/aer.90.4.847.

Center for International Development, Harvard University. (2003). Washington Consensus, available at: http://www.cid.harvard.edu/cidtrade/issues/washington.html (Accessed on January 20, 2014).

Commission on Growth and Development. (2008). The Growth Report Strategies for Sustained Growth and Inclusive Development. International Bank for Reconstruction and Development / The World Bank 2008, available at: http://cgd.s3.amazonaws.com/GrowthReportComplete.pdf (Accessed on July 19, 2014]. DOI: 10.1596/978-0-8213-7491-7.

Commission on Growth and Development. (2010). Post-Crisis Growth in Developing Countries. A Special Report of the Commission on Growth and Development on the Implications of the 2008 Financial Crisis. International Bank for Reconstruction and Development / The World Bank 2010, available at: http://www.growthcommission.org/storage/cgdev/documents/specialreport/specialreportfullversion.pdf (Accessed on June 20, 2014). DOI: 10.1596/978-0-8213-8165-6.

Council of the European Union. (2012). Council conclusions on Annual Report 2012 to the European Council on EU Development Aid Targets, available at: http://www.consilium.europa.eu/uedocs/cms_data/docs/ pressdata/EN/foraff/130239.pdf (Accessed on June 18, 2014).

Easterly, W., Ross, L. and Roodman, D. (2004). Aid Policies and Growth: Comment, *American Economic Review*. Vol. 94, No. 3, pp. 774-80. doi: 10.1257/0002828041464560.

Estonian Government. (n.d.) Strategy for Estonian Development Cooperation and Humanitarian Aid 2011–2015, available at: http://www.vm.ee/sites/ default/files/Arengukava2011-2015_ENG.pdf (Accessed on June 20, 2014).

European Bank for Reconstruction and Development. (n.d.) Directors of the EBRD, available at: http://www.ebrd.com/pages/about/who/structure/ directors.shtml (Accessed on May 26, 2014).

European Commission. (2008). Budget support 'A question of mutual trust', available at: http://ec.europa.eu/development/icenter/repository/ LM_budget_support_en.pdf (Accessed on June 10, 2014).

European Commission. (2010). Europeans, development aid and the Millennium Development Goals. Special Eurobarometer, 352, available at: http://ec.europa.eu/public_opinion/archives/ebs/ebs_352_en.pdf (Accessed on September 22, 2014).

European Commission. (2012). Solidarity that spans the globe: Europeans and development aid, 392, available at: http://ec.europa.eu/public_opinion/ archives/ebs/ebs_392_en.pdf (Accessed on July 26, 2014).

Government of the Republic of Lithuania. (2013). Republic of Lithuania Law on Development Cooperation and Humanitarian Aid. May 16 2013 no. xii-311Vilnius.

Government of the Republic of Lithuania. (2014). Development Cooperation Policy Guidelines of the Republic of Lithuania for 2014-2016. Approved by Resolution No. 41 on January 15, 2014.

Hilmarsson, H. Þ. (2011). The Baltic States and their transition from being recipient countries to becoming donor countries. Paper presented at the 9th Baltic studies conference in Europe, Södertörn University, Stockholm, 12-15 June 2011.

Koeberle, S. and Stavreski, Z. (2006). Budget Support: Concept and Issues. In Budget Support as More Effective Aid? Recent Experience and Emerging Lessons. International Bank for Reconstruction and Development. - World Bank, Washington, DC. DOI: 10.1596/978-0-8213-6463-5.

Leyser, L. (2008). Does Size Really Matter? Small Bilateral Donors and Program-Based Approaches (PBAs) – exemplified by Austria and Ireland. 12th EADI General Conference, Global Governance for Sustainable Development, available at: http://www.eadi.org/fileadmin/ Documents/Events/General_Conference/2008/paper_leyser.pdf (Accessed on March 20, 2014).

Ministry of Foreign Affairs, Estonia. (2014a). Estonian Development Co-operation - Priority Partner Countries, available at: http://www.vm.ee/? q=en/taxonomy/term/55 (Accessed June 12, 2014).

Ministry of Foreign Affaris, Estonia. (2014b). Estonian Development Cooperation Country Strategy Paper – Moldova 2014 - 2015, available at: http://vm.ee/sites/default/files/content-editors/Moldova_Country_Strategy_2014-2015.pdf (Accessed June 12, 2014).

Ministry of Foreign Affairs, Latvia. (2014). Development Co-operation Priority Countries, available at: http://www.am.gov.lv/en/ policy/DevelopmentCo-operation/info/ (Accessed on June 12, 2014).

Ministry of Foreign Affairs, Latvia. (n.d.). Latvian Development Cooperation Policy Strategy2011-2015, available at: http://www.mfa.gov.lv/ development%20cooperation%20strategy%202011-2015_eng.pdf (Accessed on June 12, 2014).

Ministry of Foreign Affairs, Lithuania. (2014). Lithuanian development cooperation with Afghanistan, available at: http://www.orangeprojects.lt/ site/newfiles/files/Lithuanian_development_cooperation_with_Afghanistan_2006-2013.pdf (Accessed on June 19, 2014)

OECD (2006a). DAC Guidelines and Reference – Series Harmonising Donor Practices for Effective Aid Delivery - Volume 2, available at: http://www.aideffectiveness.org/media/k2/attachments/Dac_2___SWAP_PFM_BUDGET_1.pdf (Accessed July 21, 2011).

OECD. (2006b). Should OECD Donors Deliver Aid Through Poor Country Governments Budgets? Available at: http://www.oecd.org/ dataoecd/16/31/36644712.pdf (Accessed on June 10, 2014).

OECD. (2011). Denmark Development Assistance Committee (DAC) Peer Review 2011, available at: http://www.oecd.org/development/peer-reviews/47866608.pdf (Accessed on June 20, 2014).

OECD. (2012). FINLAND Development Assistance Committee (DAC) Peer Review 2012, available at: http://www.oecd.org/dac/peer-reviews/PRFINLAND2012.pdf (Accessed on June 20, 2014).

OECD. (2013a). Development Co-operation Report 2013- Ending Poverty, available at: http://www.oecd-ilibrary.org/docserver/download/ 4313111e.pdf?expires=1403225248&id=id&accname=guest&checksum= C5500F14369F4311B46F222CE1F585F1 (Accessed on June 20, 2014).

OECD. (2013b). OECD Development Co-operationPeer Review - Norway 2013, available at: http://www.oecd.org/dac/peer-reviews/Norway_ FINAL_2013.pdf (Accessed on May 20, 2014).

OECD. (2014a). Development finance reporting of countries beyond the DAC, available at: http://www.oecd.org/dac/stats/non-dac-reporting.htm (Accessed on June 20, 2014).

OECD. (2014b). International Development Statistics, available at: http://stats.oecd.org/qwids/#?x=1,4&y=6&f=2:1,3:51,5:3,7:1&q=2:1+3:51 +5:3+7:1+1:7,21+4:1,10,49+6:2008,2009,2010,2011,2012,2013 (Accessed on June 13, 2014).

Rajan, R. (2005). Aid and Growth: The Policy Challenge. Finance & Development. No. 42, Vol. 4. pp. 53-55.

Reinikka, R. (2008). Donors and Service Delivery. In Reinventing Foreign Aid, Edited by William Easterly. - The MIT Press, Cambridge, Massachusetts.

Williamson, J. (2000). What Should the World Bank Think about the Washington Consensus? Available at: http://www.iie.com/publications/ papers/print.cfm?doc=pub&ResearchID=351 (Accessed May 20, 2014).

World Bank. (2009a). Country Partnership Strategy for Georgia for the period FY10-FY13, available at: http://siteresources.worldbank.org/ GEORGIAEXTN/Resources/301745-1240578037641/GE_CPS_Final.pdf (Accessed on May 12, 2014).

World Bank. (2009b). Development Policy Operations, available at: http://siteresources.worldbank.org/PROJECTS/Resources/40940- 1244732625424/Q&Adplrev.pdf (Accessed on May 12, 2014).

World Bank. (2010a). Poverty Reduction Support Credits: An Evaluation of World Bank Support, available at: http://siteresources.worldbank.org/ INTPRSC/Resources/prsc_eval.pdf (Accessed on June 15, 2014). DOI: 10.1596/978-0-8213-8305-6.

World Bank. (2010b). Program document for a proposed economic recovery development policy credit to the Republic of Moldova, available at: http://www-wds.worldbank.org/external/default/WDSContentServer/ WDSP/IB/2010/10/19/000333038_20101019233323/Rendered/PDF/5266 90revised0111010IDAR20101018312.pdf (Accessed on June 12, 2014).

World Bank. (2012). Country partnership strategy for Ukraine for the period FY12-FY16, available at: http://siteresources.worldbank.org/ UKRAINEEXTN/Resources/328532-1328450253285/full_report_ENG. pdf (Accessed on June12, 2014).

World Bank. (2013a). Doing Business 2014. Understanding Regulations for Small and Medium-Size Enterprises. International Bank for Reconstruction and Development/The World Bank. Available at: http://doingbusiness.org/~/media/GIAWB/Doing%20Business/Documents /Annual-Reports/English/DB14-Full-Report.pdf (Accessed on April 6, 2014).

World Bank. (2013b). EU11 regular economic report: promoting shared prosperity during a weak recovery in Central and Eastern Europe, available at: http://documents.worldbank.org/curated/en/2013/ 12/18672207/promoting-shared-prosperity-during-weak-recovery-central-eastern-europe (Accessed on June 12, 2014).

World Bank. (2013c). 2012 Development Policy Lending Retrospective: Results, Risks, and Reforms, available at:http://www-wds.worldbank.org/external/default/WDSContentServer/WDSP/IB/2012/1 1/07/000425962_20121107134624/Rendered/PDF/734880BR0SecM20O FFICIAL0USE0ONLY090.pdf (Accessed on April 14, 2014).

World Bank. (2013d). Mozambique Receives US$110 Million from World Bank to Help Tackle Bottlenecks for Achieving Shared Growth and Prosperity, available at: http://www.worldbank.org/en/news/press-release/2013/07/16/mozambique-receives-us-110-million-from-world-bank-to-help-tackle-bottlenecks-for-achieving-shared-growth-and-prosperity.print (Accessed on June 12, 2014).

World Bank. (2013e). Implementation completion and results report to the Republic of Armenia for Development Policy Operations i-iii, available at:http://www-wds.worldbank.org/external/default/WDSContentServer/ WDSP/IB/2013/08/19/000333037_20130819123722/Rendered/PDF/ICR2 5930Armeni0PUBLIC00Box0379801B0.pdf (Accessed on May 14, 2014)

World Bank. (2014). The Afghanistan Reconstruction Trust Fund (ARTF), available at: http://www.artf.af/ (Accessed on January 20, 2014).

Yin, R. K. (2009). Case Study Research – Design and Methods. Applied Social Research Methods Series. 4th edition. - Sage Inc. California.

Chapter 4

SMALL STATES AND THE GLOBAL TRANSITION TO CLEAN ENERGY: CAN ICELAND MAKE A DIFFERENCE IN DEVELOPING COUNTRIES IN PARTNERSHIP WITH INTERNATIONAL FINANCIAL INSTITUTIONS?[1]

SUMMARY

As the global economy grows, so does the demand for energy. Investment in clean energy projects is increasingly important to help meet these growing energy needs. Clean energy projects are also important for environmental reasons and as part of the battle against climate change. Many clean energy sources in the world are located in developing countries[2], including emerging market economies. Investors in developing countries are normally faced with higher risks than those investing in high income developed economies. Higher risks in turn reduce capital flows to developing countries. This is particularly

---

[1] An earlier version of this chapter was presented by the author in a seminar at Cornell University on March 4, 2014. The author benefited from questions asked and comments made by participants during the seminar. The Seminar was sponsored by Cornell's Earth Energy Institute, IGERT.

[2] Developing countries in this chapter means countries that are eligible for financial assistance from international financial institutions. Those developing countries include countries classified by the World Bank Group as: low income countries, lower middle income countries and upper middle income countries. Emerging market countries, which are often in the middle income category, are also classified as developing countries in this chapter.

true during times of economic and financial crisis. At the same time energy projects tend to be large and capital intensive with long repayment periods. Energy projects also often require partnership between the public and private sectors i.e., public private partnerships (PPPs). Efficient allocation of risks among the different partners in PPPs is important for success, generally results in more profitable projects, and is more likely to benefit all parties involved. This chapter will discuss public private partnerships in the energy sector in developing countries. The focus will be on cross border investments for investors from small states, with Iceland discussed as a case. Also discussed will be the characteristics of developing countries, the risk faced by investors and risk mitigation instruments offered by international financial institutions (IFIs) and export credit agencies (ECAs) to manage those risks.[3]

This chapter argues that companies from a small country like Iceland can make an important contribution to the global transition to clean energy and to the fight against climate change if IFIs offer flexible and affordable funding and risk mitigation instruments for private investors. Risk mitigation can improve the risk profile of energy projects sufficiently to attract private sector funding from international funding sources. Guarantees from an Icelandic ECA could also be important when Icelandic companies provide services and/or equipment for cross border energy investments in developing countries. This chapter also notes that while the GATT and subsequently the WTO set out rules for trade they provided few rules for cross border investments. They did nothing to manage the political risks that could hinder foreign investment. This failure is an obstacle during times when clean energy investment is needed globally and given the great unused clean energy resources in developing and emerging markets. The chapter also discusses how IFI instruments were applied in the case of Nam Theun 2 in Lao PDR[4] to attract private sector funding to a difficult business and investment environment to enable a public private partnership. This case well demonstrates what is possible if public, private and international parties make a concerted effort to promote clean energy investment under challenging circumstances in developing countries.

---

[3] The international institutions focused on are those such as the World Bank Group, and regional development banks, while the national institutions are export credit agencies (ECAs).

[4] The official name of the country is the Lao People's Democratic Republic, shortened to 'Lao PDR' in this chapter.

INTRODUCTION

As the global economy grows, so does the demand for energy. Investment in clean energy projects is increasingly important to meet these growing energy needs. Considerable clean energy sources in the world are located in developing countries, including emerging market economies. Investors in those markets often face higher risks than those investing in high income developed economies with a more favorable investment and business climate. Higher risks in turn reduce capital flows to developing countries. This is especially true during times of crisis.

This chapter discusses cross border clean energy projects in developing countries. The focus will be on cross border investment for investors from small states: Iceland, a country that has made the transition from fossil fuel to clean energy, is discussed as a case. The characteristics of developing countries will be discussed, as will the risks faced by investors and risk mitigation instruments offered by IFIs and ECAs to manage those risks.

The main research questions are: How can companies from small countries like Iceland contribute to the transition to clean energy in developing and emerging market economies? How can risks be mitigated when investing in clean energy projects in developing countries? Does the international community offer a comprehensive framework for risk mitigation for investments in developing countries?

The proposition is that small states usually have little leverage in solving disputes bilaterally with developing and emerging market countries that are often larger. Developing countries in transition typically have business and investment climates that need improvement and are being developed. Companies from small states can better manage risks in developing countries if they work in partnership with international financial institutions. IFIs have more leverage in developing countries as they often have multiple projects there and engage in policy dialogue, including on regulatory reform. Partnership with IFIs thus improves the risk profile of cross border investments from small states.

Iceland's Transition to Clean Energy

Only a few decades ago most of Iceland's energy needs came from fossil fuel: coal and oil. Most electricity and space heating is now based on clean energy. Al Gore described this transition in his book "Our Choice" as follows:

"Iceland responded to the oil shocks of the 1970s by converting to domestic resources, virtually every building in the entire country is heated by the hot water resources close to the surface of the tectonically active land" (Al Gore, 2009, p. 109).

This transition to clean energy also meant that local capacity in geothermal energy utilization was developed. Several Icelandic companies and institutions now possess considerable experience in exploring geothermal sites, including drilling as well as constructing and operating geothermal power plants. Additionally, service providers as well as research and education institutions have supported geothermal development in Iceland (see Table 4.1). There can be little doubt that these companies and institutions can also contribute to geothermal projects in developing countries. In fact, many of them are already active in some capacity in cross border operations and have been so for many years. The question is more how companies from small countries like Iceland can contribute to the transition to clean energy in developing countries in a more comprehensive way and on a larger scale. These companies tend to be small and the recent economic and financial crisis negatively affected the balance sheets of many Icelandic firms. The largest companies, Landsvirkjun and Orkuveita Reykjavíkur, are in public ownership and the government needs to clarify what role, if any, they might have in geothermal development in developing countries. Icelandic companies also do not produce much machinery or equipment that could support geothermal development in developing countries. Nevertheless, the geothermal know-how that now exists in Iceland and has been developed over several decades provides a strong platform for further engagement. Some staff members of geothermal companies have long and diverse experience and proven technical skills. Based on this capacity a geothermal cluster is being developed that could engage cross border.[5] In addition to space heating and electricity production Icelandic companies have also made progress in multiple use activities such as fish farming, greenhouses, heating of swimming pools, lagoons for tourists and so on. Some of these activities could be useful in developing countries and drying of fish is one area with high potential.

Participants in the Icelandic geothermal cluster have many challenges to overcome. Among the most difficult is the capital constraint they are faced

---

[5] Iceland Geothermal is a non profit organization established in February 2013 around an industry-driven cluster cooperation in the field of geothermal energy, See further: https://docs.google.com/file/d/0By20q4BSBHqeTy1EWTU2ZWlpTmc/edit?usp=sharing&pli=1

with as well as proper risk mitigation in developing countries. This is the main subject of this chapter.

Table 4.1. Some Icelandic companies and institutions with capacity in geothermal development. This list is only indicative and by no means exhaustive

GeoScience	ISOR, Mannvit, Vatnaskil
Technical Consulting	Mannvit, Verkís, Efla, Reykjavík Geothermal, Landsvirkjun Power, Nýsköpunarmiðstöð Íslands, Kemía
Business Consulting	KPMG, Capacent Corporate Finance, Íslandsbanki
Drilling	Jarðboranir, Ræktunarsamband Flóa og Skeiða
Construction	ISTAK, ÍAV, Loftorka, Eykt, Framtak, Héðinn, VHE, Altak, Rafal, RST Net
Energy Audit & Law Firms	KPMG, PwC, Deloitte, Lex (law firm), Logos (law firm)
Financing	Arion banki, Íslandsbanki, Landsbankinn
Geothermal Research	ISOR, Mannvit, Vatnaskil, Utilities, Universities
Research Funding	Orkusjóður, GEORG - Geothermal Research Group , Landsvirkjun Research Fund, Orkuveita Reykjavíkur Energy Fund, Rannís – Rannsóknamiðstöð Íslands
Training and Education	University of Akureyri, University of Iceland, Reykjavík University, Reykjavik Energy Graduate School of Sustainable Systems – REYST, Keilir – Atlantic Center of Excellence, Geothermal Training Programme - United Nations University (GTP- UNU)

Source: Constructed by the author.

Cross Border Engagement and the Challenging Business and Investment Environment in Developing Countries

Utilizing clean energy resources is not only a concern for Iceland. This is a global issue affecting both rich and poor countries. Many developing countries and emerging market countries in Africa, Asia and Latin America have large geothermal resources, but most are only in the early stages of development in using those resources. Future growth in demand for electricity is also likely to be strongest in those emerging regions. Transition to clean energy could be of great benefit to those regions as well as having global implications, environmentally, and in the battle against climate change. However, it is not sufficient to have the natural resources and potential growth in future demand. Funding is also needed and energy investments tend to be large, capital intensive and with long repayment periods. In addition to government and donor contributions, private sector participation is important.

However, developing countries often have challenging business and investment environments that discourage private sector cross border investment.

The World Bank publishes the so called "Doing Business" report annually. The report presents quantitative indicators that can be compared across 189 economies—from Afghanistan to Zimbabwe—and over time. In its 2014 report the World Bank ranked 189 countries (World Bank, 2013a). The best performing country is ranked 1 and the worst performing country is ranked 189. The bank uses eleven indicators[6] that are then combined into one overall indicator: Ease of doing business. Table 4.2 shows some selected indicators for the business and investment climate in some developing countries that the World Bank[7] expects will have significant additions in installed geothermal capacity in the future (World Bank, 2012, p. 31). As Table 4.2 shows, most of these countries face challenging business and investment environments. African countries tend to be low income whereas Asian and Latin American countries tend to be middle income. In most countries companies have difficulty getting electricity and they also score low on indicators that are important for cross border energy investment, such as dealing with construction permits, protecting investors, enforcing contracts and trading across borders. Investors, especially those considering long term investments, will avoid difficult business and investment environments unless risks can be managed. Proper risk mitigation for operators and investors is thus a major challenge in most of the African countries listed below as well in many developing and emerging countries in Asia and Latin America. Table 4.2 below only provides some indication for investors.

---

[6] Regulations affecting 11 areas in the life of a business are covered in the 2014 "Doing Business" report: starting a business, dealing with construction permits, getting electricity, registering property, getting credit, protecting investors, paying taxes, trading across borders, enforcing contracts, resolving insolvency, and employing workers. The employing workers data was not included in the ranking on the ease of doing business in the 2014 report.

[7] The World Bank Group represents five institutions. These are: (i) the International Bank for Reconstruction and Development, IBRD, established in 1944, (ii) the International Development Association, IDA, established in 1960, (iii) the International Finance Corporation, IFC, established in 1956, (iv) the Multilateral Investment Guarantee Agency, MIGA, established in 1988, (v) the International Centre for Settlement of Investment Disputes, ICSID, established in 1966. Four of these institutions issue insurance or guarantees, i.e., IBRD, IDA, IFC and MIGA.

Table 4.2. According to the World Bank, significant additions in installed geothermal capacity can be expected in the following African, Asian and Latin American countries

Region	Income Level	Ease of Doing Business Rank	Getting Electricity	Dealing with Construction Permits	Protecting Investors	Enforcing Contracts	Trading Across Borders
Africa							
Tanzania	Low income	145	102	177	98	42	139
Eritrea	Low income	184	95	189	115	67	170
Sudan	Lower middle income	149	113	167	157	154	155
Somalia	N/A	N/A	N/A	N/A	N/A	N/A	N/A
Malawi	Low income	171	183	173	80	145	176
Zambia	Low middle income	83	152	57	80	120	163
Burundi	Low income	140	161	126	34	177	175
Rwanda	Low income	32	53	85	22	40	162
Uganda	Low income	132	178	143	115	117	164
Congo, Dem. Rep.	Low income	183	142	90	147	177	171
Mozambique	Low income	139	171	77	52	145	131
Madagascar	Low income	148	187	157	68	160	115
Comoros	Low income	158	109	44	68	159	146
Mauritius	Upper middle income	20	48	123	12	54	12
Pacific Asia							
Malaysia	Upper middle income	6	21	43	4	30	5
Papua New Guinea	Lower middle income	113	24	165	68	168	134
Latin America							
Guatemala	Lower middle income	79	34	61	157	97	116
Honduras	Lower middle income	127	125	83	170	182	84
Panama	Upper middle income	55	16	62	80	127	11
Columbia	Upper middle income	43	101	24	6	155	94
Ecuador	Upper middle income	135	138	64	138	99	122
Bolivia	Lower middle income	162	128	136	138	131	126

Source: World Bank, 2012 and 2013a.

The "Doing Business" report does not measure the full range of factors, policies and institutions that affect the quality of the business environment in an economy or its national competitiveness. It does not, for example, capture aspects of security, the prevalence of bribery and corruption, market size and macroeconomic stability.[1] A more thorough review would be needed for a company to make a decision about cross border engagement. Nevertheless the "Doing Business" report is a useful start to begin identifying challenges in each country. Gaining a fuller understanding of the broader business environment, and a broader perspective on policy challenges requires combining insights from "Doing Business" with data from other sources, such as World Bank Enterprise Surveys.[2] Other indicators more specific to the regulatory environment for energy investment also need to be studied and assessed. Moreover, political or non commercial risks are associated with cross border investments. These will be discussed in later sections of this chapter.

Geothermal Resource Risk Constraints and IFI Support

In addition to the risks associated with cross border investments and operations, geothermal power projects also suffer from risks not found in other thermal power generation projects, including higher upfront development costs associated with uncertainty as to site capacity (Delmon, 2009). Risks associated with geothermal projects are high during the pre-survey, exploration and test drilling phases.[3] Validating geothermal resources through test drilling is capital intensive. Commercial financing for test drilling is generally hard to find and private equity and government support are often the only sources of capital to undertake test drilling. These risks are not specific to developing and emerging markets, but it is often more challenging to obtain private and public capital in these markets than in high income countries. IFIs have so far done little to mobilize funding for resource risk mitigation for geothermal projects in developing countries (see Table 4.3). They have mostly spent their resources on the less risky production phase after the more risky

---

[1] Including whether the government manages its public finances in a sustainable way.

[2] See, http://www.enterprisesurveys.org

[3] Until the first borehole has been drilled into the geothermal reservoir, developers cannot be sure about the exact parameters (temperature and flow rate) of a planned geothermal electricity project. Once drilling has taken place, in situ pump tests, temperature and hydrological measurements then reduce the resource risk and can make it easier to attract external capital (GEOELEC, 2013, p. 6).

exploratory phase is completed. Here IFIs are failing in their role to promote geothermal development in developing countries. Scaling up geothermal by addressing the resource risk through sustained international effort is being discussed at the World Bank, including raising US$500 million for exploration and drilling activity.[4] This is a modest number and little progress has been made so far. Iceland is also in the early phases of assisting selected African countries with geothermal exploration[5] in cooperation with the Nordic Development Fund and the World Bank. In Europe a European Geothermal Risk Insurance Fund is being prepared (GEOELEC, 2013).

Table 4.3. Three decades of cumulative lending for geothermal energy development (US$ million)

International financial institutions (IFIs)	Exploratory Phase	Production Phase	Technical Assistance	Total
World Bank	117	1,544	48	1,710
African Development Bank	4	124	-	129
Asian Development Bank	-	554	3	557
European Investment Bank	-	256	-	256
Inter-American Development Bank	3	403	11	416
Total	124	2,881	62	3,068

Source: World Bank, 2013b.

Private Sector Cross Border Investment in Developing Countries

Private sector funding and participation in clean energy projects is a challenge for many reasons. One of these is that the host government is often the only buyer of the electricity or hot water produced i.e., it is the so called

---

[4] On March 6, 2013, World Bank Managing Director Sri Mulyani launched the Global Geothermal Development Plan (GGDP) in Reykjavik, Iceland. The GGDP is a call to all donors and sponsors of geothermal energy to join hands in mobilizing additional concessional resources and fund a pipeline of geothermal resource validation projects. According to the World Bank this is a way to address a critical financing gap and to help scale up geothermal energy and expand clean energy access (According to an email from the World Bank on February 17, 2014).

[5] The Icelandic International Development Agency, which is an autonomous agency under the Icelandic Ministry for Foreign Affairs, has provided some assistance to selected African countries for the initial phases of geothermal development. This has been done in cooperation with the Nordic Development Fund and the World Bank. This effort is in its initial phases and on a small scale and the Icelandic contribution was under threat of being reduced due to post-crisis budget cuts in Iceland.

offtake purchaser[6]. Many developing countries with large clean energy potential have limited creditworthiness. They have low per capita income and are often going through economic and political transition. In these cases the sponsors[7] of a project might hesitate to fund the project because of uncertainty with the income stream from the investment made. Lenders, including commercial investment banks, would also often hesitate to provide loans to such projects because of uncertainty whether the project company, whose income stream is at risk, can service its loans.

One possible institutional arrangement to address this situation is to form a PPP and use the Build-Operate-Transfer (BOT) scheme. The PPP becomes a venue for the public and private sectors to cooperate on a project that would traditionally have been in the public domain. The BOT arrangement means that the project is transferred back to the government when the concession[8] agreement ends. In this situation efficient and effective risk allocation is key to success and the international community can play a constructive role, e.g., through IFIs that can offer a variety of risk mitigation instruments. Among the remedies that investors from small countries can apply to manage risks is partnership with IFIs and/or participation in a consortium with stronger partners. National institutions such as ECAs, which support trade finance (goods and services), can also play a constructive role in reducing the risks taken by private sector investors.

Ppps and Risk Allocation – Definitions and Theoretical Considerations

Public private partnerships can be a feasible platform to fund infrastructure development and to increase the efficiency of public sector service delivery. Infrastructure projects in the energy sector are often large, capital intensive and long term. Repayment periods are also often long. It can take a private investor 10 to 25 years to recover the investment and the project returns.

---

[6] An offtake purchaser is a purchaser of the product produced by a project. In the case of a power project the product produced is the electricity generated.

[7] A sponsor of a project is a party wishing to develop or undertake a project. A sponsor would normally provide financial support for the project e.g. early equity capital.

[8] A concession is the right granted by the host government for a private company to undertake a public sector project and operate it over an agreed period.

The private sector is recognized as a significant financing source for meeting developing country investment requirements, but financial markets remain largely untapped for this purpose and have yet to live up to their potential (Asian Development Bank, 2006). PPPs are one platform worth considering for the private sector to engage in infrastructure projects. Private capital, donor support (including IFIs) and public funds can be combined in a PPP project. A well designed policy and institutional framework for PPPs offers the opportunity to leverage and combine all three sources of financing and expertise without crowding out private investment. By forming a PPP both public and private sectors can share the risks and rewards of infrastructure projects.

There are many different definitions for PPPs. One definition is "any public sector service provided partially or wholly by the private sector" (Delmon, 2009, p. 601). Another definition is "co-operative institutional arrangements between public and private sector actors" (Hodge and Greve, 2009, p. 33). Yet another definition of a PPP is "the transfer to the private sector of investment projects that traditionally have been executed or financed by the public sector" (World Bank, 2008, p. 93).

To engage in cooperation, the public and private sectors can employ several different schemes[9] including the so called BOT, i.e., Build-Operate-Transfer (IMF, 2004). In BOT projects the private sector is responsible for financing, constructing and operating the project. Under this arrangement the host country grants a concession, i.e., the right for a private firm to undertake a public sector project and operate it over an agreed period. When the concession expires the ownership of the project is transferred back to the party granting the concession. For a comprehensive discussion on BOTs see Jeffrey Delmon's outstanding book on Private Sector Investment in Infrastructure (Delmon, 2009).

The partners typically involved in a BOT project are: the project company that undertakes the project, the host government (that can also be the offtake/power purchaser), the shareholders, the lenders, the grantor, the construction contractor, the operator, the offtake purchaser/power purchaser, and the input supplier.

Figure 1 below shows a typical PPP BOT contractual structure.

---

[9] PPP schemes and modalities other than Build-Operate-Transfer (BOT) include for example: Build-Own-Operate-Transfer (BOOT), Build-Rent-Own-Transfer (BROT), Build-Lease-Operate-Transfer (BLOT), Build-Transfer-Operate (BTO).

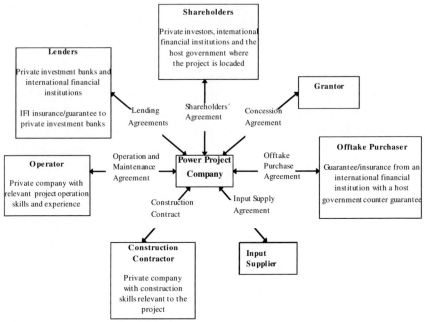

Source: Constructed by the author.

Figure 1. Typical PPP BOT contractual structure.

The project company uses the income stream from the project to service its debt and to pay returns to its investors (i.e., the equity contributors to the project company). The lenders to a BOT project might, for example, be commercial investment banks, IFIs and bilateral agencies. The IFIs and ECAs could also serve as guarantors e.g., for payment to the lenders, including commercial investment banks.

The lenders would be keen to manage their risks (i.e., only take measurable and measured risks) and would receive a fixed margin on their loan whereas the shareholders (i.e., the equity holders in the project company) maximize the profits on their equity investment. In addition to obtaining funding for the project, the project company procures the design and coordinates the construction and operation of the project in line with the requirements of the concession agreement. Project company shareholders often include firms with construction and operation experience, and with offtake purchase capabilities (Delmon, 2009, p. 98).

The offtake purchase agreement secures the project payment stream. The offtake purchaser will be looking for guaranteed long term output from the project. The credit risk associated with the offtake purchaser will be of particular concern to the project company and the lenders. This is where guarantees from host governments or IFIs, including the World Bank, become important.

Critical to the design of PPPs is the way risks are allocated between the partners in the PPP. A general principle is that risk should fall on the party that is more able to do something about it. Risks in PPP tend to be allocated on the basis of commercial and negotiating strength. The stronger party will allocate risk that it does not want to bear to the weaker party. Efficient allocation of risk will generally result in a more successful and profitable project and will benefit each of the parties involved (Delmon, 2009).

In order to minimize the market risk from the project company and the project lenders, an offtake purchase agreement, or in the case of a power project, a power purchase agreement, may be made. This is to create a secure payment stream which will be an important basis for financing the project. The offtake purchaser may also be the grantor, or a government entity such as a public utility, in which case the offtake purchase agreement and the concession agreement may be one and the same document (Delmon, 2009).

The lenders will want project risks to be allocated to project participants, i.e., the construction contractor and the operator and not the project company, which is their debtor.

The project company will enter into a contract with the construction contractor in order to divest its obligations to the grantor to design, build, test, and commission the project. Completion risk for the project should be allocated to the construction contractor. In the case of a turnkey project, completion and performance risk should be on the construction contractor.

If the main risks are associated with poor management of the service, shifting the risk to the operator could provide the right incentives to ensure that the project delivers. If risks are related to changes in policies, then the government should bear the risk. This is because the project company will not generally be able to manage political risk.

The project company will ask the government to bear those risks, not necessarily to claim compensation at a future date but to pressure the government to avoid such risks and to minimize the probability that such risks will occur.

Does an Effective International Framework Exist for Mitigating Political Risks?

When discussing international investors' efforts to manage political risks Wells (2005) discusses four options: (i) international arbitration, (ii) official political risk insurance, (iii) home government support, and (iv) official credit.

In the absence of a global investment agreement like the GATT and later the WTO, investors have turned to piecemeal solutions when protecting their rights in risky countries. According to Wells, "[t]hese agreements set out rules for trade, but they provided few rules for investment.....They did nothing to manage the political risks that could hinder foreign investment. Starting with the aborted International Trade Organization of the immediate post-World War II era, several efforts to create a similar global framework for investment came to naught. The history of failure did not encourage renewed efforts to create a comprehensive approach." Further, Wells states that "[t]he resulting system, however, was not the product of any grand design but the result of uncoordinated steps by various parties. Certainly, some of the problems of the new system derive from the lack of a single framework; even more important problems can be attributed to the lack of explicit negotiation and mutual acceptance among the affected parties" (Wells, 2005, pp. 89-90).

This failure described by Wells is especially serious if one considers clean energy projects that tend to be large, capital intensive and long term. Furthermore, energy resources are to a large extent located in developing and emerging countries that are also currently growing faster than high income industrialized countries both in terms of GDP and population, and thus energy use. When host governments cannot make credible long term commitments to foreign investors, those investors will tend to avoid these projects. This becomes especially troubling during times when there is a global need for transition to clean energy projects.

As Wells points out, "[t]he need to satisfy the demand for security grew as the international community became increasingly eager to encourage private foreign investors to build infrastructure – roads, power plants, water systems – in the developing world" (Wells, 2005, p. 89). "Without external protection, direct investors in these industries would have to be very brave, or perhaps ignorant, to enter these industries, where they would have little bargaining power once their capital was committed" (Wells, 2005, p. 89).

What Can an Investor from a Small Country Like Iceland Do?

Wells (2005) noted four options when discussing international investors' efforts to manage political risks: (i) international arbitration, (ii) official political risk insurance, (iii) home government support, and (iv) official credit.

Option (i) faces the objection that engaging in cross border investment and relying on favorable international arbitration in the event of dispute does not sound like a predictable means of mitigating political risks. Option (iii) faces the objection that home government support does not sound promising for investors from small countries. In fact, being an investor from a small country like Iceland only adds to the risks. Small countries can only be expected to have limited leverage in the event of dispute with a host government in a developing country that could be a much larger country. Options (ii) and (iv) could be a possibility for investors from small countries to consider when making a foreign investment decision, if feasible venues for cooperation with IFIs and ECAs can be found.

This chapter will focus on the official insurance that can be provided by IFIs that operate globally, such as the World Bank Group, and regionally, such as the African Development Bank, the Asian Development Bank, the European Bank for Reconstruction and Development, and the Inter-American Development Bank. These institutions are well placed to mitigate risks at competitive prices as Wells says "official insurance can be priced low, since the threat of sanctions by the organizations backing the insurance sharply reduce the chances of the events being insured against occurring" (Wells, 2005, p. 91). In terms of trade finance the role of ECAs will be discussed.

International Financial Institutions and Risk Mitigation in Developing Countries

Concerns about investment environments and perceptions of political risk often inhibit foreign investment, with the majority of flows going to a few countries leaving the world's poorest economies mostly ignored. This is especially true during times of economic and financial crisis. The limited number of investors engaging in risky environments might also be tempted to invest only when quick payback periods are possible. IFIs can have an important role to play here and a responsibility to offer effective venues and viable risk mitigation instruments. This is especially true for long term investments such as energy infrastructure.

For large infrastructure projects investors must pay considerably more attention to political risk management issues. Risk reduction can reduce the cost of funding projects and facilitate longer loan periods. Political risk insurance, especially from IFIs, can also act as an effective deterrent against host government interference with insured private investments.

IFIs offer a number of financial and risk management instruments that can be useful for PPPs.[10] These include loans, equity investments and guarantees or insurance against political risk (non-commercial risk). Among the IFIs active in this area are: (i) the World Bank Group, (ii) the European Bank for Reconstruction and Development, (iii) the Asian Development Bank, (iv) the Inter-American Development Bank, (v) the African Development Bank, (vi) the European Investment Bank, and (vii) the Nordic Investment Bank.

Iceland is not a member of the Asian Development Bank, the Inter-American Development Bank or the African Development Bank. Icelandic companies therefore do not have access to the services of all IFIs and have fewer options to form partnerships when investing in developing and emerging markets, for example, than companies from the other Nordic countries, which are members of all the above institutions.

Key risk issues can be categorized as: political, breach of contract by a government entity, market risk, and default risk.[11] Risk mitigation products can attract new financing resources, reduce costs of capital, and extend maturities by providing coverage for risks that the market is unable or unwilling to bear (Delmon, 2009). Those products can attract more private capital to invest in infrastructure. Examples of guarantee products provided by the World Bank Group are partial risk guarantees (PRGs) from the International Bank for Reconstruction and Development (IBRD) or the International Development Association (IDA) and IBRD partial credit guarantees (PCGs), International Finance Corporation (IFC) partial credit guarantees and political risk insurance (PRI) from the Multilateral Investment Guarantee Agency (MIGA) (Delmon, 2009). Those risk mitigation instruments

---

[10] In addition to these services, IFIs often engage in policy dialogue with governments of developing and emerging market economies to improve economic policy and management. This includes reforms to improve the business and investment climate for the private sector, to promote business activities, and to encourage foreign direct investment. IFIs also provide loans and credit to government-led projects in developing countries and emerging markets that are subject to international competitive bidding. This allows private sector firms to participate in bidding and potentially to benefit from public sector projects supported by IFIs.

[11] For an excellent overview of World Bank risk mitigation products, see Jeffrey Delmon Chapter 7 (Delmon, 2009).

allow investors to be compensated in the case of certain adverse events and thus reduce the risk and hence also project costs.

In the case of energy infrastructure projects World Bank guarantee products such as partial risk guarantees (PRG) can be key to success. According to the World Bank PRGs "cover commercial lenders for a private sector project against default arising from a government-owned entity failing to perform its obligations. PRGs can cover changes in law, failure to meet contractual payment obligations, expropriation and nationalization, currency transfer and convertibility, nonpayment of a termination amount, failure to issue licenses in a timely manner, other risk to the extent that they are covered by contractual obligations of a government entity, and noncompliance with an agreed dispute resolution clause. PRGs can be provided in both IBRD and IDA countries and require a government counter-guarantee" (World Bank, 2009, p. 10).

Regarding the IBRD/IDA PRGs the investor receives comfort, improved credit terms, and is not liable for loan repayment. Among the strengths of this instrument is increased government commitment to success of projects, accompanied by the benefits of an ongoing policy dialogue between the World Bank and the host government. Among the weaknesses are sovereign guarantees required in all cases, cumbersome processing and high transaction costs. The demand for this instrument is mainly limited to PPPs and sectors with heavy government engagement (World Bank, 2009, p. 74).

The five institutions of the World Bank Group also include MIGA. MIGA provides guarantees against political risks, i.e., non-commercial risks for investments in emerging markets. It also provides technical assistance and a dispute mediation service. Developing countries would hesitate to take measures that would negatively affect projects that MIGA is involved with because of the concern that it could adversely affect their relationship with the IDA and/or IBRD and possible credit or a loan (see for example West, 1999, pp. 29-30).

According to the World Bank, MIGA "offers PRI coverage to foreign direct investors for any combination of the following political risks: transfer restriction, expropriation, war and civil disturbance, and breach of contract. MIGA can insure direct equity, quasi-equity, nonequity direct, and other investments. To insure debt, however, it must have an equity link. MIGA guarantees cover new foreign-currency-denominated investments, including "new" investments to existing investments, investments by private for-profit and nonprofit organizations, and public owned investors and organizations that operate on a commercial basis. MIGA can cover any freely usable currency, which may include local currency investments/loans. Under certain circumstances, MIGA can cover investments by local investors" (World Bank, 2009, p. 10).

Regarding the MIGA PRI the investor receives comfort, improved credit terms, mediation services and compensation in the event of loss. Among the strengths are flexible coverage of all PRI risks; main product for equity investments; dispute resolution; minimal time and processing. Among weaknesses are no comprehensive coverage (commercial risk and political risk cover) and a lengthy process to change Convention limitations (World Bank, 2009, p. 74).

The Asian Development Bank and the other regional development banks also offer risk mitigation instruments that are important for private investors in emerging markets although they are not discussed in any detail in this chapter. Asian Development Bank risk mitigation instruments can, for example, cover breach of contract. For a power project a breach of this kind may result from failure by a government owned entity to make payments in accordance with the power purchase agreement between the independent power producer and the user or distributor (Asian Development Bank, 2000, p. 2). Such insurance can be critical for the success of an energy infrastructure project. According to the Asian Development Bank the majority of the PRGs that it has provided have been private sector oriented, including PRGs for PPPs (Asian Development Bank, 2006, p. 5).

The Case of the Nam Theun 2 Hydropower Project in Lao PDR

There are cases that demonstrate that IFIs and ECAs can work with governments and the private sector to mobilize funding for clean energy projects in difficult business environments where the private sector would generally hesitate to engage alone. One of those cases is Nam Theun 2 (NT2) a hydropower project in Lao PDR.

Lao PDR is one of the poorest countries in South East Asia with weak human capacity, governance, institutions and physical infrastructure. NT2 is an excellent example of how the public and private sectors can form a partnership and construct a major infrastructure project in the energy sector in a developing country with limited creditworthiness with support from IFIs and ECAs. The estimated project costs were US$1.25 million at financial close (excluding contingencies), equity 28 percent (US$350 million) and 72 percent debt (US$900 million).

The NT2 hydropower project was implemented by the Nam Theun 2 Power Company Limited (NTPC). The shareholders (equity holders) of NTPC were: Électricité de France International of France (35%), Italian-Thai Development Public Company Limited of Thailand (15%), Electricity Generating Public Company Limited of Thailand (25%) and Lao Holding State Enterprise (25%). Several IFIs provided loans to NTPC and/or guarantees to the private sector lenders: (i) multilateral institutions including the World Bank Group's IDA and MIGA, (ii) bilateral agencies, and (iii) ECAs. A consortium of 16 commercial banks supported the project.[12]

The shareholders' agreement signed by Électricité de France International, the Government of Lao PDR, Electricity Generating Public Company Limited of Thailand, and Italian-Thai Development Public Company Limited sets out the rights and obligations of the shareholders, provides for the objective, establishment, management, and operation of the project company, NTPC, and agrees on the Articles of Association of NTPC. The shareholders' agreement lasts for 45 years from signing (World Bank, 2005). In the concession agreement, the Government of Lao PDR granted NTPC a concession to develop, own, finance, construct, and operate the hydroelectric plant and related facilities, and to transfer the project to the Government of Lao PDR at the end of the concession period, i.e., after 25 years (World Bank, 2005).

NT2 is the largest ever foreign investment in Lao PDR and was the Asia Power Deal of the Year 2005. The project has an electric generating capacity of 1070 megawatts, of which 995 MW of the power was for export to Thailand and 75 MW for domestic use in Lao PDR. The power purchase agreements are between NTPC and the Electricity Generating Authority of Thailand, and between NTPC and Electricite du Laos.

A Head Construction Contract was signed between NTPC and Électricité de France International (the head contractor). This is a turnkey, price-capped engineering, procurement and construction contract (World Bank, 2005). The subcontractors are Italian-Thai Development Public Company Limited of Thailand, Nishmatsu Contracting Company of Japan, General Electric of the USA and Mitsubishi-Sumitomo Electric of Japan. The head contractor and the subcontractors are all reputable international companies.

IFIs played an instrumental role in enabling this project. In fact, the international dollar lenders to the project informed the NTPC that without

---

[12] The international commercial banks were: ANZ Bank, BNP Paribas, Bank of Tokyo Mitsubishi, Calyon, Fortis Bank, ING, KBC, SG and Standard Chartered.
The Thai commercial banks were: Bangkok Bank, Bank of Ayudhya, KASIKORNBANK, Krung Thai Bank, Siam City Bank, Siam Commercial Bank and Thai Military Bank.

political risk mitigation they would not be able to lend to the project. The Government of Lao PDR requested the World Bank Group to provide risk mitigation to support the international lending package (World Bank, 2005). IFI guarantees were thus key in lowering the project's risk profile sufficiently to attract the commercial financing needed.

Political risk guarantees were provided by MIGA (World Bank) and the Asian Development Bank. The IDA (World Bank) also provided a partial risk guarantee (PRG). The NT2 PRG is the first IDA guarantee to support hydropower development and is also the first project to use a mix of IDA, MIGA and Asian Development Bank guarantees. Debt guarantees were provided by IDA, MIGA and the Asian Development Bank supporting about US$126 million of private financing. Direct loans from IFIs were about US$144 million provided to NTPC (World Bank, 2005).

Loans were also provided by the Asian Development Bank, the EIB, the Nordic Investment Bank, Agence Francaise de Developpement, Proparco and the Export-Import Bank of Thailand. The IDA and Agence Francaise de Developpement also provided grants.

Nine International Commercial Banks and seven Thai commercial Banks helped fund the project. In addition, the NT2 project received ECA support from COFACE of France, Exportkreditnamnden (EKN) of Sweden and its equivalent (GIEK) in Norway.

The Nam Theun 2 project can be viewed as a test case for infrastructure development in the developing world. It is an excellent demonstration of what is possible if the public and private sectors, supported by IFIs, team up and join forces. The use of IFI risk mitigation instruments is particularly interesting as it demonstrates how a modest commitment through such instruments can help mobilize much larger amounts of private funding.

The NT2 project, which was the world's largest private sector cross border power project financing, and the largest private sector hydropower project financing, would be too large for participation by Icelandic firms, except if they provided only technical assistance or advisory services, or maybe participated as subcontractors. Lessons learned from this landmark project would nevertheless be a valuable study for all companies that intend to participate in infrastructure projects in developing and emerging market economies. In 2010 two senior managers from the World Bank published a book with comprehensive discussion about the lessons learned from Nam Theun 2 (see Porter and Shivakumar, 2010).

How Can International Financial Institutions Support Cross Border Geothermal Engagement In Developing Countries?

If Icelandic companies that are a part of a geothermal exporting cluster engage in cross border investment in developing and emerging markets, capital shortages and risk mitigation will be among the key challenges that they face. How could they possibly solve this problem, and in partnership with whom?

Among the most obvious partners to help solve that problem are the IFIs discussed above that often have a strong presence in developing countries and can offer financial instruments such as equity, loans, or guarantee/insurance instruments to support investment projects. The involvement of IFIs could also facilitate participation by private international investment banks, ECAs, as well as potential co-sponsors providing equity capital.

As discussed above the institutions of the World Bank Group include the IBRD and IDA which work with host governments (requiring government guarantees) as well as the IFC and MIGA that support private sector investment (without government guarantees). As also mentioned above, there are IFIs with regional focus such as the African Development Bank, the Asian Development Bank, the European Bank for Reconstruction and Development, the Inter-American Development Bank, and the European Investment Bank.

As Table 4.4 shows, IFIs offer funding in the form of loans and equity as well as guarantees and political risk insurance that can help mobilize funding from other sources, including e.g., loans from private sector commercial banks as well as equity participation from private sector companies.

Capital shortages for cross border energy investments in developing countries is not only a problem for potential Icelandic investors. This is a global problem. It is widely known that investment needs in clean energy in emerging markets and developing countries are huge. The IFC, for example, estimated that electricity sector investment needs in developing countries from 2007 to 2030 will be US$7.9 trillion (IFC, 2009). This is about half of the Gross National Income of the U.S.A. in 2009 when this estimate was done (World Bank, 2010).

IFIs contribute billions of dollars to private sector investment in developing countries every year and part of those funds goes to clean energy investments (see Table 4.5). However, even if all the IFI funds were used for clean energy investments this would only be sufficient to fund a small fraction of the global investment needs for clean energy. This is why pooling funds from the public and private sectors and donors, including IFIs, is necessary.

Table 4.4. International financial institutions and their financial products

Institution	Major Products
Asian Development Bank	Loans, equity, guarantees, advisory services, and syndications.
African Development Bank	Loans, equity, commercial and political risk guarantees, syndications, and technical assistance.
European Bank for Reconstruction and Development	Loans, equity, guarantees, securitized finance, advisory services, and syndications.
European Investment Bank	Loans, equity, guarantees, and technical assistance.
Inter-American Development Bank. Non- sovereign Guaranteed Operations.	Loans, guarantees, grants, technical assistance, and syndications.
International Finance Corporation – World Bank Group	Loans, equity, guarantees, securitized finance, advisory services, and syndications.
Multilateral Investment Guarantee Agency – World Bank Group	Political risk insurance guarantees.

Source: International Finance Corporation, 2011.

Table 4.5. International financial institutions and annual private sector commitments, 2010

Institution	Annual Private Sector Commitments, 2010
Asian Development Bank	$4.3 billion in support of private sector development, of which $1.9 billion was approved for direct assistance to private sector companies and projects.
African Development Bank	$1.9 billion (fiscal year ending December 31, 2010).
European Bank for Reconstruction and Development	$8.9 billion (fiscal year ending December 31, 2010).
European Investment Bank	€3.69 billion (fiscal year ending December 31, 2010) outside the European Union.
Inter-American Development Bank. Non sovereign Guaranteed Operations.	$1.2 billion (calendar year 2010).
International Finance Corporation – World Bank Group	$12.7 billion (fiscal year ending June 30, 2010) for own account, plus $5.4 billion of mobilization.
Multilateral Investment Guarantee Agency – World Bank Group	$2.1 billion (fiscal year ending June 30, 2010).

Source: International Finance Corporation, 2011.

The international community increasingly emphasizes clean energy investment for environmental reasons and as part of the battle against climate change. To promote those investments the international community uses IFIs. Table 4.6 shows that there is a clear focus on clean and renewable energy, and climate action among most IFIs. Some institutions (the African Development Bank, and IFC and MIGA from the World Bank Group) do not mention this specifically, but presumably those kinds of investments would fall under infrastructure investments that they as well as all the other IFIs mention as key private sector focus areas.

Table 4.6. International financial institutions and key private sector focus areas

Institution	Key Private Sector Focus Areas
Asian Development Bank	*Infrastructure*, capital markets, and financial sectors, **with increasing focus on clean and renewable energy**, frontier markets, and underserved economies.
African Development Bank	*Infrastructure*, financial sector, industry, agribusiness, services, regional integration, and inclusive growth.
European Bank for Reconstruction and Development	Industry, commerce and agribusiness, natural resources, **renewable energy**, *infrastructure*, financial institutions, and SMEs.
European Investment Bank	*Infrastructure*, **energy, climate action,** financial markets, SMEs, microfinance, and industry.
Inter-American Development Bank. Nonsovereign Guaranteed Operations.	*Infrastructure*, **energy,** transport, water and sanitation, industry, agribusiness, natural resources, financial institutions, capital markets, trade finance, health care, education, tourism, corporate governance, corporate social responsibility, and **climate change.**
International Finance Corporation – World Bank Group	Frontier markets and International Development Association countries, sustainability, *infrastructure*, agribusiness, health and education, financial markets, and SMEs.
Multilateral Investment Guarantee Agency – World Bank Group	International Development Association and conflict-affected countries, *infrastructure*, and South-South investment projects.

Source: International Finance Corporation, 2011.

Partnership with private investors has for a long time been a central part of IFI support to the private sector. Most IFIs limit their participation in a project investment to well under 50 percent, thus requiring partnership with other investors. The structure of IFI finance substantially leverages the capital provided by governments. Not only do IFIs borrow significantly from outside to support their operations, but they also invest in projects alongside private financiers and sponsors. Indicatively, the net result is that one dollar of capital supplied to an IFI by governments can lead to \$12 of private sector project investment (IFC, 2011).

The Nam Theun 2 Project in Lao PDR, discussed above, is an excellent example of a successful leveraging of multilateral guarantee mechanisms in a difficult business and investment environment. The risk mitigation instruments used by the World Bank Group were IDA PRG and MIGA PRI. The Asian Development Bank also provided a guarantee (for more detail see World Bank, 2005).

If Icelandic companies sponsor a geothermal project in an emerging market, or maybe more likely, form a consortium with investors from other countries to sponsor a project, an IFI such as the World Bank would be an ideal partner to help mobilize funds. Guarantees to facilitate participation by private investors could be important here. However, Icelandic companies have so far not been successful in working with the IFIs that Iceland is a member of, i.e., the World Bank Group and the EBRD. In fact, Icelandic companies, banks and the government are novices in the field of international development cooperation and lack knowledge and experience in doing business with IFIs. Furthermore, unlike the other Nordic countries, Iceland is not a member of the regional development banks, i.e., the Asian Development Bank, the Inter-American Development Bank and the African Development Bank.

IFIs generally need to demonstrate that their financing is essential, beyond what commercial finance would provide on its own, and that they can add value through risk mitigation and improved project design that leads to better overall development outcomes. They need to ensure that they crowd in investment and do not harm development of private financial markets. Most IFIs recognize this need, and many call their special role "additionality," that is, the value they bring to a project beyond what private sector financial institutions could typically offer (IFC, 2011).

All the IFIs are large and carry out extensive feasibility studies before they move on with a project. They are bureaucratic and project approvals take time. It is doubtful whether these long processing times fit well with the Icelandic mentality.[13]

---

[13] The president of Iceland described this well when he was praising the Icelandic banks that collapsed shortly after his speech. When talking about the Icelandic approach the president said "On numerous occasions I have also emphasized how Icelandic society, including our history and traditions, has produced a modern business culture that has proven to be very favourable when meeting the competitive challenges of our times" (Grímsson, 2006, p. 3). And then the president goes on to describe some of those qualities of modern Icelandic business culture and talks about "The inclination to focus on results rather than a process: to go straight to the task and do the job in the shortest time possible" (Grímsson, 2006, p. 4).

IFI participation can help projects in developing countries in two ways: (1) making them more commercially viable through, for example, better finance, improved risk mitigation, advice; and (2) improving their developmental outcomes by, for example, providing the advice and standard setting that lead to better operations, products, and services; stronger environmental, social, and corporate governance activities; or projects that are more inclusive (IFC, 2011). IFIs also tend to provide finance with longer maturities, which is generally beyond the risk appetite of private capital (IFC, 2011).

IFIs clearly can be catalysts to support PPP projects, including in the energy sector; however, as stated above they tend to be bureaucratic and this can cause problems and be costly for the private sector.

The World Bank Group and the Effectiveness of Its Risk Mitigation Instruments

The effectiveness of the risk mitigation instruments offered by IFIs and the performance of those institutions require constant review and scrutiny. In 2009 the World Bank Group (WBG) issued a report entitled: "The World Bank Group Guarantee Instruments 1990-2007. An Independent Evaluation" (World Bank, 2009). Unfortunately no such evaluation has been done since then. As part of the evaluation the Independent Evaluation Group at the Bank conducted a survey in 2008 to solicit views among its staff about the use and effectiveness of guarantee instruments (World Bank, 2009). A survey questionnaire was sent to 363 staff, of whom 206 responded.

Among the information that the survey revealed is that WBG staff are familiar with their own products, but not with the guarantee products of other WBG institutions. For example only one-fifth of IFC[14] staff were familiar with

---

This would not fit well with the long preparation time often used by international financial institutions. The president goes on to say: "The absence of bureaucracy and our lack of tolerance for bureaucratic methods. Perhaps because there are so few of us, we have never really been able to afford extensive bureaucratic structures" (Grímsson, 2006, p. 4). This approach proved to be extraordinarily expensive for Iceland in the case of the banking sector that eventually failed. If Icelandic investors want to gain the trust of international financial institutions and other reliable partners, this behavior must change. They need to learn.

[14] The International Finance Corporation, IFC, is the private sector arm of the World Bank Group, WBG.

IBRD/IDA[15] products. In fact, IFC staff were not familiar with the products of IBRD, IDA or MIGA.

According to the survey more than 85 percent of WBG staff felt that the most critical benefits of WBG guarantee instruments were enhanced image of financial soundness and improved rates and tenors. Other benefits included e.g., WBG's role as an honest broker and securing other investors (World Bank, 2009).

It is also notable how few guarantees and insurances have been issued from an institution as large as the World Bank Group. A high proportion of staff felt that changes are needed to improve the WBG's guarantee instruments (World Bank, 2009). Interestingly enough, most WBG staff felt that reducing the time and cost of processing guarantees and improving marketing were important for improving WBG guarantee instruments. Furthermore, staff reported that clients proceeding with a project without a guarantee and long processing time were the main reason for dropped guarantee projects. Eighty percent of IFC staff reported that droppages occurred because the cost of the guarantee was too high for the client (World Bank, 2009).

IBRD, IDA and MIGA staff reported that project sponsors/investors most frequently originated a request for guarantees. IFC staff reported that host governments and staff of another WBG institution are least likely to originate IFC guarantees.

On May 7, 2008 the Committee on Development Effectiveness at the World Bank considered the Independent Evaluation Group evaluation. Several speakers called for greater collaboration among WBG institutions based on their comparative advantages, and strengthening the coherence of the products offered, including pricing. They also called for more coordinated WBG efforts for marketing, increased staff knowledge of guarantee products, and appropriate staff incentives (World Bank, 2009, p. xxviii). Comments were also made about the need for the WBG to think about a "single Window" for guarantee products (World Bank, 2009, p. xxvi).

As already mentioned, no evaluation by the Independent Evaluation Group has taken place at the World Bank since 2009, [16] making it difficult to assess if the effectiveness of World Bank Group guarantee instruments has improved since 2009.

Multilateral as well as bilateral financial organizations can be a catalyst to support PPP projects, including in the energy sector. A recent book published

---

[15] The IBRD and the IDA are the public sector arms of the WBG.
[16] According to an email from Jayasankar Shivakumar and Pankaj Gupta, WBG, dated July 13. 2013.

by the World Bank, entitled "Public Private Partnerships in Europe and Central Asia – Designing Crisis-Resilient Strategies and Bankable Projects", comments very cautiously that "working with these institutions may also lengthen the project development process, given specific requirements in terms of environmental and social safeguards requirements and stringent procurement procedures" (Cuttaree and Mandri-Perrott, 2011, p. 59). Another recent book also published by the World Bank entitled: "Doing a dam better: the Lao People's Democratic Republic and the story of Nam Theun 2 (NT2)", is more critical when discussing World Bank cooperation with the private sector. The authors simply state that: "The bad news is that the World Bank is seen as a high-cost/high-hassle partner of last resort. There is therefore a critical need to reduce the costs the private sector incurs for doing business with the World Bank. Doing so will require the World Bank to better understand the constraints under which the private sector works" (Porter and Shivakumar, 2010, p. 22). These comments are especially notable given that the authors have both served as World Bank country directors.

From the above, it seems that a key institution like the World Bank has some way to go to find an optimal trade-off between excessive safeguards and efficient use of its financial instruments for capital mobilization. This is especially unfortunate given the urgency to construct more clean energy projects in developing countries.

The Need for Ifis to Make More Use of Their Guarantee Powers in Developing Countries

The ongoing debate about the role of IFIs increasingly recognizes the importance of making greater use of the risk mitigation potential inherent in their unique multilateral structure (Asian Development Bank, 2006). The World Economic Forum (WEF)[17] has, for example, argued strongly for IFIs to better use guarantee and risk mitigation instruments and capabilities to attract increased commercial investment in development projects. In 2006 the WEF issued a report entitled "Building on the Monterrey Consensus: The Untapped Potential of Development Finance Institutions to Catalyze Private

---

[17] The World Economic Forum's Financing for Development Initiative comprises more than 200 global experts from financial institutions, corporations, governments, international organizations, universities, and nongovernmental organizations, who offer their views on improving the effectiveness of efforts to stimulate private sector investment in developing countries.

Investment". In this report the WEF specifically asserted that: "…the weight of DFI [development finance institutions] activities should shift over time from direct lending to facilitating the mobilization of resources from the world's large private savings pools – international and domestic – for development – oriented investment through: wider use of risk mitigation instruments to alleviate part of the risk faced by investors; and stronger direct support for capacity building to strengthen the enabling environment for investment" (World Economic Forum, 2006, p. 9).

Furthermore the WEF argued that development financial institutions should "…adapt their services, culture and capital allocation to the imperative of "crowding in" domestic and foreign private investment by placing much more emphasis on such risk mitigation instruments as partial guarantees as transitional strategy and on capacity building" (World Economic Forum 2006, p. 10) and that "an international consensus has emerged, embodied by the Monterrey Consensus, that a deeper partnership between the public and private sector is needed if we are to achieve common development objectives" (World Economic Forum, 2006, p. 10). In its final recommendations the WEF says: "The overwhelming majority of expert participants in the project recommended a major expansion of risk mitigation activity by DFIs…" (World Economic Forum, 2006, p. 15).

The WEF thus sent a very clear signal to the IFIs. And the IFIs are listening. In its report entitled "Review of ADB's Credit Enhancement Operations" the Asian Development Bank takes a clear note of the WEF's views and refers to their 2006 report several times (Asian Development Bank, 2006).

While there is a clear need for risk mitigation in developing countries for sectors like the energy sector, it seems that IFIs, including the WBG, have some way to go to make those instruments widely used. IFIs need to do a better job in coordinating risk mitigation activities within themselves and spend more effort in marketing those products and to make them more efficient and more cost effective for the private sector and shorten their processing time.

Export Credit Agencies and Their Role in Risk Mitigation to Support Cross Border Trade Finance

Most developed countries have established export credit agencies (ECAs) to help finance export of their national goods and services as well as cross border investments. These agencies can provide guarantees in connection with projects involving deliveries of equipment and/or services to the project from the home country. This applies generally speaking to all ECAs supporting the export industry in their home country. In Iceland such an agency exists and is called *Tryggingardeild útflutnings* (TRÚ). ECAs can provide guarantees against both commercial and non-commercial risks in developing countries. These instruments can be quite suitable for supporting overseas investments in developing countries and emerging markets, including energy investments. TRÚ was to work in partnership with the Swedish ECA Exportkreditnamnden (EKN) which would assist the Icelandic agency to assess risks in host countries. Under Icelandic law TRÚ can provide guarantees and insurances up to 130 million SDR. This is a sizable amount of money. To keep the story short: TRÚ services have never been used by Icelandic exporters or cross border investors.

Developing and emerging countries are increasingly important to the Nordic countries for export and they all have ECAs to support their cross border trade. In contrast Icelandic exporters and investors are not using the risk mitigation instruments that are available from TRÚ at all. In the case of Nam Theun 2 discussed above ECAs from Norway, Garanti-instituttet for eksportkreditt (GIEK) and Sweden (EKN) supported the project.

For more discussion about the role of ECAs in supporting cross border trade, including during times of crisis, as well as economic justifications for the existence of ECAs, see Dinh and Hilmarsson (2012a, 2012b and 2012c) and Hilmarsson and Dinh (2013).

Overview of Some Sources of Funding for Cross Border Geothermal Energy Projects

This final section provides an overview of some possible sources of funding for cross border geothermal projects at an early, middle and late stage of project development. As discussed earlier in this chapter, high upfront development costs are associated with geothermal energy projects.

Table 4.7. Overview of potential sources of funding for cross border geothermal projects

Stage of project development	Early	Middle	Late
Activities	Exploration Initial drilling	Resource confirmation Field development Production drilling	Power plant Construction Commissioning
Risk of failure	*High risk*	*Medium risk*	*Low risk*
Potential funding sources	Balance sheet financing from sponsors Private equity from shareholders/investors Government cost sharing, concessional loans, grants, loan guarantees Donor grants, IFIs and bilateral donors Concessional loans/funds from international donors, including IFIs* (e.g., World Bank IDA terms)	Balance sheet financing or corporate bonds from sponsors Public equity Construction debt Loan guarantee by government Long term loan from IFIs* Guarantees from IFIs against non commercial risk to facilitate commercial lending ECAs**/trade finance. Guarantees and insurance against commercial and non commercial risks. Buyer or Supplier credits. Direct loans	Long term loans from commercial sources/investment banks Long term loan from IFIs* Guarantees from IFIs to attract commercial loans (larger loan allocation, longer term, lower interest rate) ECAs**/trade finance. Guarantees and insurance against commercial and non commercial risks. Buyer or Supplier credits. Direct loans

*IFIs: International Financial Institutions: Lending, equity, guarantees, grants and policy reform.

**ECAs: Export Credit Agencies: Guarantees for trade finance and loans.

Source: Constructed by the author.

At the initial phase risks are high but at the middle stage risks are medium and at the late stage the risks are low and projects may become bankable. Table 4.7 below provides an indication as to what funding sources and risk mitigation instruments might be feasible at each of the three stages of geothermal project development. Exploration and initial drilling costs are especially difficult for developing countries with small fiscal budgets and a weak tax base. Unfortunately, as shown in Table 4.3, IFIs have been avoiding this high risk at the early phase of geothermal development. Here they could and should do much more offering, for example, grants and concessional loans. Other donors should also get involved with grants or subsidized loans. During the middle and especially the late stage of project development IFIs should make more use of their guarantee and insurance instruments for capital mobilization attracting for example loans from international investment banks. Guarantees and insurance instruments could also attract equity contributions from international investors and investment funds.

IFIs should be able to price guarantee and insurance instruments lower than the private sector because they often engage with governments in developing countries on multiple projects and programs, which gives them as multilateral institutions leverage *vis-à-vis* developing country governments. An example of additional risk mitigation is to allow the host governments to own a stake in the geothermal power plant, which gives them an incentive to help ensure project success.

As discussed above, IFIs, including the World Bank Group, have so far made little use of their guarantee powers to mobilize funding for clean energy projects. High costs and bureaucracy are cited as major reasons, not only by outside observers, but also by staff and managers within the World Bank. ECAs can also play an important role in facilitating trade of goods and services from providers in developed countries to geothermal projects in developing countries.

CONCLUSION

Iceland can play a constructive role in developing countries by sharing its transition experience from fossil fuel to clean energy and could be an example for other countries to follow. Icelandic companies have a proven record in building and operating geothermal power plants. Several service providers, research and education institutions in geothermal energy could also contribute to the transition to geothermal energy in developing countries.

Most of the future increase in demand for electricity is likely to come from developing and emerging market economies. This is also where most of the clean energy resources are located. This offers a tremendous opportunity for developing countries, but is also a challenge, including with funding. Sufficient private funds will not flow into these countries unless the risk profile of energy projects can be reduced. This is especially true during times of financial and economic crisis.

To fill the tremendous energy infrastructure gap in developing countries the public and private sectors need to work in partnership, including via PPPs. Such partnerships can be supported by IFIs. For large energy project partnerships, pooling public, private and donor funds should not crowd out the private sector. Instead they offer the potential to crowd in private funds to risky markets that would not get private investment without proper risk mitigation.

In the absence of a global investment agreement, like the GATT and subsequently the WTO on trade, investors have turned to piecemeal solutions when protecting their rights in risky countries. This failure to create a global framework for investment is especially serious if one considers clean energy projects, which tend to be large, capital intensive and long term.

IFIs can be important partners not only with direct funding, i.e., loans and equity investments, but also increasingly through risk mitigation instruments. IFIs need to provide instruments that are more flexible and more cost effective for the private sector and with a shorter processing time. Better coordination is needed between World Bank Group institutions providing guarantees/ insurances, as indeed is better marketing of those instruments. In a recent World Bank publication, discussed in this chapter, two World Bank staff members who have been country directors describe the World Bank as a high-cost/high-hassle partner of last resort. They also argue that the World Bank needs to better understand the constraints under which the private sector works. Clearly the bank needs internal reform in order to achieve its potential in mobilizing private sector capital via its financial instruments, especially guarantees and insurance products.

ECAs can also play a constructive role in supporting exporters of equipment and services to developing and emerging markets by providing guarantees and insurance against commercial and non-commercial risk to facilitate longer term lending and at more affordable cost.

If Icelandic companies participate in energy projects as sponsors/investors in emerging market economies they should make serious efforts to develop a comprehensive risk identification and mitigation strategy before they engage.

This could be done by forming an international consortium with participation of IFIs that Iceland is a member of and with support of the Icelandic ECA.

The government of Iceland should increase its capacity in cooperating with those IFIs it is a member of. It should also carry out feasibility studies that could help in the decision making process of applying for membership in regional development banks. This could help strengthen the bargaining position of Icelandic companies *vis-à-vis* IFIs and enable them to select from a larger menu of financial and risk mitigation instruments in emerging markets than they presently can. Access to IFIs is also even more important for Icelandic companies than for companies from larger countries, as Iceland does not have wide representation in emerging markets through embassies and business representatives.

The government should also investigate why Icelandic companies have not been using the services of the Icelandic ECA, TRÚ. The services of TRÚ could be an important export promotion tool for Icelandic exporters especially during times of crisis.

The Nam Theun 2 project is an excellent example of successful leveraging of multilateral guarantee mechanisms in a difficult business and investment environment. ECAs also provided significant support by using their instruments to facilitate cross border trade finance for Nam Theun 2.

This chapter shows that the global system to support cross border investment in developing and emerging markets is fragmented and the international community offers only piecemeal solutions, e.g., via IFIs such as the World Bank and regional development banks. However, internal evidence from the World Bank suggests that it is difficult for the private sector to use the instruments offered. The World Bank has so far hesitated to use its guarantee powers in any significant way and thus does less to help mobilize as much private sector capital to developing and emerging countries as it could. This is especially unfortunate for investment in clean energy infrastructure where investments tend to be large, capital intensive and with long repayment periods. IFIs are well suited to mitigating non-commercial risks in emerging markets e.g., because of their global nature and because they often engage in policy dialogue with host governments and can facilitate regulatory reform often needed in emerging markets. IFIs including the World Bank have also so far done little to help fund the high upfront development costs for geothermal projects in developing countries. Here they should team up with other development institutions with grants and concessional lending to help make geothermal projects in developing countries bankable.

IFIs have failed to provide efficient and effective support for cross border infrastructure investment in developing countries. Among the results is underinvestment in clean energy investment globally. In spite of all the talk from IFIs about clean energy and the battle against climate change, so far they have little to show when it comes to capital mobilization for clean energy projects.

REFERENCES

Asian Development Bank. (2000). Review of the Partial Risk Guarantee of the Asian Development Bank, available at: http://www.adb.org/sites/default/files/pub/2000/prg.pdf (Accessed on June 1, 2014)

Asian Development Bank. (2006). *Review of ADB's Credit Enhancement Operations*, available at: http://www.adb.org/sites/default/files/credit-enhancement-operations-2006.pdf (Accessed on June 9, 2014)

Cuttaree, V. and Mandri-Perrott C. (2011). Public-Private Partnerships in Europe and Central Asia – Designing Crisis-Resilient Strategies and Bankable Projects. The World Bank, 2011.

Delmon, J. (2009). *Private Sector Investment in Infrastructure. Project Finance, PPP Projects and Risk.* 2nd edition, Kluwer Law International, the Netherlands.

Dinh, T. Q. and Hilmarsson H. Þ. (2012a). What are the Economic Justifications for the Existence of Export Credit Agencies and How Can They Facilitate Cross Border Trade to Emerging Market Economies? *Journal of Regional Formation and Development Studies*, 2012, 6, p. 15-25, Klaipeda.

Dinh, T. Q. and Hilmarsson, H. Þ. (2012b). Private Sector Export to Emerging Market Economies During Times of Crisis: How Can Export Credit Agencies Help? *Review of International Comparative Management*, Volume 13, Issue 1, March 2012, p. 167-180.

Dinh, T. Q. and Hilmarsson. H. Þ. (2012c). How Can Private Companies Use the Financial Services and Risk Mitigation Instruments Offered by Export Credit Agencies in Emerging Markets? Proceedings. Project Development - Practice and Perspectives. First International Scientific Conference on Project Management in the Baltic Countries. February 8-9, 2012, Riga, University of Latvia, p. 14-25.

GEOELEC. (2013). European Geothermal Risk Insurance Fund, EGRIF, available at: http://www.geoelec.eu/wp-content/uploads/2011/09/D-3.2-GEOELEC-report-on-risk-insurance.pdf (Accessed on June 12, 2014)

Gore, A. (2009). Our Choice – A Plan to Solve the Climate Crisis. Melcher Media, New York.

Grímsson, Ó. R. (2006). Icelandic ventures: Can the success continue? Speech made at the Kaupthing Seminar in Helsinki on May 24, 2010, available at: http://www.forseti.is/media/files/06.05.24.Helsinki.Conference.pdf (Accessed on June 15, 2014)

Hilmarsson, H. Þ. and Dinh T. Q. (2013). Export credit agencies, cross border trade, times of crisis, and increased value added in emerging economies' industrial sectors. Conference article presented at the 55th Annual Meeting of the Academy of International Business, July 3 to 6, 2013, Istanbul, Turkey.

Hodge, G. A. and Greve, C. (2009). PPPs: The Passage of Time Permits a Sober Reflection. Institute of Economic Affairs, Blackwell Publishing, Oxford, Vol. 29. Issue 1, 33- 39.

International Financial Corporation, IFC. (2009). Financing of Renewable Energy: IFC's Perspective. Presentation made in Washington D.C. in November 2009. Washington: World Bank.

International Financial Corporation, IFC. (2011). International Finance Institutions and Development Through the Private Sector, available at: http://www.miga.org/documents/IFI_report_09-13-11.pdf (Accessed on June 15, 2014).

International Monetary Fund. (2004). *Public Private Partnerships.* IMF, Washington, DC, available at: http://www.imf.org/external/np/fad/2004/pifp/eng/031204.pdf (Accessed on June 15, 2014).

Porter, I. C. and Shivakumar, J. (2010). *Doing a dam better: the Lao People's Democratic Republic and the story of Nam Theun 2 (NT2).* Washington D.C.-The World Bank, available at: http://documents.worldbank.org/curated/en/2010/01/13240425/doing-dam-better-lao-peoples-democratic-republic-story-nam-theun-2-nt2 (Accessed on June 2, 2014).

Wells, L. T. (2005). The New International Property Rights. Can the Foreign Investor Rely on Them. In International Political Risk Management. Looking to the Future, Theodore H. Moran and Gerald T. West, Eds. The World Bank Group – Multilateral Guarantee Agency.

West, G. T. (1999). Political Risk Investment Insurance: A Renaissance. *Journal of Project Finance*, 5(2), 27-36.

World Bank. (2005). Project Finance and Guarantees – IDA Guarantee Paves Renewed Interest in Private Hydropower – Nam Theun 2 Project, available at: http://siteresources.worldbank.org/INTGUARANTEES/ Resources/Lao_NamTheun2_Note.pdf (Accessed on June 8, 2014)

World Bank. (2008). *Capital Matters*, Vietnam Consultative Group Meeting Hanoi, 2008, available at: http://siteresources.worldbank.org/ INTVIETNAM/Resources/387318- 1235543674588/vn_devreport09_front.pdf (Accessed on June 7, 2014)

World Bank. (2009). *The World Bank Group Guarantee Instruments 1990- 2007. An Independent Evaluation.* The World Bank Washington, D.C.

World Bank. (2010). World Development Indicators Database, available at: http://siteresources.worldbank.org/DATASTATISTICS/Resources/GNI.p df(Accessed on June 2, 2014).

World Bank. (2012). Geothermal Handbook: Planning and Financing Power Generation. *Washington DC: World Bank Group, Energy Sector Management Assistance Program,* available at: http://www.esmap.org/ sites/esmap.org/files/DocumentLibrary/FINAL_Geothermal%20Handboo k_TR002-12_Reduced.pdf (Accessed on June 19, 2014).

World Bank. (2013a). Doing Business 2014 - Understanding Regulations for Small and Medium-Size Enterprises, available at: http://doingbusiness.org /~/media/GIAWB/Doing%20Business/Documents/Annual- Reports/English/DB14-Full-Report.pdf (Accessed on June 2, 2014)

World Bank. (2013b). Global Geothermal Development Plan, available at: http://www.esmap.org/sites/esmap.org/files/ESMAP_Paris_Geothermal_E nergy_KEF_Optimized.pdf (Accessed on June 12, 2014).

World Economic Forum. (2006). *Building on the Monterrey Consensus: The Untapped Potential of Development Finance Institutions to Catalyze Private Investment,* available at:http://allafrica.com/download/ resource/main/main/idatcs/00010787:aaea4ab2ef18167851a5fde8ad0778d 2.pdf (Accessed on June 6, 2014).

Chapter 5

SMALL STATES IN A GLOBAL ECONOMY. DISCUSSION, LESSONS LEARNED, AND CONCLUSION

In an era of globalization no country can be an island disconnected from the rest of the world and small states are now firmly integrated into the global economy. The discussion in this book shows that the experiences of small states can be valuable, including Iceland's transition to clean energy and the economic and political transition of the Baltic States. At the same time small states can be vulnerable, including during global crisis, and cannot take for granted that the international community will take their interests and well being into consideration.

This book focused on several issues of global importance, how small states are affected, why they can be vulnerable and how their experiences can be beneficial internationally. The issues discussed include the 2008 global economic and financial crisis; governance issues and vulnerabilities in small states with small institutions and limited administrative capacity; contributions to international development cooperation; and how small states can contribute to global issues such as the transition to clean energy.

This final and concluding chapter will discuss what lessons can be learned from the challenges small states are faced with in a global world and how they can contribute constructively to the development and well being of other countries globally. The following overview (see Table 5.1.), was provided in the introduction to this book as a summary of its organization. This final chapter will discuss some lessons learned and conclusions for each chapter.

The discussion is based on the questions asked in the introduction to the book as well as the propositions that were spelled out for consideration.

Table 5.1. Small states and multilateralism. Partnership with international financial institutions (IFIs). The table shows broadly the organization of the book by chapter, issues discussed, countries analyzed and potential benefits for small states when participating in the activities of those multilateral institutions

Chapter 1	Chapter 2	Chapter 3	Chapter 4
Crisis and economic policy response. Austerity vs. growth	Crisis, dishonesty and incompetence. Domestic issues with international implications	Participation in international development cooperation and development effectiveness	Clean energy projects. Technical assistance, advisory services, and cross border investment
Countries discussed			
Iceland and Latvia	Iceland	Baltic States and Nordic countries	Iceland
Potential benefits from partnering with IFIs			
Financial assistance, technical assistance and advisory services from IFIs during times of crisis		Increase in development effectiveness by participating in policy dialogue in partnership with IFIs in priority countries	Funding and risk mitigation in developing and emerging markets via partnership with IFIs. Use of IFI funding and risk mitigation instruments

Source: Constructed by the author.

Chapter 1

The objective of this chapter was to analyze the challenges faced and action taken by the governments of Iceland and Latvia during the 2008 crisis. To what extent was the response to the crisis the choice of the domestic governments in Iceland and Latvia exercising strong government "ownership"? To what extent were actions taken shaped by external actors, including economic interests, such as bank owners from other countries and international organizations such as the IMF and the EU? Were the policy outcomes favorable for those small states if one considers economic and social performance?

The proposition considered was the following: It is beneficial for small states to be members of multilateral institutions such as the EU when crisis hits since small states have limited resources and human capacity to deal with crisis situations and are likely to receive support and assistance from international organizations should things go wrong domestically. Small states can also benefit during a crisis from being part of a group such as the Nordic Baltic group since they can receive support from friendly countries in such a group.

As discussed in chapter 1 Iceland and Latvia were both severely affected by the 2008 global economic and financial crisis but their policy response was different, in Latvia's case with a fixed exchange rate, and in Iceland with a flexible exchange rate and heavy depreciation. Both countries adjusted and made sacrifices, implementing painful fiscal budget cuts.

Post crisis both countries are enjoying GDP growth well beyond the EU and Euro area and unemployment has gone down although long term unemployment is still high in Latvia.

In contrast to the above proposition one can argue that Iceland benefited from not being a member of the EU when the crisis hit and Latvia suffered from EU membership and its intention to join the Euro area (Latvia adopted the Euro in January 2014). This is because Latvia maintained a peg with the Euro while Iceland managed to improve its competitiveness by depreciating its local currency, the Krona, as did Finland and Sweden in the early 1990s, for example. Iceland had a locally owned banking system that the international community did not want to support, and thus had to fall, while Latvia had a foreign banking system that foreign investors and the EU insisted on rescuing, and perhaps had to save. Iceland benefited from not serving EU interests while Latvia suffered from interference by the EU, whose main interest was to serve the Euro area, and the foreign owners of their banks, mainly from Scandinavia.

Furthermore, the 2008 global economic and financial crisis shows that while small states can benefit from cooperation with international organizations and other states, such as the Nordic countries, they can be vulnerable if the interests of those institutions and countries are different from their own interests. Iceland could react to the crisis according to its own interest while Latvia had to take the interests of the Euro area into account given its ambitions to adopt the Euro, which it did in January 2014. Latvia also had to serve the interest of the Nordic countries that owned the Latvian banking system while the locally owned banking system in Iceland fell. A group of countries, in this case the Nordic countries, especially Sweden, strongly influenced how the Baltic States reacted to the crisis. Membership in international organizations can thus be a disadvantage for small states during times of crisis. Interference by larger more powerful states can also be a mixed blessing.

The two countries compared in this chapter, Iceland and Latvia, are in many ways different, for example, with large differences in level of development, income, history, location, institutions, social welfare system, and so on. Nevertheless, they are interesting comparator cases as they were both hit hard by the crisis, but responded very differently in terms of economic policy and with different economic and social outcomes. While this study focuses on Iceland and Latvia the results can be interesting for other small countries. Moreover, the fact that these two countries responded so differently to the crisis makes a comparative case study feasible. Important lessons can be learned about the effects of different policy responses on economic recovery in small countries.

The Case of Iceland

During the 2008 crisis Iceland tried to use a bilateral approach, to rescue its banking system, making contact with major central banks as well as the Nordic central banks. When that did not yield the intended results Iceland made unilateral moves, including the Emergency Act, which is unusual for small states. Historically Iceland seems not to place much trust in multilateral institutions and has tended to pursue bilateral relations rather than international relations within international organizations.

Iceland does not use international organizations as a protection forum from larger and more powerful states in the same way as do the Baltic States, including Latvia. Iceland is not a member of the EU and has not been very active within NATO. Support for NATO operations mainly seems to have had the purpose of pleasing the USA when a US defense force was based in Iceland and part of Iceland's strategy was to keep a credible defense force in the country, especially air defense. That defense force is now gone.

Consistent with its limited emphasis on cooperation within international organizations Iceland has not developed strong units in its ministries to become an active participant in those international organizations, depending more on bilateral arrangements. The so called Cold War is an example of how Iceland uses a bilateral relationship, namely with the USA, to push its agenda. At that time the US had a military base in Iceland that it wanted to keep.

If bilateral relations have not yielded the desired results Iceland has not hesitated to take unilateral decisions and confront larger nations. This was done against the UK during the Cod Wars and again against the UK and the

Netherlands during the Icesave dispute. During the Cod Wars Iceland unilaterally extended the boundaries of its territorial waters and protected vital national fisheries resources.

Iceland uses loose international frameworks rather than formal integration, is a member of EFTA and has access to the EU common market through the EEA. Iceland also attaches importance to Nordic cooperation, with what could be called "a young brother mentality", sometimes naively assuming that the other Nordic countries will come to its rescue during times of crisis. The Nordic countries, however, were hesitant to come to Iceland's aid during the 2008 crisis and were not keen to support Iceland during the Cod Wars.

Iceland was isolated during the 2008 crisis and external actors, including "friendly" nations and international organizations, were not interested in rescuing its locally owned banking system. Internal actors, i.e., the people of Iceland via two national referendums, twice rejected settlements with the UK and the Netherlands. This proved to be beneficial for Iceland as it meant that Icelandic taxpayers were not made responsible for the fall of private banks. This also enabled Iceland to better protect its welfare system during the crisis.

In line with its limited interest in operating via multilateral organizations, Iceland was reluctant to approach and work with the IMF during the 2008 crisis. Its cooperation with the IMF, however, proved to be successful and the IMF was overall well regarded in Iceland as, in addition to funds and advice, it provided much needed credibility. Iceland was also reluctant to trust the EFTA Court until it ruled in its favor against the Netherlands and the UK in the Icesave dispute.

Icelandic governments are less restricted in their scope of action, both domestically and internationally, than they would have been within the EU system. Iceland has historically opposed powerful states during times of crisis and does not hesitate to take unilateral decisions contrary to the general norms and rules of the international system, including during the Cod Wars and the 2008 crisis. As Thorhallsson puts it when discussing Iceland's behavior during the Cod Wars "Icelandic governments have taken radical unilateral decisions concerning the extension of 'Icelandic waters' and been successful in their approach. This contradicts the small-state literature concerning the vulnerability of small states, their reactive nature and the importance they allegedly attach to working within multilateral organizations" (Thorhallsson, 2005, p.133). Also as Ingebritsen states, "...Iceland's determined defense of its establishment of an Exclusive Economic Zone to protect their vital fisheries significantly enhance their reputations as principled actors in international relations – willing to challenge opponents and to rely on innovative strategies against superior might" (Ingebritsen, 2006, p. 86).

This challenges assumptions concerning the relative capacity of smaller powers in international relations. Relying on unilateral decisions seems a risky strategy in international relations for small states but it seems to have worked well during the 2008 crisis and the Cod Wars. One big difference was that during the Cod Wars, Iceland could utilize its membership in NATO and the strategic importance of the Keflavík NATO base as a means of seeking to resolve the conflict. During the 2008 crisis the Cold War was over and the US Defense Force gone so US support was not forthcoming when requested.

During the Cod Wars the British and the West Germans agreed to take the dispute to the International Court of Justice for resolution. Consistent with the limited faith that Iceland has in international organizations the Icelandic government questioned the jurisdiction of the court. Iceland also did not show much interest in the EFTA Court during the 2008 crisis until it ruled in its favor in the Icesave dispute with the Netherlands and the UK.

As a small state Iceland has been able to punch above its weight and successfully defend vital interests against larger, powerful states in the international system without being a member of the EU and without taking full part in its integration. This strategy is not without risks but it has worked during critical times.

Iceland can learn a few lessons from the 2008 economic and financial crisis and it needs to decide how to participate in international organizations including during times of crisis. Unilateral decisions have at times proven successful, and may also be feasible in the future, but during the 2008 crisis Iceland was successful in cooperating with the IMF and the ruling of the EFTA Court was favorable for Iceland. Iceland needs to rethink its relationship with the USA post Cold War given that the USA did not make credible efforts to come to Iceland's aid during the 2008 crisis. It also needs to reconsider its relationship with the Nordic countries. Preserving a good political and cultural relationship with the Nordic countries is important, but relying on them during times of crisis is naïve. Iceland also needs to build and strengthen relationships with new allies in Asia, the fastest growing region in the world economically and a rising political and military power. In terms of bilateral relations Iceland needs to diversify by having multiple allies in different regions.

The Case of Latvia

Latvia's approach to the 2008 global economic and financial crisis was more in line with what the small states theory, discussed in the introduction to this book, suggests a small state would do, i.e., rely on the multilateral system for support. International organizations were very much involved in managing the crisis response in Latvia, especially the EU and the IMF. The World Bank and EBRD could also support Latvia because Latvia, unlike Iceland, was classified as a middle income developing country when the crisis hit.

Latvia's behavior during the crisis also needs to be viewed in light of its history. Less than 25 years ago it was part of the Soviet Union and the country suffered from the legacy of Soviet economic structures upon independence and during its transition. Latvia uses international organizations, especially the EU and NATO, as a protection mechanism from larger and more powerful states, most notably Russia.

If one considers Keohane's categorization discussed in the introduction to this book, Latvia would fall into the "system-ineffectual" category: a small state that simply adjusts to the international system and cannot change it (Keohane, 1969). It chooses firm EU integration, including Euro area membership, seeking economic benefits and stability. It also seeks security through EU and NATO membership.

Like some Eastern and Central European countries, Latvia imported a foreign banking system during its transition from the Soviet system. The Baltic banking systems are dominated by Nordic-headquartered banks and reliance on parent bank funding is high suggesting strong financial linkages with the Nordic countries. Added to this are strong links in trade and investment. These inter-linkages were in many ways useful during Latvia's transition from the Soviet system, and could be valuable during times of crisis, but they also make the Baltic States, including Latvia, more vulnerable as Nordic banking interests, mainly Swedish, took control in Latvia during the crisis. More diversified ownership of the banking system in Latvia could be useful for Latvia and the Nordic countries.

Latvia's reliance on the multilateral system during the 2008 crisis was mainly on the EU. The Scandinavian countries as a group also played an important role. The IMF, which recommended modest depreciation hoping for improved competitiveness and faster economic recovery for Latvia, was marginalized during the crisis and pushed into a corner by the EU and foreign banking interests, supported by Scandinavian governments. The peg with the Euro required implementation of a radical austerity program with high human costs. This is confirmed by data from Eurostat, which measures poverty, social exclusion as well as income distribution. The data show that Latvia compares poorly not only with Iceland but also with other transition countries at a similar income level. This illustrates that international norms and rules, in this case EU policy on fiscal discipline and exchange rate policy, do not always benefit small international players.

In addition to the high human costs, Latvia's austerity program also resulted in lower contributions to defense. This is a concern especially during increasing geopolitical tensions surrounding Ukraine that could lead to disruption in financial, trade and commodity markets.

Latvia's experience during the crisis shows that the small-state literature cannot take it for granted that multilateral cooperation within international organizations constitutes the best framework for small states to secure their interest.

Among the lessons learned from the 2008 crisis is that Latvia needs to develop a more independent capacity in engaging multilaterally and bilaterally. It should be more ambitious than merely being part of an EU/Nordic bandwagon. It urgently needs to find ways to protect its vulnerable social systems and ensure further social cohesion. This is important not only for economic growth and prosperity, but also for security. Latvia should also place more emphasis on strengthening its own security systems instead of relying blindly on NATO and the EU.

As a small state Latvia needs to consider options to diversify its banking system. Strong inter-linkages make both the Scandinavian and Baltic States more vulnerable during times of crisis and can be dangerous for small states.

In conclusion, neither Iceland nor Latvia appears to have had ownership over their reform programs during the 2008 economic and financial crisis. Pre-crisis the government of Iceland tried to rescue the banking system and failed as the foreign central banks approached refused to rescue the Icelandic banks. After the fall of the banking system the government tried to achieve a settlement on the Icesave issue but the Icelandic nation rejected it twice in national referendums.

In Latvia, EU and foreign banking interests were heavily involved in designing the policy response. Both countries are currently enjoying healthy economic growth. The human costs during the crisis in Latvia are much higher than in Iceland, and remain a serious concern. In Iceland balance sheet problems for families and corporates remain, causing controversy and increasing uncertainty.

Chapter 2

The objective of this chapter was to address the following questions: Did the Icelandic government take appropriate action when the Icelandic banks expanded with investments and operations overseas? Was inaction a problem? Can the government be charged with attempting to fake reality? Is it possible that the government was honest but incompetent and therefore not trustworthy?

Similarly, did the international community, including the European Union, take appropriate action when the Icelandic banks expanded with investments and operations overseas? Was inaction a problem? Can the international community be charged with attempting to fake reality, i.e., pretend that Iceland had responsibilities that it did not have? Is it possible that the international community was honest but demonstrated incompetence and is therefore not trustworthy? Put differently, during the crisis a failure of European integration was exposed, but larger countries, the UK and the Netherlands, supported by the EU tried to use force to have a small country suffer the consequences.

The proposition considered was: Small countries like Iceland benefit from being members of multilateral arrangements such as the European Economic Area and generally benefit from European integration and open access to markets, including financial markets. When crisis hits, small states such as Iceland also benefit from being part of a group of nations like the Nordic countries and are likely to receive assistance from nations with whom it has friendly political relations.

As discussed in the introduction to this book, conventional small states theory suggests that small states benefit from working with international organizations and participating in the international system. As also discussed, Iceland has a preferred bilateral approach and does not place much trust in multilateral institutions. Iceland is not a member of the EU, but is part of the EEA. It has favored the less restricted structure of decision making within EFTA and the EEA compared to the supranational character of the EU.

Economic theory suggests that there can be benefits from economic integration, including gains from trade. However, there are also risks. Pre crisis the EEA agreement allowed cross border banking expansion from Iceland without host country supervision. Being part of the European Economic Area allowed Icelandic banks, which had recently been privatized, access to the European market and they expanded aggressively.

It is clear that the government of Iceland made mistakes when this banking expansion took place pre crisis. It is now known that the government could not adequately support the banks during times of crisis and when the 2008 global crisis hit the Ministry of Finance did not have fiscal capacity to support the banks, nor did the Central Bank of Iceland have adequate reserves to serve as a lender of last resort. The government chose to turn a blind eye to the problem and treated a financial problem as a problem of perception and an image crisis. As discussed in chapter 2 the government of Iceland showed negligence during the crisis and could be charged with dishonesty. That the government was incompetent and did not understand the risks involved is also a possibility as hinted at by the governor of the Swedish Riksbank.

The actions and the responsibility of the international community during the crisis in Iceland have been less researched. During the crisis flaws in the European integration system became evident. Banks could, for example, expand cross border without host country supervision. Instead of assisting Iceland during the crisis the international community failed Iceland. The UK and the Netherlands, supported by the EU, tried to force Iceland to undertake obligations that the EFTA Court later ruled it did not have. This shows that a multilateral organization like the EU is prepared to take hostile action against small nations if it is in the interests of some of its larger member states. In this sense being part of an arrangement such as the EEA can be risky for small states that have less institutional capacity than do larger states to defend themselves in the event of dispute.

Iceland tried to use its bilateral relations to rescue its banking system, contacting major central banks individually. This included the Federal Reserve, the Bank of England, and the European Central Bank. The Nordic central banks were also contacted. It is now known that those central banks coordinated their reactions among themselves when responding to the Central Bank of Iceland and decided not to assist Iceland during the crisis. It can be argued that the international community behaved dishonestly against Iceland during the crisis by pretending that Iceland had responsibilities that it did not have. Additionally, some level of incompetence within the EU has become evident as serious flaws in its financial integration surfaced during the crisis, also severely affecting EU countries.

The discussion in this chapter can have a wider relevance than that for Iceland only. This is especially true for small countries with a large banking sector, using their own currency, and with limited fiscal space to support their banks during a crisis. Important lessons can also be learned, both regarding the mode of privatization for banks, as well as on policy response during times of economic and financial crisis.

Small states can benefit from working with international organizations and from being a member of such integration arrangements as the European Economic Area. There can be no doubt that access to this market was, and still is, critically important for Iceland. During times of crisis small states can, however, be vulnerable if larger states try to use their strength in international organizations to impose costs on them. The UK and the Netherlands used their membership in the EU to pressure the EU to take a stand against Iceland during the crisis. The IMF was also taken hostage by the UK and the Netherlands during the crisis when Iceland sought its assistance. Small states can benefit from involvement by multilateral courts like the EFTA Court. During the Icesave dispute the EFTA Court ruled in Iceland's favor, in spite of potential pressure from larger states.

Among the lessons learned from the 2008 crisis is that small states such as Iceland can become vulnerable if relying on international relations to solve their problems. The EU became hostile towards Iceland when the interests of its own member states were at stake, in this case the Netherlands and the UK. In spite of global financial markets, small states can become isolated when crisis hits.

The government of Iceland was criticized by the international community but did not receive sufficient advice or support to deal with a very difficult situation that to a large extent was not only due to mistakes in Iceland, but failure in European economic integration as well. The Federal Reserve in the USA did not get involved in rescuing the Icelandic banking system, reflecting weak relations between Iceland and the USA post Cold War. Iceland was deliberately isolated by the UK's activation of its antiterrorist legislation. Aggression from the UK towards Iceland was not a total surprise, given their historical relationship. During the so-called Cod Wars, when Iceland was expanding its fishing territory, the UK sent its navy into Icelandic waters. During the 2008 crisis the UK and the Netherlands tried to force the Icelandic government to have Icelandic taxpayers bail out UK and Dutch depositors beyond the amounts their Icesave accounts had been insured for. The Nordic Countries were at best passive bystanders when this went on, but sometimes supported the larger states against Iceland.

The government of Iceland was brought to its knees by the UK and the Netherlands during the Icesave dispute and reached two settlements with their governments that were agreed to by the Icelandic parliament, the Althingi. The president of Iceland, however, refused to sign the legislation. This in turn triggered two national referendums. In both referendums the Icelandic nation rejected the demands from the UK and the Netherlands. Finally, Iceland was taken to the EFTA Court where Iceland won the case brought against it by the Netherlands and the UK. It can be argued that the behavior of the UK and the Netherlands before and after the crisis was dishonest and in the end, not only damaging for Iceland, but also for their own citizens. They pretended that Iceland had an obligation that the EFTA Court ruled that it did not have. They used strong-arm tactics against Iceland, acting like colonizers against a colony.

Iceland was on its own and isolated until the collapse of its banks. Iceland should not rely on "friendly" nations during times of crisis. It needs to rethink its future relationship with the UK and the Netherlands including a possible submarine cable to supply the UK with electricity. History shows that Iceland cannot trust the UK during times of crisis. The UK tends to take extreme actions during disputes including sending in its navy during the Cod Wars and using anti terrorist legislation during the 2008 financial crisis. Iceland also needs to rethink and reconsider its relationship with the Nordic countries post crisis. It is now known that those countries closely coordinated with the UK during the crisis in line with their own self interest, not fully considering Iceland's interest.

Among the lessons learned is also that engagement with international organizations can be beneficial for small states. Iceland, for example, managed to establish good cooperation with the IMF which helped with restoring Iceland's credibility. The EFTA Court also helped set the record straight on the Icesave issue. Iceland needs to rethink its emphasis on bilateral relations and build more capacity to work with international organizations as this may be beneficial, at least in some cases.

In retrospect, Iceland benefited from not receiving assistance from major central banks, including the Bank of England, the European Central Bank, and the Federal Reserve in rescuing its banking system when the 2008 crisis hit. Bailing the banks out at taxpayers' cost would have brought government debt to an unsustainable level.

The government of Iceland twice tried to reach a settlement with the UK and the Netherlands. Each time, the president activated the constitution, allowing a public referendum to take place. Two national referendums refusing a sovereign guarantee for the Icesave deposits stopped the government from making a settlement with the UK and the Netherlands. Had a settlement been reached on Icesave it would have reduced the government's capacity to defend the welfare system.

Chapter 3

The objective of this chapter was to assess what role small states can play in assisting their partner countries in implementing economic transition and achieving economic growth and poverty reduction. The countries focused on were mainly the Baltic States as participants in multilateral institutions and providers of bilateral assistance to the partner countries they have selected. How should the Baltic States assist their partner countries in the future? How can the Baltic States best share their transition experience with less advanced transition countries? Should they focus on small bilateral projects or should they work in partnership with other bilateral and multilateral donors? Should they engage in budget support operations and participate in policy dialogue or concentrate on small projects, or some combination of both?

The proposition considered was as follows: Small states can increase their development effectiveness by cooperating with international financial institutions and by engaging in policy dialogue with their priority countries in partnership with IFIs and other countries. Small countries can further increase their development effectiveness by providing technical assistance to support policy actions that they consider important for their priority countries.

According to conventional small states theory, discussed in the introduction to this book, small states would be expected to favor multilateralism, working through international organizations, rather than engaging bilaterally. In the area of international development cooperation the Baltic States do not emphasize multilateral participation as the theory predicts. Their development budgets are currently so small that they are to a large extent used to pay mandatory contributions to international organizations. The Baltic States have also not developed sufficient institutional capacity to actively participate in or shape the policies of those institutions. Nor have they been active in policy dialogue with their own partner countries. After paying their mandatory share to international organizations, little room is left for bilateral activities. This is especially the case for Latvia.

Looking at their partner country choice the Baltic States have mostly selected middle income countries in Europe and Central Asia. This narrow regional focus is in line what small states theory would predict. This focus makes sense for the Baltic States as their transition experience is recent and most relevant to middle income countries in Europe and Central Asia.

This book argues that the Baltic States could increase their development effectiveness by more actively sharing their transition experience with their priority countries and channeling their aid more to support policy reform accompanied with relevant technical assistance in areas where they have recent experience. This would require working more in partnership with international development organizations in their partner countries as well as in small groups of bilateral donors. The small bilateral projects that the Baltic States currently support can only have limited development impact in their priority countries unless they are also linked to overall policy reform efforts in those countries.

While small states can increase their development effectiveness by working with international organizations and participating in policy dialogue with partner countries, the bureaucratic nature of those institutions can be an obstacle. The Baltic States tend to use their participation in international development organizations to reach a larger number of countries without much participation in policy dialogue and sharing of their transition experience. In contrast, the Scandinavian countries (Denmark, Norway and Sweden) are active in advising their partner countries on policy reform and in influencing the policies of international organizations. The Baltic States can learn from the Scandinavian countries here, but to be more effective advisors on policy reform they need to strengthen their institutional capacity.

The development cooperation of the Baltic States has a narrow regional focus which is understandable for small states, but they also to focus too much on their own narrow self interest. What is in this for us? Part of their contributions to economic development seems mainly to serve their own security concerns. Contributions to Afghanistan are a good example. Such contributions help improve their standing in NATO. All the Baltic States contribute far less to international development cooperation that the EU expects them to do. Their bilateral budgets are small, embarrassingly small in the case of Latvia.

To a large extent the Baltic States fail to share their transition experience when participating in international development cooperation. The current emphasis on small projects and their low profile in international organizations reduces the impact the Baltic States could have in their priority countries. The Baltic States often hesitate to engage in policy dialogue with their priority countries in partnership with international financial institutions and other donors and lack confidence in their ability to influence multilateral decisions.

To become more effective participants globally in international development cooperation, the Baltic States need to fulfill their financial commitment. This means that their financial contributions need to increase substantially. They also need to strengthen their institutional capacity to engage in dialogue with international development organizations as well as to participate meaningfully in policy dialogue with their partner countries. This can be achieved via participation in budget support operations in partnership with other donors and international organizations where the Baltic States can offer advice based on their own transition experience. Working in small donor groups, such as with the Nordic countries, could help move the Baltic States from the "system-ineffectual" category as classified by Keohane and discussed in the introduction to this book, to the "system-affecting" category (Keohane, 1969). In addition to strengthening their capacity through working with international financial institutions, they should also consider membership in the regional development banks.

While the Baltic States should develop their own approaches in international development cooperation, they could benefit and learn lessons from the approaches of the Nordic countries, most notably Denmark, Norway and Sweden. Their generous contributions and global focus in development cooperation has greatly contributed to their international prestige. In spite of their smallness they have developed sufficient capacity to keep a high profile in multilateral institutions. Their financial contribution to international development cooperation exceeds what the international community, including the EU and the UN, expects them to do. Given their large development budget, contributions to multilateral institutions take a relatively small share of their total development budget so they also have large bilateral programs.

The Nordic countries now focus primarily on low income countries in Sub-Saharan Africa. The development instruments they use include investment projects, technical assistance as well as budget support.[1] This active and high profile participation in international organizations has enabled those countries to become "system-affecting" states as classified by Keohane, i.e., small states that can as a group influence the international system (Keohane, 1969). The Scandinavian countries, Denmark, Norway and Sweden, have been keen to engage in policy dialogue with priority countries in partnership with international financial institutions and other donors. These partnerships have enabled them to 'punch above their weight' in terms of global influence which would be impossible for them to achieve alone.

Among the lessons learned from this chapter is that the Baltic States can benefit from studying the international development cooperation practices of the Scandinavian countries: Denmark, Norway and Sweden. The Baltic States should make credible medium term plans to fulfill their financial commitments

---

[1] Iceland is an exception with its relatively small development budget and it also does not participate in budget support operations.

in international development cooperation. They should increase their capacity to work with international development institutions and with small donor groups such as the Nordic Countries. When working with partner countries the Baltic States should engage in policy dialogue and provide technical assistance that can support policy reform in their partner countries. By helping partner countries implement policy reform the Baltic States can better share their own experience and increase the development effectiveness of their programs.

Chapter 4

The objective of this chapter was to answer the following questions: How can companies from small countries like Iceland contribute to the transition to clean energy in developing and emerging market economies? How can risks be mitigated when investing in clean energy projects in developing countries? Does the international community offer a comprehensive framework for risk mitigation for investments in developing countries?

The proposition considered was: Small states usually have little leverage in solving disputes bilaterally with developing and emerging market countries that are often larger. Developing countries in transition typically have business and investment climates that need improvement and are being developed. Companies from small states can better manage risks in developing countries if they work in partnership with international financial institutions. IFIs have more leverage in developing countries as they often have multiple projects there and engage in policy dialogue, including on regulatory reform. Partnership with IFIs thus improves the risk profile of cross border investments from small states.

Several Icelandic companies and institutions have proven capacity in utilizing geothermal energy and could transfer that know-how to developing countries on a larger scale than they currently do. In the absence of a global investment agreement, like the GATT and subsequently WTO on trade, investors have turned to piecemeal solutions when protecting their rights in risky countries. This failure to create a global framework for investment is especially serious if one considers clean energy projects that tend to be large, capital intensive and long term. Nevertheless, it is clear that by cooperation with IFIs Icelandic companies can better mitigate the risks of cross border engagement, especially investments. This is because private companies from small countries such as Iceland have little leverage in developing countries especially in the event of dispute with the host governments in those countries.

Cooperation with IFIs could also help with funding of projects since IFIs can both provide loans and contribute equity capital. Their risk mitigation instruments can help in mobilizing capital from private sector players, including international investment banks. Better risk management helps ensure larger loan allocation and longer term lending in challenging business environments.

While Icelandic companies could improve the risk profile of their cross border energy projects by cooperating with international financial institutions, IFIs themselves have so far done little to promote clean energy projects in developing countries. IFIs tend to be bureaucratic and the costs of forming partnerships with their participation can be high. The funding and risk mitigation instruments of IFIs make IFIs ideal partners for companies from small states but the bureaucracy and high costs of cooperation are among obstacles for cooperation. IFIs have also done very little so far in using their risk mitigation instruments to mobilize capital for clean energy projects in developing countries.

There is no doubt that Iceland is a global leader in utilizing clean energy for electricity production and space heating. Iceland's transition to clean energy is impressive, including several modern geothermal power plants that have received international attention. In addition to space heating and electricity production Iceland has also been successful in generating added value via multiple use activities such as using geothermal energy for fish farming, greenhouses, swimming pools, lagoons to attract tourists, and so on. Developing countries could also learn from this experience.

As discussed in the introductory chapter to this book, and contrary to small states theory, the tendency in Iceland has been to engage in bilateral cooperation rather than to cooperate multilaterally within international organizations. Iceland has so far showed little interest in cooperating with international financial institutions in clean energy. Iceland has limited capacity in working with IFIs and has allocated only modest resources in building up a foreign service capable of taking an active part in international organizations. Low capacity in cooperating with the World Bank and the EBRD, however, means that the government cannot advise the private sector how to engage in cooperation with IFIs. Furthermore, Iceland is not a member of regional development banks which also could be important multilateral partners.

Iceland as a global leader in geothermal utilization can set a good example internationally, including in developing countries. Iceland needs to build its capacity in cooperating with international financial institutions in clean energy by establishing a specialized unit within the Ministry of Foreign Affairs with sufficient long term staff and institutional memory. It also needs to decide if companies in public ownership, such as Landsvirkjun and Orkuveita Reykjavíkur, can participate in energy projects in developing countries, and if so, under what circumstances. There is a need to explore the feasibility for Iceland to become a member of regional development banks. This could help strengthen the bargaining position of Icelandic firms that seek to engage in geothermal development in developing countries and need to form partnerships with IFIs. The government should also investigate why Icelandic companies have not shown interest in the instruments of the Icelandic export credit agency.

As discussed in chapter 4 several companies and institutions in Iceland have a proven record in constructing and operating geothermal power plants. The largest companies, however, are as stated above in public ownership and other companies tend to be small with limited funding capacity and a small number of staff. Production of equipment for geothermal development in Iceland is also limited. The current experience of Icelandic companies in geothermal development in developing countries is mostly related to small projects. Icelandic companies lack the funding and tools for risk mitigation to engage in cross border investment. Icelandic companies have so far showed little interest in and have limited capacity for working with international financial institutions. They have low capacity to form international consortiums and manage public private partnerships in the energy sector in developing countries.

Many Icelandic companies and institutions that have geothermal expertise are now in the process of forming a geothermal cluster and an entity called Iceland Geothermal has now been established. This entity could become a platform for cooperation and coordination for cross border engagement for Icelandic companies. Iceland Geothermal would need to possess some knowledge about the instruments offered by IFIs and be able to advise companies how to form partnerships with IFIs and use the services of ECAs. It is also important to develop capacity among Icelandic companies as to forming and managing consortiums for geothermal projects.

As stated above Iceland is a member of the World Bank Group and the European Bank for Reconstruction and Development but not a member of regional development banks, the African Development Bank, the Inter-American Development Bank and the Asian Development Bank. All those institutions emphasize clean energy investments in their public communications. IFIs have the funding and risk mitigation instruments needed for capital mobilization. They also often engage in policy dialogue, including regulatory reform, in developing countries. IFIs also have capacity in forming international consortiums.

In spite of all this IFIs have so far done little to engage on the ground in clean energy projects in developing countries and their portfolio in geothermal energy is tiny. IFIs have avoided taking the risks of investing in the early phases of geothermal development as shown in chapter 4. They have also made little use of risk mitigation instruments for capital mobilization. The World Bank has been described by its own managers as a "high-cost/high-hassle partner of last resort." This state of affairs is unacceptable for a leading global institution like the World Bank Group.

IFIs including the World Bank need to show results on the ground for clean energy projects. They need to show more willingness to take risks including investing in the early development phase of geothermal projects. IFIs also need to make more use of risk mitigation instruments to help with capital mobilization of clean energy projects. There is also a need to improve the marketing of their instruments available for clean energy investments and make an effort to reduce the costs which the private sector incurs when cooperating with IFIs.

Among the lessons for Iceland to learn from this chapter is that although Iceland has strong technical competence in the area of geothermal development, and has been successful in its own transition to clean energy, it does not have advantages in funding or risk mitigation for large and long term projects in developing countries. Its advantages in this area are more technical than commercial. Iceland should build more capacity to cooperate and form partnerships with IFIs in this area to improve the risk profile of cross border engagement. Increased capacity in cooperating with IFIs could also provide a platform for Iceland to influence the policies of IFIs and help implement much needed institutional and policy reform within those institutions.

REFERENCES

Ingebritsen, C. (2006). *Scandinavia in world politics*. Rowman & Littlefield Publishers.

Keohane, R. O. (1969), Lilliputians'Dilemmas: Small States in International Politics. International Organizations, Vol. 23, No. 2 (Spring, 1969), pp. 291-310.

Thorhallsson, B. (2005). What features determine small states' activities in the international arena? Iceland's approach to foreign relations until the mid-1990s. *Stjórnmál og stjornsýsla – Veftímarit, Stofnun stjórnmála og stjórnsýslu,* Háskóli Íslands. 1:1, 107-140. Available at: http://www.irpa.is/article/view/861/pdf_4 (Accessed on April 1, 2014).

BOOK ENDORSEMENTS

In this book Professor Hilmarsson makes an important contribution to the study of small states in a global economy. His empirical evidence casts doubt on some of the conventional wisdom concerning optimal foreign policy strategies. The study examines small states during the 2008 global financial crisis, the contribution of small states to economic development and transition to markets, and their potential in the transition to clean energy. Hilmarsson uses his extensive knowledge of Iceland and the Baltic States to explore empirically the effectiveness for small states of multilateralism, bilateralism, unilateralism, and cooperation with international organizations, including international financial institutions. The evidence shows that no single strategy fits all circumstances. Strategies such as working closely with a group of larger nations (or not doing so), can bring benefits but also costs when relationships involve conflict of interest. Hilmarsson, with his broad academic background and experience, work on three continents as a staff member of the World Bank Group, and advisor to Iceland's foreign minister, was well placed to make a substantial contribution to the burgeoning small states literature.

Thráinn Eggertsson,
Professor of Economics,
University of Iceland and Adjunct Professor,
Hertie School of Governance, Berlin

Professor Hilmarsson has rescued small states like Iceland from the simplistic, stereotypical explanations of their behavior that dominates so much international analysis. Rather than repeating sophism based on discredited notions of "national character" like the so called "Viking spirit," his book offers a riveting, detailed account of the decisions that went into pre- and post-crises response in Iceland. In his comparison of Iceland and Latvia, he shows how Latvia, as an EU member state, had few options beyond meeting outside demands with fixed exchange rates and an austerity program, which resulted in high human costs. Iceland had more options to explore, but met international resistance as it sought financial assistance from major central banks. As its currency depreciated and the banks fell, Iceland acted unilaterally with emergency legislation and succeeded surprisingly well in protecting its welfare system. He also analyzes how small states can make important global contributions, for instance through sharing their experience in transitioning to clean energy and to market-based economies. I will be recommending this book to all of my friends and colleagues who have been misled by recent popular media treatment of the Icelandic and Latvian economic and political situations and want to better understand how small states actually operate in the global arena.

Dr. Elisabeth Ida Ward, Director,
Scandinavian Cultural Center,
Pacific Lutheran University, USA

This is an important contribution to the small states literature. In this book Professor Hilmarsson shows how small states like Latvia and Iceland can become vulnerable during times of economic and financial crisis, especially when confronted by larger states and international organizations, including international financial institutions. He also demonstrates how small countries can make contributions of global importance: the Baltic States through their international development cooperation when assisting less advanced transition countries and Iceland through assisting emerging countries in their transition to clean energy. The ideas in this book are likely to prompt discussion and debate.

Professor Dr. Erika Sumilo,
Head of the Department of International
Economics and Business,
University of Latvia

Professor Hilmarsson provides an excellent analysis of how small states respond differently to an economic and financial crisis. In Iceland the government was isolated during the 2008 crisis, all its major banks fell and the currency depreciated sharply. Nevertheless Iceland managed to protect its welfare system and the economy is recovering remarkably well. Latvia received strong international assistance during the crisis mainly from the EU as well as the Nordic countries which had and still have strong interests in the Baltic financial sector. Latvia now enjoys strong economic growth but unemployment and income inequality remain a concern. In this book Professor Hilmarsson also shows how the Baltic States can increase the effectiveness of their development programs by engaging in policy dialogue with less advanced transition countries in Europe and Central Asia. He further shows how Iceland can contribute to the transition to clean energy in developing and emerging market economies in partnership with international financial institutions. This is an important contribution and I strongly recommend it to anyone interested in the economic and financial literature focusing on small states.

Dr. OEC., Associate Prof. Ramona Rupeika-Apoga,
University of Latvia, Latvia

In this book Professor Hilmarsson offers an interesting analysis of a wide range of small states issues. This includes how small states can help solve some of the world's greatest problems, including the transition to clean energy and the transition to a market economy. It also shows that small states do not react uniformly to international financial crises. Some emphasize close cooperation with international organizations while others are more likely to pursue bilateral relations or even act unilaterally. No single formula can explain the behavior of small states in the international arena.

Professor Ligita Šimanskienė,
Klaipėda University, Lithuania

ABOUT THE AUTHOR

Hilmar Þór Hilmarsson is a Professor at the University of Akureyri, School of Business and Science, Iceland. Dr. Hilmarsson teaches courses on international business and macroeconomics. He received his cand. oecon. degree in Economics from the University of Iceland in 1987, an MA in Economics from New York University in 1989, and a Ph.D. in public administration and economic development from the American University in Washington, D.C. in 1992. He served as a Specialist and Coordinator with the World Bank Group in Washington D.C. from 1990 to 1995, at the World Bank office in Riga from 1999 to 2003 and the World Bank office in Hanoi from 2003 to 2006. From 1995 to 1999 he served as a Special Advisor to the Minister for Foreign Affairs in Iceland. Dr. Hilmarsson has published over 50 scholarly articles and book chapters and has lectured and made presentations in more than 30 universities in Europe and the USA, including the American University in Washington DC, Aalborg University, Cornell University, Georgetown University, Klaipeda University, Stockholm School of Economics, University of California Berkeley, University of California Los Angeles, the University of Latvia, the University of Mauritius, the University of Porto, the University of Tartu, the University of Washington, Vytautas Magnus University, the University of York, and Yale University. He has travelled to about 60 countries. He was a Visiting Professor at Stockholm School of Economics in Riga during the fall semester 2013 and a Visiting Scholar at the University of Washington in Seattle in the spring semester 2014.

He can be contacted at Hilmar@unak.is

INDEX

A

accountability, 90
adjustment, 2, 18, 19, 20, 31, 51
adverse event, 123
Afghanistan, 78, 79, 80, 92, 94, 104, 106, 112, 156
Africa, xxii, xxiii, 80, 90, 111, 113, 157
African Development Bank, 75
Agence Francaise de Developpement, 126
agencies, xx, 72, 84, 88, 93, 96, 101, 108, 118, 125, 134, 141
arbitration, 120, 121
Armenia, 78, 79, 92, 95, 106
Asia, xxii, xxiii, 111, 112, 113, 125, 148, 155
Asian Development Bank, 82, 92, 124, 126, 130, 134
assessment, 46, 52, 53, 56, 57, 94, 96
assets, 9, 21, 30, 31, 40, 45, 47, 51, 54
audit, 88, 90
austerity programs, 17, 18
Austria, 76, 80, 95, 104
authority(ities), xv, xxi, 3, 7, 12, 15, 23, 33, 36, 39, 40, 44, 47, 49, 51, 52, 54, 56, 57, 58, 65, 93
Azerbaijan, 78, 79

B

balance sheet, 10, 12, 15, 16, 21, 26, 46, 50, 51, 54, 56, 110, 150
Baltic States, vii, x, xvii, xix, xx, xxi, xxiii, xxv, xxvii, 8, 9, 15, 20, 28, 66, 71, 72, 73, 74, 75, 76, 77, 78, 79, 80, 81, 82, 83, 84, 85, 86, 87, 88, 89, 90, 91, 92, 93, 94, 96, 97, 98, 100, 101, 102, 103, 143, 144, 145, 146, 149, 150, 155, 156, 157, 163, 164, 165
Bangladesh, 80
Bank of England, x, xxiv, 3, 11, 27, 34, 48, 59, 65, 66, 152, 154
Bank of International Settlements (BIS), xv
bankers, 43, 55
banking, x, xvii, xxiv, 1, 3, 4, 5, 8, 9, 11, 12, 14, 15, 16, 27, 28, 29, 33, 34, 35, 36, 37, 38, 39, 40, 41, 42, 43, 44, 46, 47, 48, 49, 50, 51, 52, 53, 54, 56, 58, 59, 60, 61, 62, 64, 65, 66, 67, 131, 145, 146, 147, 149, 150, 151, 152, 153, 154
banking sector, 8, 9, 15, 34, 37, 41, 42, 44, 47, 48, 54, 58, 61, 64, 65, 131, 152
bankruptcy, 12
banks, x, xxiii, xxiv, xxv, 1, 5, 7, 8, 9, 10, 11, 12, 13, 14, 15, 16, 27, 28, 30, 33, 34, 35, 37, 38, 39, 40, 41, 42, 43, 44, 45, 46, 47, 48, 49, 50, 51, 52, 53, 54, 55, 56, 57, 58, 59, 60, 61, 63, 64, 65, 66, 67, 75, 82,

108, 116, 118, 127, 130, 136, 137, 139,
  145, 146, 147, 149, 150, 151, 152, 154,
  157, 159, 160, 164, 165
bargaining, 120, 139, 160
barriers to entry, 98
basic needs, 14
Beijing, 84
Belarus, 78, 79, 92, 94
Belgium, 76, 80
beneficiaries, 90
benefits, xxvii, 4, 22, 88, 92, 123, 132, 144,
  149, 151, 163
bilateral, 81, 83, 104
bilateral agencies, 118, 125
bilateral aid, 88
bilateral currency swap arrangement, 59
bilateral development cooperation, x, xxv
bilateral relationship, 146
bilateralism, xx, 163
Bolivia, 80, 113
bonds, 136
borrowers, 15, 16
Bosnia, 80
Bretton Woods institutions, xx, 72, 75
Britain, xix, 13, 43, 62
budget allocation, 74
budget cuts, 2, 27, 115, 145
budget support, xxvi, 72, 73, 75, 80, 87, 88,
  89, 90, 91, 92, 93, 94, 96, 97, 98, 101,
  102, 155, 157
Build-Operate-Transfer (BOT), 170
Bulgaria, 23, 24, 26, 76
bullying, 46
bureaucracy, 131, 137, 159
Burkina Faso, 90
Burundi, 113
business environment, 47, 74, 114, 124, 159
business model, 45, 57, 58, 67
buyer, 115

C

cabinet, 6, 28, 34, 36, 41, 48, 49, 51, 53, 58,
  64
Cairo, 84

capacity building, 85, 89, 95, 134
capital adequacy, 45
capital controls, 3, 10
capital flows, 16, 107, 109
capital intensive, x, xxvi, 108, 111, 114,
  116, 120, 138, 139, 158
capital markets, 129
capital mobilization, 133, 137, 140, 160,
  161
capitalism, 48
case studies, 36, 77
case study, ix, 2, 36, 77, 146
catalyst, 132
categorization, xxi, 149
Central Asia, xix, 32, 78, 79, 93, 101, 133,
  140, 155, 165
central bank(s), ix, x, xxiii, xxiv, 5, 11, 12,
  27, 34, 39, 49, 57, 59, 60, 65, 66, 146,
  150, 152, 154, 164
Central Bank of Iceland (CBI), 36, 40, 44,
  48, 49, 51, 52, 53, 56, 57, 59, 60
Central Europe, 149
central planning, 93
challenges, xi, xxiv, xxvii, 2, 5, 27, 71, 73,
  85, 110, 114, 127, 130, 143, 144, 148
Chamber of Commerce, 42, 64, 68, 69
Chicago, xiii, xiv, 43, 71
China, xix
citizens, 22, 33, 39, 61, 62, 86
civil society, 85
clarity, 7, 58
clean energy, ix, x, xvii, xviii, xix, xx, xxiii,
  xxvi, 63, 68, 107, 108, 109, 110, 111,
  115, 120, 124, 127, 128, 133, 137, 138,
  139, 140, 143, 158, 159, 160, 161, 163,
  164, 165
clients, 54, 132
climate change, xix, 107, 108, 111, 129, 140
CNN, 53
coal, 109
Coast Guard, 63
Cod Wars, 34, 63, 65, 146, 147, 148, 153,
  154
COFACE, 126
cohesion funds, 24

Cold War, 11, 63, 66, 146, 148, 153
collaboration, 92, 132
commerce, 129
commercial, 15, 48, 114, 116, 118, 119,
    122, 123, 124, 125, 126, 127, 128, 130,
    133, 135, 136, 138, 139, 161
commercial bank(s), 15, 48, 125, 127
commercial risks, 123, 135, 139
Commission on Growth and Development,
    99, 100, 102
commodity, 150
commodity markets, 150
communities, 48
community, x, xvii, xviii, xxi, xxiii, xxiv,
    xxv, xxvi, 3, 33, 34, 35, 39, 44, 46, 54,
    60, 65, 80, 84, 91, 100, 109, 116, 120,
    128, 139, 143, 145, 151, 152, 153, 157,
    158
comparative advantage, 72, 87, 88, 91, 132
compensation, 119, 124
competitiveness, 17, 24, 92, 114, 145, 149
concession agreement, 118, 119, 125
concessional terms, 82
conference, xiii, 1, 10, 71, 94, 103
conflict, 129, 148, 163
conflict of interest, 163
Congo, 80, 113
consensus, xviii, 7, 87, 98, 133, 134, 142
constituents, 8
constitution, 7, 13, 154
construction, 112, 117, 118, 119, 125
construction contractor, 117, 119
consumption, 17, 19
contractual structure, 117, 118
cooperation, ix, x, xviii, xix, xx, xxi, xxiii,
    xxv, xxvii, 28, 72, 74, 75, 76, 77, 78, 79,
    81, 82, 83, 84, 86, 87, 88, 91, 95, 100,
    101, 104, 110, 115, 117, 121, 130, 133,
    143, 144, 145, 146, 147, 150, 154, 155,
    156, 157, 158, 159, 160, 163, 164, 165
coordination, 50, 52, 66, 87, 91, 94, 138,
    160
corporate governance, 131
corruption, 6, 42, 69, 97, 114

cost, 4, 8, 12, 18, 19, 27, 28, 52, 122, 132,
    133, 134, 136, 138, 154, 161
Council of the European Union, 84, 103
credentials, 96
credit rating, 40, 48, 50
creditworthiness, 116, 124
crises, xviii, 29, 42, 46, 48, 164, 165
criticism, 34, 48, 52, 62
Croatia, 76
cross-ownership, 43
crowding out, 117
culture, 3, 37, 130, 134
currency, 2, 8, 10, 11, 14, 15, 16, 17, 26, 37,
    40, 44, 59, 60, 67, 123, 145, 152, 164,
    165
current account balance, 19
current account deficit, 17, 19, 42
curriculum vitae (CV), 42
Cyprus, 76
Czech Republic, 5, 9, 23, 24, 26, 76

D

danger, 39, 53, 64, 65
debt(s), 2, 10, 13, 16, 26, 27, 34, 35, 40, 48,
    62, 66, 90, 118, 123, 124, 136, 154
debtors, 14
deficits, 17, 19
democracy, 13, 62, 67, 85
democratization, 85
Denmark, xvii, xix, xx, xxi, 11, 41, 43, 60,
    72, 74, 75, 80, 81, 82, 83, 84, 90, 100,
    104, 156, 157
deposits, 39, 40, 154
depreciation, 2, 3, 8, 9, 10, 11, 14, 16, 17,
    18, 26, 27, 145, 149
deregulation, 98
devaluation, 8, 9, 14, 15, 16, 28
developed countries, 134, 137
developing countries, x, xxvi, xxvii, 82, 86,
    89, 98, 107, 108, 109, 110, 111, 112,
    114, 116, 122, 127, 131, 133, 134, 135,
    137, 138, 139, 140, 158, 159, 160, 161
development, vii, xv, xvi, xxii, xxiii, xxviii,
    5, 8, 31, 37, 68, 71, 72, 73, 75, 78, 79,

81, 82, 83, 84, 85, 87, 89, 91, 92, 93, 94, 95, 96, 97, 98, 99, 101, 102, 103, 104, 105, 106, 112, 115, 117, 121, 122, 124, 125, 126, 127, 128, 129, 130, 132, 133, 134, 140, 141, 142, 160

development assistance, xvi, 76, 80, 81, 88, 90

Development Assistance Committee (DAC), 104

development banks, xxiii, 7, 8, 75, 82, 108, 124, 130, 139, 157, 159, 160

development budgets, 74, 82, 84, 155

development cooperation, x, xix, xxi, xxv, 74, 76, 77, 78, 82, 83, 84, 86, 87, 88, 91, 95, 100, 101, 104, 156, 157, 158

development policy, 72, 75, 91, 95, 105

direct investment, xv

direct observation, 36, 77

directors, 10, 47, 53, 103, 133, 138

dishonesty, x, xxiv, xxvii, 6, 34, 38, 57, 64, 65, 66, 144, 152

distribution, 23

division of labor, 58, 65, 97

Doha, 84

domestic economy, 15

domestic resources, 110

dominant strategy, 45

donor country(ies), 8, 72, 74, 84, 87, 95, 96, 98, 101, 103

donors, xx, xxvi, xxviii, 72, 75, 80, 87, 88, 89, 90, 91, 92, 95, 96, 97, 100, 101, 115, 127, 136, 137, 155, 156, 157

downsizing, 42, 49, 58, 64

DPO, xv, 92

drying, 110

E

early warning, 49

earnings, 43

East Asia, 124

Eastern Europe, 106

economic crisis, 138

economic development, xxiii, 3, 20, 21, 74, 79, 85, 93, 98, 156, 163, 167

economic growth, xxv, 2, 4, 20, 21, 26, 27, 35, 37, 73, 75, 76, 83, 87, 98, 99, 101, 102, 150, 155, 165

economic growth rate, 76

economic indicator, 22

economic integration, x, xxiv, 50, 151, 153

economic performance, 20

economic policy, xxvii, 98, 100, 122, 144, 146

economic progress, 20

economic reforms, 73, 102

economic well-being, 21

economics, xvii, 36, 37

Ecuador, 113

education, 10, 14, 25, 42, 43, 52, 54, 94, 95, 98, 99, 110, 129, 137

education reform, 95

EFTA Court, 13, 34, 62, 63, 66, 67, 147, 148, 152, 153, 154

Eksportkreditt (Norway), xv

Exportkreditnämnden (EKN) (Sweden), xv, 126

electricity, x, xxvi, 63, 65, 109, 110, 111, 112, 114, 115, 116, 127, 138, 154, 159

emergency, 14, 65, 164

emerging markets, xxvii, 55, 108, 114, 122, 123, 124, 127, 135, 138, 139, 144

emigration, 18, 25

employment, 19

energy, ix, x, xvii, xviii, xix, xx, xxiii, xxvi, xxvii, 47, 53, 55, 63, 65, 68, 93, 107, 108, 109, 110, 111, 112, 114, 115, 116, 120, 121, 123, 124, 127, 128, 129, 131, 132, 133, 134, 135, 137, 138, 139, 140, 143, 144, 158, 159, 160, 161, 163, 164, 165

energy prices, 63

engineering, 125

England, 3, 11, 34, 59, 65

environment(s), 29, 30, 47, 51, 56, 74, 85, 87, 98, 99, 108, 112, 114, 121, 130, 134, 139

environmental impact, 6

equality, 23

equipment, 108, 110, 135, 138, 160

equity, 29, 114, 116, 118, 122, 123, 124, 125, 127, 128, 136, 137, 138, 159

Eritrea, 113

Estonia, xvii, 5, 8, 9, 20, 73, 74, 75, 76, 78, 79, 80, 81, 82, 83, 84, 85, 86, 87, 94, 101, 104

ethics, 36, 38

Ethiopia, 80

EU11 countries, 20, 76, 80, 91, 100

EU15 countries, 20, 84, 91

Euro, 2, 4, 5, 8, 9, 10, 11, 12, 15, 16, 18, 20, 23, 27, 28, 34, 40, 60, 66, 73, 76, 83, 85, 93, 94, 145, 149

Euro area, 2, 4, 10, 11, 12, 15, 18, 20, 27, 28, 34, 66, 73, 76, 145, 149

Euro area countries, 76

Europe, xix, xxii, xxiii, 2, 4, 13, 23, 24, 29, 32, 40, 42, 47, 50, 55, 62, 65, 78, 79, 101, 103, 106, 115, 133, 140, 155, 165, 167

European Bank for Reconstruction and Development (EBRD), xv, xxii, 5, 8, 9, 71, 73, 75, 100, 130, 159

European Central Bank (ECB), x, xv, xxiv, 11, 34, 48, 59, 152, 154

European Commission (EC), xv, 10, 20, 21, 24, 29, 31, 86, 89, 92, 103

European Economic Area (EEA), xv, 36, 50, 147, 151, 152

European integration, xxv, 35, 36, 61, 62, 101, 151, 152

European Investment Bank (EIB), xv, 115, 122, 127, 128, 129

European market, 50, 151

European Parliament, 29

European Union (EU), ix, x, xv, xix, xxii, xxiv, xxv, 2, 3, 4, 5, 8, 9, 10, 11, 13, 14, 16, 18, 19, 20, 21, 22, 23, 24, 25, 26, 27, 28, 36, 45, 46, 49, 57, 62, 63, 66, 71, 73, 74, 76, 77, 80, 81, 83, 84, 85, 86, 90, 91, 93, 100, 101, 103, 144, 145, 146, 147, 148, 149, 150, 151, 152, 153, 156, 157, 164, 165

evidence, 11, 36, 51, 56, 77, 97, 98, 139, 163

exchange rate, 2, 9, 10, 14, 15, 16, 17, 27, 28, 98, 99, 145, 150

exchange rate policy, 2, 150

exchange rates, 164

exclusion, 23, 150

expertise, 96, 97, 117, 160

export, xv, xvi, 15, 19, 100, 108, 125, 134, 135, 139, 160

export market, 15

export promotion, 100, 139

exporters, 135, 138, 139

export-led growth, 17, 18, 28

exports, 2, 17, 20, 31

exposure, 15, 16

expropriation, 123

external financing, 89

F

families, 150

farmers, 13, 62

Faroe Islands, 3, 4

FDI inflow, 98

Federal Reserve, x, xxiv, 11, 27, 34, 48, 60, 61, 152, 153, 154

Federal Reserve Bank of New York, 60

fiduciary risks, 97

financial crisis, ix, xvii, xviii, xx, xxiii, 1, 2, 21, 26, 33, 35, 40, 41, 45, 46, 58, 63, 71, 73, 76, 86, 100, 108, 110, 121, 143, 145, 148, 149, 150, 153, 154, 163, 164, 165

financial instability, 42

financial institutions, xi, xvi, xxiii, xxvi, 7, 36, 52, 54, 57, 73, 75, 76, 88, 89, 93, 97, 98, 109, 115, 128, 129, 130, 131, 133, 134, 155, 156, 157, 158, 159, 160, 163, 164, 165

financial instrument, 127, 133, 138

financial markets, xxv, 36, 45, 46, 47, 50, 117, 129, 130, 151, 153

financial regulation, 42

financial sector, 4, 10, 16, 33, 35, 42, 43, 44, 48, 129, 165

financial soundness, 132

financial support, 27, 89, 116

financial system, 15, 35, 40, 42, 43, 52, 54, 64
Finland, xx, 16, 17, 18, 31, 72, 75, 76, 80, 81, 82, 83, 90, 145
fish, 110, 159
fisheries, 63, 147
fishing, 153
fixed exchange rates, 164
Fjármálaeftirlitið (FME), xv, 40
flaws, 39, 61, 152
force, xxi, xxv, 17, 27, 36, 40, 49, 146, 151, 152, 153
foreign aid, 72, 74
foreign banks, 9, 12, 15
foreign direct investment (FDI), 122
foreign exchange, 48, 59, 65
foreign investment, 9, 44, 108, 120, 121, 125
foreign policy, xxi, 63, 163
formula, xxii, 82, 99, 165
fossil fuel, 109, 137
France, xix, 76, 80, 125, 126
freedom, 42
freezing, 46, 47
funding, xi, xxvi, xxvii, 8, 16, 40, 42, 45, 46, 63, 92, 94, 95, 96, 100, 108, 114, 115, 118, 122, 124, 126, 127, 135, 136, 137, 138, 144, 149, 159, 160, 161
funds, 24, 59, 83, 89, 97, 101, 117, 127, 130, 136, 137, 138, 147

G

G10, 60
Garanti-instituttet for eksportkreditt (GIEK), 135
Gaza Strip, 80
GDP per capita, 22
General Agreement on Tariffs and Trade (GATT), xv, 108, 120, 138, 158
Georgia, xviii, 78, 79, 87, 92, 93, 105
geothermal power, 110, 114, 137, 159, 160
Germany, xix, 76, 80
Glitnir, 35, 45, 50, 54

global economy, ix, xi, xvii, xviii, xxvii, 71, 73, 100, 107, 109, 143, 163
global scale, 35
globalization, ix, 143
GNP, xvi, 21
goods and services, 116, 134, 137
governance, ix, xx, 6, 85, 93, 98, 124, 129, 143
government budget, 16, 17
government policy, 51
governments, ix, xxiii, xxiv, 1, 2, 5, 7, 13, 28, 39, 61, 62, 66, 89, 94, 96, 99, 100, 119, 120, 122, 124, 127, 129, 132, 133, 137, 139, 144, 147, 149, 153, 158
governor, 59, 60, 152
grants, 117, 126, 128, 136, 137, 139
Great Depression, 48
Greece, 76, 80
greenhouses, 110, 159
Gross Domestic Product (GDP), xv, xviii, 2, 8, 9, 17, 18, 19, 20, 21, 22, 23, 25, 26, 27, 29, 40, 41, 44, 62, 120, 145
growth, xxvii, 2, 4, 17, 18, 19, 20, 22, 23, 25, 26, 27, 33, 40, 47, 48, 49, 50, 54, 56, 76, 87, 98, 99, 100, 106, 111, 129, 144, 145
growth rate, 18, 20, 23
guarantees, 119, 122, 123, 125, 126, 127, 132, 134, 135, 138
Guatemala, 113
guidelines, 51, 84, 87, 100
Guinea, 80, 113

H

Haiti, 80
harmonization, 87, 90, 91, 96
health, 2, 10, 14, 19, 26, 27, 56, 85, 95, 98, 99, 129
health care, 14, 98, 129
high income countries, 73, 114
history, ix, xix, xxiv, 3, 47, 50, 65, 66, 120, 130, 146, 149
homes, 11
Honduras, 113

honesty, 37, 38, 39, 69
host, x, xxiv, 115, 116, 117, 119, 120, 121,
    122, 123, 127, 132, 135, 137, 139, 151,
    152, 158
host country, x, xxiv, 117, 151, 152
host government, 115, 116, 117, 119, 120,
    121, 122, 123, 127, 132, 137, 139, 158
hostility, 65
housing, 15
human, xviii, xxiv, 5, 18, 24, 26, 28, 85,
    124, 145, 149, 150, 164
human development, 27, 85
human rights, 85
humanitarian aid, 83
Hungary, 9, 76

I

Iceland Chamber of Commerce, 42, 64, 68,
    69
Icelandic banks, x, xxiv, xxv, 9, 11, 12, 27,
    33, 34, 35, 40, 42, 43, 44, 45, 46, 47, 49,
    50, 53, 54, 57, 60, 61, 64, 65, 130, 150,
    151
Icesave, 3, 12, 13, 28, 34, 61, 62, 66, 147,
    148, 150, 153, 154
imbalances, 41, 42, 43, 51
in transition, xxvii, 4, 6, 109, 158, 164
income, x, xix, xxvi, 3, 4, 5, 8, 14, 15, 16,
    20, 21, 22, 23, 24, 25, 26, 28, 31, 33, 41,
    71, 73, 74, 75, 76, 78, 79, 80, 81, 83, 85,
    91, 98, 101, 107, 109, 112, 113, 114,
    116, 118, 120, 146, 149, 150, 155, 157,
    165
income distribution, 16, 21, 22, 23, 24, 98,
    150
income inequality, 4, 24, 26, 28, 165
incompetence, x, xxiv, xxv, xxvii, 36, 64,
    66, 144, 151, 152
independence, xxi, 71, 73, 149
Independent Evaluation Group, 89, 96, 131,
    132
industrial sectors, 141
industrialized countries, 120
industry(s), 19, 90, 110, 120, 129, 135

inequality, 23, 24
inflation, 16, 41, 99
infrastructure, 47, 50, 98, 116, 117, 120,
    121, 122, 123, 124, 126, 129, 138, 139,
    140
infrastructure investment, 129, 140
insanity, 14, 28
institution building, 101
institutional reforms, 65, 98
institutions, ix, xx, xxii, xxiii, xxiv, xxv, 3,
    5, 7, 15, 34, 42, 47, 56, 57, 58, 62, 65,
    72, 75, 76, 81, 82, 88, 92, 93, 101, 108,
    110, 111, 112, 114, 116, 121, 122, 123,
    124, 125, 127, 129, 131, 132, 133, 134,
    137, 138, 139, 143, 144, 145, 146, 151,
    155, 156, 157, 158, 160, 161
insurance, xv, xvi, 19, 40, 56, 112, 120, 121,
    122, 124, 127, 128, 136, 137, 138
integration, 66, 85, 147, 148, 149, 152, 153
Inter-American Development Bank, xxii,
    xxiii, 75, 82, 115, 121, 122, 127, 128,
    129, 130, 160
interest groups, 7
interest rate, 16, 51, 56, 61, 98, 136
interest rates, 16, 51, 56, 61
interference, 7, 122, 145
international affairs, xxi
International Bank for Reconstruction and
    Development (IBRD), xvi, 31, 68, 91,
    102, 103, 106, 112, 122
International Development Association
    (IDA), 82, 122
international development cooperation, ix,
    x, xviii, xix, xx, xxi, xxiii, xxv, xxvii, 72,
    74, 75, 76, 77, 81, 83, 86, 87, 100, 101,
    130, 143, 144, 155, 156, 157, 164
International Finance Corporation (IFC),
    122
International Financial Institutions (IFIs), x,
    xx, xxiii, xxvi, xxvii, 7, 36, 71, 73, 75,
    76, 88, 89, 97, 98, 101, 107, 108, 109,
    121, 127, 131, 136, 144, 155, 156, 157,
    158, 159, 160, 163, 164, 165
international investment, 127, 137, 159

International Monetary Fund (IMF), ix, xvi,
    xx, xxii, xxiii, xxiv, 1, 3, 4, 5, 6, 7, 8, 9,
    10, 12, 14, 15, 16, 18, 19, 23, 27, 28, 30,
    40, 46, 47, 59, 61, 68, 75, 91, 93, 117,
    141, 144, 147, 148, 149, 153, 154
international relations, 146, 148, 153
international trade, 85, 99
internationalization, 42
investment(s), xv, xxvii, 9, 17, 44, 48, 63,
    73, 90, 93, 97, 98, 99, 108, 109, 112,
    114, 116, 117, 118, 120, 121, 122, 125,
    127, 128, 129, 130, 133, 134, 136, 137,
    138, 139, 140, 144, 149, 157, 158, 160
investment bank, 44, 48, 116, 118, 127, 136,
    137, 159
investors, 1, 9, 16, 108, 109, 112, 116, 118,
    120, 121, 122, 123, 124, 127, 129, 130,
    131, 132, 134, 135, 136, 137, 138, 145,
    158
Ireland, 12, 27, 75, 76, 80, 95, 104
Italy, xix, 76, 80

J

Japan, 42, 125
jurisdiction, 148

K

Kaupthing, 35, 45, 47, 50, 54, 67, 141
Kenya, 80
Korea, 87
Kyrgyzstan, 78, 79

L

labor market, 19, 31
Landsbanki, 35, 43, 44, 45, 47, 50, 54
Lao PDR, 108, 124, 125, 126, 130, 133,
    141, 142
Latin America, 111, 112, 113
Latvia, vii, ix, xiii, xvii, xviii, xx, xxiii,
    xxiv, xxvii, 1, 2, 3, 4, 5, 6, 7, 8, 9, 10, 11,
    12, 14, 15, 16, 17, 18, 19, 20, 22, 23, 24,

25, 26, 27, 28, 29, 30, 31, 73, 74, 75, 76,
    78, 79, 81, 82, 83, 84, 85, 86, 101, 104,
    140, 144, 145, 146, 149, 150, 155, 156,
    164, 165, 167
laws, 53, 65, 99
lawyers, 37
lead, 7, 89, 95, 130, 131, 150
leadership, xvii, 13, 50, 62, 96
legislation, 3, 7, 38, 62, 88, 153, 154, 164
lender of last resort, 40, 44, 56, 58, 67, 152
lenders, 16, 117, 118, 119, 123, 125
lending, 50, 51, 72, 93, 96, 101, 115, 126,
    134, 136, 138, 139, 159
liberalization, 42, 47, 98
liquidity, 40, 44, 52
Lithuania, xvii, 20, 73, 74, 75, 76, 78, 79,
    80, 81, 82, 83, 85, 86, 94, 101, 103, 104,
    165
loan guarantees, 136
loans, 15, 16, 116, 122, 124, 125, 126, 127,
    136, 137, 138, 159
local authorities, 88
local government, 9, 85
Luxembourg, 75, 76, 80, 84

M

Macedonia, 75
machinery, 110
macroeconomic management, 99
macroeconomic policy(ies), 41, 51, 91
macroeconomics, 167
majority, 7, 13, 28, 62, 86, 121, 124, 134
Malawi, 80, 90, 113
Malaysia, 113
management, 45, 51, 73, 89, 90, 97, 102,
    119, 122, 125
mania, 46
manic, 48
market economy, 85, 93, 165
market-based economies, 164
marketing, 132, 134, 138, 161
Mauritius, xiii, 113, 167
measurements, 20, 114

media, 29, 30, 31, 46, 53, 54, 67, 68, 69, 104, 106, 141, 142, 164
mediation, 123, 124
membership, 4, 8, 80, 82, 97, 101, 139, 145, 148, 149, 153, 157
methodology, 36, 77
migration, 2, 25
military, xviii, xix, xxi, 146, 148
minimum wage, 19
models, 88
Moldova, xviii, 78, 79, 87, 92, 93, 104, 105
monetary policy, 16, 17, 42
moral hazard, 10
Mozambique, 80, 90, 106, 113
multilateral, xvi, xxii, 81, 82, 96, 112, 122, 128, 129, 132, 141
multilateral institutions, xx, xxii, xxiv, xxv, 5, 75, 81, 82, 92, 93, 125, 137, 144, 145, 146, 151, 155, 157
Multilateral Investment Guarantee Agency, xvi (MIGA), 96, 112, 122, 128, 129
multilateralism, xx, xxvii, 144, 155, 163

N

Nam Theun 2 (NT2), 108, 124, 125, 126, 130, 133, 135, 139, 141, 142
Namibia, 80
national character, 164
national income, xix, 20
national interests, 7
NATO, xxii, 63, 71, 73, 80, 100, 146, 148, 149, 150, 156
natural rate of unemployment, 19
natural resources, 111, 129
negotiating, 4, 119
negotiation, 120
Nepal, 80
Netherlands, ix, xxiv, xxv, 3, 11, 12, 13, 28, 33, 36, 61, 62, 63, 66, 75, 76, 80, 84, 92, 93, 140, 147, 148, 151, 152, 153, 154
neutral, 96
NGOs, 7
Nicaragua, 80
Nobel Prize, 19, 20, 37, 62

non commercial risks, 114, 136
nonprofit organizations, 123
Nordic countries, xx, xxi, xxv, xxvii, 3, 4, 9, 12, 15, 27, 34, 36, 59, 60, 63, 66, 72, 74, 75, 77, 80, 91, 100, 101, 122, 130, 135, 144, 145, 147, 148, 149, 151, 154, 157, 165
Norway, xv, xvii, xix, xx, xxi, 11, 43, 60, 72, 74, 75, 80, 81, 82, 83, 84, 90, 100, 105, 126, 135, 156, 157

O

obstacles, 159
officials, 6, 33, 34, 35, 36, 38, 39, 50, 53, 57, 58, 59, 61, 62, 65, 67, 94
offtake, 116, 117, 118, 119
offtake purchaser, 116, 117, 118, 119
oil, 109
open economy, 20
operations, xxv, xxvi, 11, 15, 35, 49, 52, 53, 58, 59, 61, 64, 65, 72, 73, 75, 91, 92, 93, 97, 98, 101, 102, 110, 114, 129, 131, 140, 146, 151, 155, 157
opportunities, 54
Organization for Economic Cooperation and Development (OECD), xvi, 3, 5, 8, 12, 23, 30, 33, 48, 62, 68, 80, 81, 82, 83, 87, 89, 97, 104, 105
overseas development assistance, 90
overseas investment, 33, 135
ownership, xxiv, 1, 3, 5, 6, 7, 10, 12, 15, 28, 43, 63, 87, 88, 89, 91, 110, 117, 144, 149, 150, 160

P

Pacific, xiii, 113, 164
Pakistan, 80
Panama, 113
Parliament, 34, 36
partial risk guarantees (PRG), 123
participant observation, 77

participants, xiv, xxv, 1, 33, 71, 75, 107, 119, 134, 155, 156
partner countries, xxv, 74, 75, 78, 79, 80, 85, 87, 88, 91, 92, 93, 95, 97, 98, 100, 101, 155, 156, 157, 158
payback period, 121
per capita income, 24, 25, 26, 74, 75, 116
pipeline, 115
planned economies, 71
platform, 51, 56, 110, 116, 117, 160, 161
Poland, xix, 3, 4, 9, 76
policy, xv, xvii, xxi, xxiv, xxvi, xxvii, 2, 3, 4, 5, 8, 9, 10, 16, 21, 24, 27, 28, 37, 38, 44, 46, 49, 51, 56, 63, 72, 73, 74, 75, 76, 77, 80, 84, 85, 87, 88, 89, 90, 91, 92, 94, 96, 98, 99, 100, 101, 102, 104, 105, 109, 114, 117, 122, 123, 136, 139, 144, 145, 146, 150, 153, 155, 156, 157, 158, 160, 161, 163, 165
policy choice, 28
policy dialogue, xxvi, xxvii, 72, 75, 76, 80, 88, 89, 90, 94, 96, 98, 100, 101, 109, 122, 123, 139, 144, 155, 156, 157, 158, 160, 165
policy issues, 73, 102
policy makers, 37, 51, 77, 99
policy making, 56
policy options, 44
policy reform, 72, 89, 90, 136, 155, 156, 158, 161
policy responses, 2, 4, 46, 146
policymakers, 10, 20, 23
political risk, xvi, 108, 119, 120, 121, 122, 123, 124, 126, 127, 128
political risk insurance (PRI), 122
political system, 54
politics, xxviii, 161
pools, 110, 134, 159
population, xviii, xix, 24, 25, 26, 28, 120
portfolio, 161
Portugal, 76, 80
potential benefits, xxvii, 144
poverty, xxv, 4, 22, 23, 24, 28, 73, 75, 84, 94, 98, 99, 102, 149, 155
poverty alleviation, 99

poverty reduction, xxv, 73, 75, 94, 98, 102, 155
power generation, 114
power plants, 110, 120, 137, 159, 160
power purchaser, 117
PR campaign, 34, 42, 57, 64
predictability, 90
president, 6, 12, 13, 21, 28, 29, 30, 31, 36, 54, 55, 57, 59, 62, 64, 68, 130, 153, 154
prestige, 95, 157
Prime Minister (PM), xvi, 14, 15, 16, 53
principles, 84, 88, 90
priority countries, xxvi, 76, 78, 79, 91, 93, 95, 155, 156, 157
private banks, 13, 35, 39, 63, 66, 147
private investment, 117, 122, 134, 138
private sector, 7, 16, 44, 65, 73, 96, 99, 108, 111, 116, 117, 122, 123, 124, 125, 126, 127, 128, 129, 130, 131, 133, 134, 137, 138, 139, 159, 161
private sector investment, 127, 133
privatization, x, xxiv, 2, 41, 47, 48, 50, 98, 153
probability, 65, 119
procurement, 87, 89, 93, 125, 133
procurement systems, 87
productive capacity, xviii
profit, 88, 110, 123
profitability, 21, 42
Programme-Based Approaches (PBAs), 95
project, 58, 63, 73, 87, 88, 90, 95, 97, 98, 101, 102, 114, 116, 117, 118, 119, 123, 124, 125, 126, 129, 130, 132, 133, 134, 135, 136, 137, 138, 139
project approach, 73, 87, 90, 98, 101, 102
project company, 116, 117, 118, 119, 125
project sponsors, 132
promoter, 20
property rights, 98
proposition, 5, 36, 75, 109, 145, 151, 155, 158
prosperity, 23, 106, 150
protection, 19, 40, 90, 120, 146, 149
prudential regulation, 42
public administration, xvii, 36, 37, 101, 167

public awareness, 100
public capital, 114
public debt, 26
public domain, 44, 116
public finance, 92, 114
public investment, 90
public policy, 24
public sector, 37, 116, 117, 122, 132
public service, 37
public support, 86, 95, 100

R

rating agencies, 48
reactions, x, xxiv, 56, 59, 152
real estate, 14, 43
reality, xxv, 7, 8, 34, 35, 38, 39, 49, 50, 52, 53, 57, 64, 65, 66, 151
recession, 15, 41
recovery, 2, 5, 8, 17, 19, 20, 26, 27, 29, 46, 105, 106, 146, 149
recovery plan, 5
reform(s), ix, xxiii, xxvii, 1, 3, 5, 6, 7, 8, 10, 19, 24, 25, 26, 27, 28, 73, 89, 90, 91, 93, 95, 98, 100, 101, 109, 136, 138, 139, 150, 156, 158, 161
regional development banks, xxiii, 75, 124, 159
regional integration, 129
regions of the world, xix
regulations, 39, 46, 58, 65
regulatory framework, 46
rejection, 38
relevance, 4, 37, 78, 152
relief, 10
renewable energy, 129
reputation, 40, 50
requirements, 85, 117, 118, 133
reserve currency, 45
reserves, 8, 11, 48, 56, 58, 59, 65, 152
resistance, 164
resolution, 56, 123, 124, 148
resources, xviii, xxiv, 5, 6, 72, 76, 88, 89, 95, 99, 108, 111, 114, 115, 120, 122, 134, 138, 145, 147, 159

response, xvii, xxiv, xxvii, 2, 5, 6, 8, 11, 27, 39, 48, 50, 54, 56, 59, 60, 63, 144, 145, 149, 150, 153, 164
restructuring, 26
retail, 44
rewards, 117
rights, 120, 125, 138, 158
risk(s), xi, xvi, xxvi, xxvii, 7, 10, 16, 22, 23, 24, 26, 40, 41, 44, 46, 50, 53, 55, 58, 59, 61, 64, 65, 97, 108, 109, 111, 112, 114, 116, 119, 120, 121, 122, 123, 124, 126, 127, 128, 130, 131, 133, 134, 135, 136, 137, 138, 139, 141, 144, 158, 159, 160, 161
risk allocation, 116
risk aversion, 46
risk management, 16, 122, 159
risk mitigation, xi, xxvi, xxvii, 58, 65, 108, 109, 111, 112, 114, 116, 121, 122, 124, 126, 127, 130, 131, 133, 134, 135, 137, 138, 139, 144, 158, 159, 160, 161
risk mitigation instrument, xxvii, 108, 109, 116, 121, 122, 124, 126, 130, 131, 133, 134, 135, 137, 138, 139, 144, 159, 160, 161
risk profile, xxvii, 108, 109, 126, 138, 158, 159, 161
risk taking, 55
Romania, 9, 23, 24, 26, 76
rule of law, 14, 42, 63
rules, 39, 53, 65, 84, 108, 120, 147, 150
rural areas, 93
Russia, 3, 149
Rwanda, 90, 113

S

safety, 17
sanctions, 121
savings, 134
scaling, 88
Scandinavia, xxviii, 14, 28, 145, 161
Scandinavian countries, ix, x, xvii, xix, xx, xxi, xxii, xxiii, xxv, 3, 8, 9, 26, 72, 74, 75, 81, 82, 89, 149, 156, 157

school, 77, 95
science, xvii, 36, 37
scope, 88, 90, 147
seafood, 47
secondary data, 36, 77
securities, 40, 45
security, 114, 120, 149, 150, 156
seminars, xiii, xvii, 33
service provider, 110, 137
services, xxvii, 3, 96, 108, 122, 124, 126,
    128, 129, 131, 134, 135, 138, 139, 144,
    160
settlements, 28, 66, 147, 153
shareholders, 117, 118, 125, 136
shock, 45, 48, 52
single market, 62
Slovakia, 23, 26, 76
small states, ix, x, xi, xvii, xviii, xix, xx,
    xxi, xxiii, xxiv, xxv, xxvii, xxviii, 5, 35,
    36, 72, 75, 77, 82, 84, 89, 90, 95, 108,
    109, 143, 144, 145, 146, 147, 148, 149,
    150, 151, 152, 153, 154, 155, 156, 157,
    158, 159, 162, 163, 164, 165
social exclusion, 4, 22, 23, 24, 28, 150
social fabric, 2, 19, 27
social indicator, 26
social problems, 4
social responsibility, 129
social safety nets, 92
social welfare, 146
society, 2, 6, 22, 25, 26, 28, 130
solution, 60, 65
Somalia, 80, 113
South Korea, xix
Soviet Union, 23, 25, 71, 73, 149
Spain, xix, 76, 80
Special Investigation Commission (SIC),
    xvi, 3, 8, 10, 11, 12, 31, 34, 38, 40, 50,
    51, 52, 53, 54, 56, 57, 58, 59, 64, 65, 69
specialists, 37
speech, 13, 38, 54, 62, 67, 130
spending, 14, 84
spillover effects, 28
sponsors, 115, 116, 127, 129, 132, 136, 138
stability, 35, 68, 79, 99, 114, 149

stabilization, 98
staff members, 110, 138
stakeholders, 15, 91
state(s), ix, x, xi, xvii, xviii, xix, xx, xxi,
    xxiii, xxiv, xxv, xxvi, xxvii, xxviii, 2, 4,
    5, 6, 8, 9, 10, 11, 12, 15, 16, 17, 21, 30,
    35, 36, 38, 41, 42, 47, 48, 50, 51, 52, 61,
    63, 65, 69, 72, 75, 76, 77, 81, 82, 83, 84,
    85, 87, 89, 90, 93, 94, 95, 108, 109, 120,
    133, 143, 144, 145, 146, 147, 148, 149,
    150, 151, 152, 153, 154, 155, 156, 157,
    158, 159, 161, 162, 163, 164, 165
strategic planning, 87
structural adjustment, 87
structure, xxii, 103, 117, 118, 129, 133, 151
Sub-Saharan Africa, 80, 157
Sudan, 80, 113
supervision, x, xxiv, 40, 42, 46, 47, 49, 51,
    56, 58, 65, 151, 152
supervisor(s), 45, 46, 49, 56, 57
supplier, 117
sustainability, 22, 129
sustainable development, 99
sustainable economic growth, 73, 102
sustainable energy, 47
Sweden, xv, xvii, xix, xx, xxi, 3, 11, 12, 16,
    17, 18, 31, 43, 60, 66, 72, 74, 75, 80, 81,
    82, 83, 84, 90, 93, 100, 126, 135, 145,
    156, 157

T

tactics, 35, 61, 63, 66, 154
Tajikistan, 78, 79
Tanzania, 80, 90, 113
target, 76, 81, 83
tax base, 98, 137
tax cuts, 10
tax rates, 47
tax reform, 98
taxes, 13, 14, 19, 51, 62, 112
taxpayers, 4, 12, 26, 27, 61, 66, 147, 153,
    154
teachers, 13, 62

technical assistance, xxvi, xxvii, 72, 73, 76, 89, 95, 96, 97, 101, 102, 123, 126, 128, 144, 155, 156, 157, 158
technology, 85
temperature, 114
tensions, 63, 150
territorial, 147
territory, 63, 153
terrorism, 3
terrorist attack, 47
Thailand, 125, 126
threats, 39
tourism, 129
trade, 6, 7, 98, 108, 116, 120, 121, 129, 133, 135, 136, 137, 138, 139, 141, 149, 150, 151, 158
trade liberalization, 98
trade-off, 133
traditions, 130
training, xvii
transaction costs, 88, 99, 123
transition, ix, x, xvii, xviii, xix, xx, xxiii, xxv, xxvi, xxvii, 4, 6, 63, 73, 75, 77, 78, 79, 85, 88, 89, 93, 94, 96, 100, 101, 102, 103, 108, 109, 110, 116, 120, 137, 143, 149, 150, 155, 156, 157, 158, 159, 161, 163, 164, 165
transition economies, 73, 102
transition experience, xvii, xix, xx, xxvi, 75, 85, 88, 89, 93, 94, 101, 137, 155, 156, 157
transparency, 7, 43, 90, 93
Treasury, 50
Trust Fund, 80, 94, 106
trustworthiness, 39
Tryggingardeild útflutnings (TRÚ), xvi, 135, 139
Turkey, 141

U

Uganda, 80, 90, 113
Ukraine, xviii, 78, 79, 92, 93, 106, 150
unacceptable risk, 93

unemployment, 2, 4, 18, 19, 24, 25, 26, 27, 28, 145, 165
unemployment insurance, 19
unemployment rate, 19, 26
unilateralism, 163
unions, 19
United Kingdom (UK), ix, xvi, xxiv, xxv, 3, 11, 12, 13, 28, 33, 36, 47, 55, 59, 61, 62, 63, 65, 66, 80, 93, 146, 147, 148, 151, 152, 153, 154
United Nations (UN), xvi, xxii, 74, 81, 84, 93, 157
United States of America (US/USA), xvi, 11, 34, 42, 43, 47, 60
universities, xiii, xviii, 48, 133, 167
university education, 25
USSR, xvi, xix
Uzbekistan, 78, 79

V

value added tax (VAT), xvi, 93
variables, xviii
venue, 116
Vietnam, xix, 80, 97, 142
Viking, 43, 164

W

wages, 8
war, 123
Washington, xiii, 29, 59, 87, 98, 99, 102, 103, 105, 141, 142, 167
Washington Consensus, 98, 99, 102, 105
water, 8, 110, 115, 120, 129
water resources, 110
wealth, 25, 43
welfare, xxii, 3, 16, 17, 20, 21, 28, 35, 147, 154, 164, 165
welfare system, xxii, 16, 28, 147, 154, 164, 165
West Bank, 80
workers, 25, 112

World Bank, xiii, xvi, xvii, xx, xxii, xxiii, 3, 5, 6, 7, 8, 9, 20, 21, 23, 24, 29, 31, 32, 47, 68, 71, 73, 74, 75, 76, 77, 79, 80, 82, 87, 88, 89, 90, 91, 92, 93, 94, 96, 97, 101, 102, 103, 105, 106, 107, 108, 112, 113, 114, 115, 117, 119, 121, 122, 123, 124, 125, 126, 127, 128, 129, 130, 131, 132, 133, 136, 137, 138, 139, 140, 141, 142, 149, 159, 160, 161, 163, 167
World Economic Forum (WEF), xvi, 132, 133, 134
World Trade Organization (WTO), xvi, 71, 73, 100, 108, 120, 138, 158

World War II, 120

Y

Yale University, xiii, 1, 167
yield, 37, 146
youth unemployment, 24

Z

Zimbabwe, 112